EDUQAS

AS AND A LEVEL MUSIC

Study Guide

**PWYLL AP SIÔN,
ADRIAN COLBORNE,
PAULA GARDINER,
DR TOM PANKHURST,
ERIC PHILLIPS,
JAMES REEVELL,
PETER REYNOLDS** &
JAN RICHARDS

with examiner tips from Alun Guy

Editor: Sarah Lambie, Consultant: Huw Thomas
Design: Fresh Lemon Australia

ISBN: 978-1-78558-347-6

RHINEGOLD
EDUCATION

EXCLUSIVELY DISTRIBUTED BY

HAL•LEONARD

Contact us:
Hal Leonard
7777 West Bluemound Road
Milwaukee, WI 53213
Email: info@halleonard.com

In Europe, contact:
Hal Leonard Europe Limited
42 Wigmore Street
Marylebone, London, W1U 2RY
Email: info@halleonardeurope.com

In Australia, contact:
Hal Leonard Australia Pty. Ltd.
4 Lentara Court
Cheltenham, Victoria, 3192 Australia
Email: info@halleonard.com.au

You should always check the current
requirements of your examination,
since these may change.

Contents

The authors

Pwyll ap Siôn (Composing) is Professor of Music at Bangor University. A composer and musicologist, his music has been performed by BBC National Orchestra of Wales and Welsh National Opera. He has published books on Michael Nyman and Steve Reich, writes regularly for *Gramophone* magazine, and has served as examiner for WJEC composition at AS and A level.

Adrian Colborne (AOS C: Musical Theatre) is head of performing arts at Cowbridge comprehensive school and has worked as an examiner for WJEC for ten years. He currently sets questions for the new AS and A Level specifications for Eduqas and WJEC, areas of study B, C and D.

Paula Gardiner (AOS D: Jazz) originally trained as a classical guitarist. She calls herself 'the accidental bassist' despite becoming one of Wales' best known jazz musicians as composer and double bassist. She specialises in composing jazz scores for drama, including theatre, radio and film. Paula is Head of Jazz at The Royal Welsh College of Music and Drama.

Alun Guy (Examiner tips: Performing) has spent his professional music career since graduating from Cardiff University teaching, examining and traversing the world as a conductor and an adjudicator.

Dr Tom Pankhurst (AOS E: Into the 20th Century) is Head of Music at King Edward VI, Stourbridge. His specialisms are in analysis and twentieth century music. He has published an undergraduate text book on Schenkerian analysis which, like his websites on Schenker and Bach Chorales, are widely used in the UK and abroad.

Eric Phillips (Performing) is Head of Music at Whitchurch High School, Cardiff and Principal Examiner for AS and A level performing for WJEC and Eduqas. Eric was awarded an MBE for services to music and education in the 2013 Queen's Birthday Honours.

James Reevell (AOS B: Rock & Pop) is a Subject Leader for Visual and Creative Arts teaching Music and Music Technology in a sixth form college in the North West of England. He studied Music at the University of Durham and is an experienced examiner, running regular nationwide A level training events and specialising in Popular Music and Music Technology.

Peter Reynolds (AOS F: Into the 21st Century) founded the contemporary music ensemble 'PM' and composed the shortest opera on Earth, *Sands of Time*; a 3 minute 34 second-long piece. He studied and lived in Cardiff and was the artistic director of the Lower Machen Festival in Monmouthshire from 1998 to 2009. Passing away in October 2016, he will be remembered for his composition and his writings and programme notes about contemporary music.

Jan Richards (AOS A: The Western Classical Tradition) has taught across Cardiff and the Vale of Glamorgan in three secondary schools and a sixth form college, working for 35 years as a Head of Performing Arts. An author of teacher resources from KS3-5, she has also been involved in developing the new specifications for GCSE and AS/A Level (WJEC and Eduqas). She is currently the principal examiner for composition at both GCSE and A level, and has recently published a text book for GCSE Music.

Introduction

Congratulations! You have chosen to study a really exciting and rewarding subject for AS and/or A Level, and the long-term benefits you'll gain from what you learn are enormous.

Whether you plan to go on and study music further, at university or a conservatoire, or to become a professional musician – a composer, performer, conductor or teacher, or simply to enjoy music as a hobby alongside another professional life, what you learn on this course will give you a broad but also detailed understanding of this extremely rewarding and enjoyable subject. The course will introduce you to music from different periods of history and different genres, and you will learn how those things fit together, where influences can be found from composer to composer, and what the structural elements are that go to make up Western music, both classical and other popular forms.

Music AS and A Level are not entirely or even mostly practical: there are significant written exams worth 40% in both courses. The written exam is called Component 3: Appraising, and the majority of this book is aimed at helping to prepare you for it, beginning on page 35.

Although this book takes you through all the parts of your course, your teacher will be your main guide: it is also important to note that where there are **set works** to study, we have not in great detail explored them here. This is because extensive notes on the set works are available on the Eduqas website, written in some cases by the same writers who have written the chapters of this book. Go to www. eduqas.co.uk/qualifications/music/as-a-level/ and choose 'Digital Resources' to find them.

How is the course structured?

There are several ways to take this course: you may be planning to take only the AS (Advanced Subsidiary) Level, in one year; you may be planning to take the AS in year 12 followed by the A Level in year 13, or you may plan to do the two-year 'linear' A Level which spreads out your study and cuts out the AS altogether.

This book caters for all of those options, and navigating it is easy. Since the A Level course consists of extensions on information already learned for the AS Level, **all** students should read the AS sections of this book – they form the foundation of the vast majority of your course. Pages or sections of pages which apply only to A Level students and constitute extensions to the information learnt at AS are marked 'A Level extension' and coloured **purple**.

At the end of each chapter in Component 3, there are practice exam questions. These pages are marked out with coloured backgrounds according to whether they are for AS Level (blue), or A Level (**purple**). You will find the answers from page 284.

The AS Level course is divided into three components.

Component 1: Performing accounts for 30% of your AS Level and is assessed by a visiting examiner.

Component 2: Composing accounts for 30% of your AS Level and is externally assessed by the exam board.

Component 3: Appraising accounts for 40% of your AS Level. It is a written exam lasting 1 hour and 30 minutes and is divided into **two** parts:

1. **Area of Study A: The Western Classical Tradition** – this is a compulsory area of study and focuses on the development of the symphony from 1750-1830. You will choose **one** set work from a choice of two for detailed analysis.

2. **Area of Study B, C or D** – You will choose only **one** of these areas of study, they are Rock & Pop, Musical Theatre and Jazz.

The A Level course is divided into three components.

Components 1: Performing, and **Component 2: Composing**, add up to a total of **60%** of your final A Level grade, but you can choose whether you would like to do more performing or more composing.

If you choose **Option A**:

- Performing will be worth 35% – and your performances will last a total of 10-12 minutes.
- Composing will be worth 25% – and your compositions will last a total of 4-6 minutes.

If you choose **Option B**:

- Performing will be worth 25% – and your performances will last a total of 6-8 minutes.
- Composing will be worth 35% – and your compositions will last a total of 8-10 minutes.

Choose your options based on what you are best at, and what you most enjoy. Your teacher will also help you to decide.

Component 3: Appraising accounts for 40% of your A Level. It is a written exam lasting 2 hours and 15 minutes and is divided into **three** parts:

1. **Area of Study A: The Western Classical Tradition** – this is a compulsory area of study and focuses on the development of the symphony from 1750-1900. You will choose one set work for detailed analysis, and one for general study.

2. **Area of Study B, C or D** – You will choose only **one** of these areas of study, they are Rock & Pop, Musical Theatre and Jazz.

3. **Area of Study E or F** – You will choose only **one** of these areas of study, they are based on periods of musical history: Into the Twentieth Century, and Into the Twenty-first Century. Each area of study includes **two** set works.

How am I marked?

Your final, overall mark for the AS and/or A Level will be a grade from A*-E, with A* being the best available grade. Although GCSE grades are now numbered from 9-1, A Levels still have lettered grades.

For each component, your teacher or an external examiner will mark your work according to how well you have met certain 'Assessment Objectives', often shortened to 'AOs'.

They will look at how you:

AO1   Interpret musical ideas through performing, with technical and expressive control and an understanding of style and context.

AO2   Create and develop musical ideas with technical and expressive control and coherence.

AO3   Demonstrate and apply musical knowledge.

AO4   Use analytical and appraising skills to make evaluative and critical judgements about music.

Not all AOs apply to each component: AO1 cannot be used in the written exams of Component 3, for example, because there is no performance involved, while AO2 applies only to Component 2: Composing. Don't worry, your teacher will ensure that you are working towards meeting these objectives throughout your course.

Using this book to help with your course

Because there are options along the way for both AS and A Level, there will be whole chapters of this book which don't apply to you. You are of course welcome to read them to enhance your more general understanding of music, but they won't help you directly in the exam, so focus on the sections which you are studying.

All students should read the chapters on Performing (page 8), Composing (page 18), and Component 3, Area of Study A: The Western Classical Tradition (page 36). If you are working towards your AS Level, there will then be one further chapter for you to study, and if you are doing the A Level, there will be two.

It is essential, however, that within each area of study you also research and study beyond the information provided in this book. This is designed as an introduction but you must read and listen around the subject as your teacher advises too.

To do well in your course, you can **never** listen to and analyse too many pieces of music for practice.

Throughout this book, you will find **green words** like these, which indicate that a full explanation of their meaning is given in the **glossary** from page 302). It is very important to become familiar with these technical terms and to use them when you are writing your exam answers.

There is lots of work to do, but music is an incredibly rewarding subject, so don't forget to enjoy it!

Component 1

Performing
at AS and A Level

Performing is an essential part of your musicianship to develop at AS and A Level, and can account for up to 35% of your marks for the qualification (at AS level, performance is worth 30% and at A Level the exact percentage will depend upon options which are explained in the table below). Your performances will be assessed by a visiting examiner.

In this chapter we will explain the requirements for the performing component at AS and then at A Level, and then we will share some top tips for your preparation and how to gain the highest marks for your performance. Be sure to read all the sections which apply to your course.

Here is a breakdown of how Component 1: Performing fits in to your course at AS and at A Level. At A Level, as you can see, you can choose to weight your assessment more heavily in favour of performing or composing, depending on where your greater interest and skills lie.

Performing options (all assessed by a visiting examiner)			
	AS Level	**A Level Option A**	**A Level Option B**
Performing time	6 to 8 minutes	10 to 12 minutes	6 to 8 minutes
Standard (levels of difficulty)	Grade 5	Grade 6	Grade 6
% of whole examination	30%	35% (if you take this option your composing will be worth 25%)	25% (if you take this option your composing will be worth 35%)

Performing options (all assessed by a visiting examiner)			
Total number of marks for this component	72 marks	108 marks	72 marks
No. of pieces	Minimum of 2 pieces	Minimum of 3 pieces	Minimum of 2 pieces
Solo/Ensemble	Solo **or** ensemble **or** a combination of both	One piece <u>must</u> be a solo. The others can be solo or ensemble	Solo **or** ensemble **or** a combination of both
No. of links with areas of study	One piece must link with an area of study	Two pieces must link with two <u>different</u> areas of study	One piece must link with an area of study
Areas of study	■ The Western Classical Tradition (which includes **Baroque**, **Classical** and **Romantic** music) ■ Rock and Pop ■ Musical Theatre ■ Jazz	■ The Western Classical Tradition (which includes **Baroque**, **Classical** and **Romantic** music) ■ Rock and Pop ■ Musical Theatre ■ Jazz ■ Into the 20th Century ■ Into the 21st Century	■ The Western Classical Tradition (which includes **Baroque**, **Classical** and **Romantic** music) ■ Rock and Pop ■ Musical Theatre ■ Jazz ■ Into the 20th Century ■ Into the 21st Century

Performing at AS Level

At AS Level, performing and composing are both worth 30% of the examination. You will be required to perform a minimum of two pieces for 6 to 8 minutes at Grade 5 standard. However, you DO have a choice as to whether you perform as a soloist or as a member of an ensemble, or a combination of both.

Performing at A Level

There are **two** options for Performing at A level:

■ **Option A** means that your performing is worth 35%, and composing worth 25%. You will be required to perform a minimum of **three** pieces, for 10 to 12 minutes, at Grade 6 standard. For this option, one piece **must be a solo**. You may perform the other pieces as a soloist or as a member of an ensemble.

■ With **option B**, 25% of your grade depends on your performing, and 35% on your composing. You will be required to perform a minimum of **two** pieces, for 6 to 8 minutes, at Grade 6 standard. In this option you may perform as a soloist or as a member of an ensemble, or a combination of both.

PERFORMING

How will my performing be assessed?

A visiting examiner will come to assess your performance. During your performance, they will be looking and listening for:

- Accurate **pitch** and **rhythm**
- Use of an appropriate **tempo**
- **Fluency** – whether you are able to maintain the appropriate tempo throughout your piece, without hesitations and without stopping
- Other performance directions followed, e.g. **dynamics**, phrasing, expression markings
- Technique
- Good **intonation**
- Tone quality and projection of sound
- Expression and interpretation
- Empathy with other performers (in ensembles)
- Communication with the audience (i.e. the examiner).

Technique

In addition to the general points listed above, the examiner will also be looking out for more specific techniques which are linked with your particular instrument or with singing, such as:

Voice:

- Diction
- **Articulation**
- Breath control and support
- Vocal techniques including **vibrato**
- Be aware of projection and communication, do not rely too heavily on your music.

Bowed Strings:

- Bow control
- LH/RH co-ordination
- Dexterity
- Playing techniques e.g. vibrato.

Plucked Strings:

- LH/RH co-ordination
- Dexterity
- Playing techniques e.g. use of pedals.

Woodwind:

- Breath control, phrasing, articulation
- Dexterity
- Playing techniques e.g. double tonguing.

Brass:

- Breath control, phrasing, articulation
- Lip flexibility
- Playing techniques e.g. double tonguing.

There are many elements which combine to make a good performance

Piano:

- RH/LH co-ordination
- Balance between musical parts and touch
- Dexterity
- Playing techniques e.g. pedalling.

Electronic Keyboard/Organ:

- Use of a variety of voices, tones, or stops
- RH/LH co-ordination
- Dexterity
- Pedalling
- Manual and pedal co-ordination (where appropriate).

Percussion:

- Stick or mallet dexterity
- Control over a variety of instruments
- Damper or pedal control
- Playing techniques e.g. damping.

Drum Kit:

- Stick dexterity
- Hands and feet co-ordination
- Control over **dynamics**
- Playing techniques e.g. single or double strokes, flams, drags and so on.
- Be particularly aware of the need for contrast in your pieces, and remember that you are not allowed to use click-tracks.

Choosing music for your performance

- Choose music which will best demonstrate your ability and skills as a performer
- Choose music which has some **contrast** within it. Drummers and guitarists should be very careful to choose music which contains some **dynamic** contrast
- Don't forget that one of your pieces must reflect the musical characteristics of one of the areas of study
- You may choose to perform **one** of your own compositions, but make sure that the piece you choose allows you to demonstrate your highest performing skills
- You may **improvise**, but if you choose to, you must perform an improvisation to a stimulus of your own choice, e.g. a chord sequence, or a scale; and a copy of the stimulus and a lead sheet must be provided for the examiner.

Think carefully about levels of difficulty for your pieces. Each piece is marked out of 36. If you perform a piece which is below the standard (the standard at AS level is **Grade 5** and at A Level, **Grade 6**) – the maximum marks you can achieve will be lowered.

At **AS level** the maximum marks are:

Grade 3 and below	31 / 36
Grade 4	32/36
Grade 5 and above	36/36

and at **A Level**:

Grade 4 and below	31 / 36
Grade 5	32/36
Grade 6 and above	36/36

There is an advantage in performing **one grade above** the required standard, e.g. playing Grade 6 pieces at AS or Grade 7 at A Level. A raw mark of 33/36 will actually achieve full marks, if your piece is above the required standard. However, **don't** be over-ambitious in your choice of music. There is nothing to be gained by performing music which is Grade 8 or Diploma standard. You should only perform pieces of this standard if you have complete control, under examination conditions, of your performance.

TIPS FROM A VISITING EXAMINER

I think that your main consideration when showcasing your talents to the examiner is to perform music that you are **comfortable** with and doesn't stress you out too much when performing under pressure.

Some students I have examined over the years have chosen to perform a series of very short pieces from the same musical period and compositional style. **Try to avoid this!** This doesn't really give you much opportunity to impress the examiner with ability to interpret a variety of musical styles and genres.

You may be tempted to include Grade examination pieces in your programme because you have already worked on them. If you are still happy and confident with these pieces then that's fine. **However, a note of caution!** I've witnessed so many performances of Grade examination pieces which lacked freshness, sparkle and musicality because the performer has simply grown weary of them.

Choosing what instrument to play

If you play an unusual or non-standard instrument – an instrument for which there is no graded music examination – your teacher should contact the exam board for advice well before the examination is due to take place.

You are not restricted to one instrument or voice but there is no advantage in performing on more than one instrument, so do not perform on a second instrument or sing unless the standard of your second instrument is as good as your first!

Solo or ensemble performances

You must perform a minimum of two pieces. Except in A Level option A, where one solo performance is compulsory, you can choose to perform as a soloist, as a member of an ensemble, or a combination of both.

Solo performance

A solo performance may be accompanied or unaccompanied but *not* conducted. The accompaniment can be live or on a backing track. When using a backing track, ensure that the balance between your instrument or voice and the backing track is correct, and agreeable to the examiner.

If you are using backing tracks, as well as balance it is also very important to familiarise yourself with tempo variations.

Ensemble performance

If you would like to perform as a member of an ensemble, give careful thought to your choice of music. Discuss this option with your teacher and instrumental or vocal tutor before you make your final choice of piece.

In an ensemble performance, you must perform a significant individual part. This **must not be doubled by any other performer.** The performance may be accompanied or unaccompanied but *not* conducted. The accompaniment can be live or on a backing track, but as with solo performances, when using a backing track, ensure that the balance between your instrument or voice and the backing track is correct and agreeable to the examiner.

An ensemble must consist of **two or more performers** (not including the accompanist). The maximum number of performers allowed is eight.

Having chosen your programme, you need to prepare to peak at the right time – just like athletes. Remember in your planning to take into account the other members of ensembles, and accompanists.

Playing in front of family and friends periodically is good practice for being psychologically prepared for the big day. It hardens the nerves and builds up 'bottle' in readiness for the visiting examiner.

One very successful centre I have visited invites tutors from other centres to listen to the students some two months before the exam. These tutors write a critique of the performances, as well as recording them. This means that when the big day arrives, the fear factor has gone, leaving only nervous energy – which in fact we all need when performing!

Practice

Once you've chosen your pieces it is important to do the right kind of practice. Simply playing your piece through from beginning to end repeatedly is not enough.

Highlight the awkward passages in a piece, spending time practising them. If the problems persist it could be:

- Breathing points if you are a vocalist
- Fingering on the piano or guitar
- Upper and lower octaves on woodwind or brass
- Hand positions or string crossing on a string instrument.

Once you are able to identify problematic passages, you can work out solutions. Remember that the most difficult passages will determine the overall tempo of your performance.

Try recording yourself or your ensemble at home without making any mistakes, then ask friends and teachers for constructive feedback.

Also make sure to acquaint yourself in advance with the examination venue, piano, microphones, amps and acoustics.

On the day

Normally, external examiners will visit centres during March or April. They will write a brief report of your performance, which will also be recorded.

A copy of the music for all pieces performed must be provided for the examiner. Where this is not possible, a detailed lead sheet must be provided. The part you are performing must be included on the lead sheet, so if you are singing, the vocal line (not simply the words) must be included; if you are playing the guitar, chord symbols or tab must be included; and if you are playing drums, drum notation must be included on the lead sheet. In addition, ensure that the copies of music or lead sheets provided for the examiner are fully accurate, with no bars cut-off and with repeats or cuts marked in.

The examiner will give you time for brief instrumental fine-tuning with the piano or other instruments in an ensemble.

How will I be assessed?

First of all, it is **vital** that your total performance lasts the appropriate length of time.

For **AS Level** and for **A Level Option B** this is **at least six minutes** and up to eight.

For **A Level Option A**, this is **at least ten minutes** and up to twelve.

If your performance falls short of these minimum times, you will receive **no marks**.

The following table explains how the examiner will mark your performance at both AS and A Level. Band 4 is the highest and Band 1 is the lowest. The use of the term 'assured' refers to a performance which is confident and convincing.

What are your examiners looking and listening for?

The assessment criteria for performing

Band	Accuracy	Band	Technical control	Band	Expression and interpretation
	Pitch and rhythm		**Technique**		**The performance is:**
4	Fully secure	4	Assured	4	Persuasive
3	Mostly secure	3	Appropriate	3	Competent
2	Sometimes inaccurate	2	Inconsistent	2	Inconsistent
1	Inaccurate throughout	1	Insecure	1	Limited and lacking in conviction
	An appropriate tempo		**Intonation**		**Communication**
4	Sustained throughout	4	Secure	4	Effective
3	Mostly maintained	3	Mostly secure	3	Mostly effective
2	Irregular at times	2	Inconsistent	2	Inconsistent
1	Frequent hesitations	1	Insecure	1	Limited
	Performance directions		**Tone quality and projection**		**Rapport with other performers (in ensemble performances only)**
4	Followed accurately throughout	4	Well developed	4	A high level of rapport is present
3	Mostly followed accurately	3	Developed	3	Rapport is present most of the time
2	Followed inconsistently	2	Inconsistent	2	Some sense of rapport
1	A limited response	1	Limited	1	Little or no rapport

A visiting examiner's guide to giving your best performance

Technical control

The examiner will expect to hear all notes played or sung correctly, including **melody**, **harmony**, chords and **rhythm**. **Intonation** with vocal and instrumental playing is so important. String instruments (including the harp and classical guitar) are often difficult to tune. The same applies for tuning woodwind and brass instruments.

Show the examiner that apart from musical excellence, your programme planning projects stylistic organisation and an appreciation of the music content and blending of periods. I always want the performer to communicate to me the power and vitality or pathos of the music.

Expression and performance visualisation

In terms of expression, musical theatre singers like to use **rubato** sparingly at times to convey feeling in their interpretation. The ability to connect and express the mood of the music is so important. Many singers lose marks due to lack of breath support from insufficient control of the diaphragm. Apart from good vocal technique and intonation, the examiner will look for performance visualisation using the eyes, the body and facial expression.

Interpretation

This is where the examiner wants to experience a truly musical performance. Try to find out if your piece was composed for a particular event – is it **programmatic**? You can amplify the inner feelings of the composer by playing with soul, excitement and style. You can go to YouTube to hear a broad range of performances with a variety of interpretations, tempi and **dynamics**. This can be beneficial, but ultimately you yourself must decide how to interpret your chosen composition and communicate it to the examiner. Musical theatre, pop and jazz singers in particular should avoid copying performances you have watched on the internet.

Articulation

The word **articulation** applies to most instrumental and vocal performances. This is probably one of the most frequently used words by examiners and music tutors. It refers to the ways in which notes are played in relation to each other, such as **staccato**, **legato**, **tenuto** and **accented**. I hear many **allegro** passages, especially in brass and woodwind, where the sound quality is weakened due to poor articulation technique. The examiner will be looking for clarity and crisp tone, particularly with flautists and trumpeters who choose to play Mozart and Haydn, for example.

Fluency

A confident performance is generally a fluent performance. However a hesitation or a stumble will probably be noted by the examiner as 'lacking in **fluency**'. So if you choose a J.S. Bach Prelude and Fugue for your piano programme you must be reasonably confident of fluency throughout. Similarly if you choose to play the Saint-Saëns composition *The Swan* on the cello you must aim for the fluency of the swan gliding gracefully along.

Dynamics

The examiner will be particularly interested in the way that you react to the composer's expressive markings. Some composers such as the **Impressionist** Debussy in his piece *Syrinx* have added many **dynamic** markings for the performer. However **Baroque** composers such as Vivaldi, Handel and Bach weren't so liberal in their dynamic markings. Ask your tutors to help you by adding dynamic markings to your copy (not forgetting the examiner's copy, of course). When a phrase is immediately repeated – as in Vivaldi's trumpet concerto – it might be a good idea to play the first phrase forte and the repeated phrase piano to obtain an echo effect. Don't be afraid to edit and add your own dynamics to pieces in this way.

Tempo

Don't worry about your **adagio** being too slow or your **allegro** too fast: these markings are often added by editors. Practising with a metronome is not recommended, the examiner will not be too hard on you if you are a little too fast or too slow. The main thing is to settle on a tempo with which you are comfortable and which is appropriate to the style of the music performed. Vocalists and woodwind and brass players have to judge the tempi carefully because of breath control. Similarly with the bowing patterns of string players: many performances run into difficulties when technically difficult passages occur because the opening tempo is too fast. The speed of the most difficult passages should be your overall tempo.

Technology

I assess an ever-increasing number of performances using backing tracks, mainly from the musical theatre, rock and pop repertoire. The standard of these tracks is excellent overall and can significantly enhance a performance. It is important that you structure your performance to match nuances on the track such as **rubato** and ritenuti. Try to have a sound and balance check using the equipment or speakers in the venue where the examination will be held: you may even need a microphone. It is imperative that the balance is sorted out well in advance with your teacher or a technician. The same rigour applies equally to drummers and guitarists. Have a spare amp, FX box and plenty of jack-leads on standby just in case.

Ensemble performing

Often the best ensembles are put together by peripatetic staff who are professional performers themselves. Don't leave ensemble choices until the week before the exam date, as a bolt-on to your solo performances. You should be performing proper ensemble music where possible, presenting worthwhile musical challenges which stretch, and allowing performers to empathise with each other: examiners will be on the look-out for manufactured ensembles where, for example, a drum kit and bass guitar have simply been added to a vocalist's piano part – it is harder to find the empathy and interaction looked for between a pop solo singer and guitar, drums and synths. If you are going to perform as part of an ensemble, tune up in the rehearsal area, and fine-tune when in the examination room.

To gain really good marks you have to do far more than just perform your own part well. You are working as a team, which means demonstrating your awareness of other members of the ensemble. This awareness is called empathy. You also need to show interaction and the ability to achieve a unified tone and harmonic balance within the group. Knowing that no conductor is permitted, you yourself must take responsibility, showing control and musical understanding. Communication and interplay between members is of great importance. The examiner will want to see evidence of this interaction in your performance.

Component 2

Composing
at AS and A Level

Whether you've already completed your first symphony or are just starting out, expressing yourself creatively through composition is an essential part of being a musician. After all, most of the world's greatest composers were also fine performers, so composing and performing have always gone together.

As with everything else, the more you put into creating your composition, the more you'll get out. Give composition a chance and it will form an enjoyable and exciting part of your studies. The task in hand is definitely achievable, and with a bit of time, thought and effort, there's no reason why you can't produce compositions of real quality for your portfolio.

So what's the deal? Your composition portfolio accounts for 30% at AS level. A Level is a little different. Depending on which option you choose, it will account for either 25% (Option A) or 35% (Option B). Whichever exam you're taking you will need to submit a portfolio of pieces by a specific date (normally this happens soon after Easter), so it's important to keep on top of things and not leave your composition tasks until the last minute. You must also hand in a composition log, detailing your process. Your work will then be assessed externally.

This chapter will explain the requirements for the composition component at AS and then at A Level. We will then share with you some top tips on sources of inspiration, the compositional 'process', getting started, and other details on how to go about obtaining the highest possible mark for your composition portfolio. As most of these tips relate to both AS and A level, we have included them together, but be sure to read the sections which specifically apply to your course too.

Here is a breakdown of how Component 2: Composition fits in to your course at AS and at A Level. At A Level, as you can see, you can choose to weight your assessment more heavily in favour of composing or performing, depending on where you consider your main strengths lie.

Composition options (all assessed externally)

	AS Level	A Level Option A	A Level Option B
Total duration	4½ to 7 minutes	4 to 6 minutes	8 to 10 minutes
% of whole examination	30%	25% (if you take this option your performance will be worth 35%)	35% (if you take this option your performance will be worth 25%)
Total number of marks for this component	72 marks (36+36)	72 marks (36+36)	108 marks (36+36+36)
No. of compositions	2 compositions	2 compositions	3 compositions
Type of composition	1. Western Classical Tradition; 2. Free Composition	1. Western Classical Tradition; 2. Free Composition	1. Western Classical Tradition; 2. Reflects a different area of study to WCT; 3. Free Composition
No. of links with areas of study	1. Must link with a brief set by WJEC; 2. Brief set by you	1. Must link with a brief set by WJEC; 2. Brief set by you	1. Must link with a brief set by WJEC; 2. & 3. Brief set by you
Areas of study	■ The Western Classical Tradition (which includes **Baroque**, **Classical** and **Romantic** music) ■ Rock and Pop ■ Musical Theatre ■ Jazz	■ The Western Classical Tradition (which includes **Baroque**, **Classical** and **Romantic** music) ■ Rock and Pop ■ Musical Theatre ■ Jazz ■ Into the 20th Century ■ Into the 21st Century	■ The Western Classical Tradition (which includes **Baroque**, **Classical** and **Romantic** music) ■ Rock and Pop ■ Musical Theatre ■ Jazz ■ Into the 20th Century ■ Into the 21st Century

Composing at AS Level

At AS Level, performing and composing are both worth 30% of the qualification, so for every hour you practise towards your performance, you should – in theory – be spending the same amount of time composing! You will need to compose **two** pieces which add up to between 4½ and 7 minutes, with the first piece reflecting the Western Classical Tradition and the second piece being in a style of your own choosing.

You could, of course, submit one piece of around 1½ and another around 4½ minutes but generally this is inadvisable because the examiner will be looking for things such as development of musical ideas, sufficient thematic transformation, formal balance, and so on.

Ask yourself the questions: is there sufficient development of ideas in my piece? Does it contain a thoroughly worked-out musical structure? If the answer is 'no' then you need to develop your composition further. For a piece of around 1½ minutes to tick all the right boxes it would need to be something like Chopin's 'Minute Waltz'!

Remember: the guidelines are very strict on portfolios that fall under the minimum length, with marks being deducted incrementally for submissions which are under-length. Do consult the assessment criteria on a regular basis and try to put yourself in the examiners' shoes.

Composing at A Level

There are **two** options for Composing at A level:

- **Option A** means that your portfolio will be worth 25%, and performing worth 35%. As with AS level, you will be required to compose **two** pieces totalling 4–6 minutes, with the first piece reflecting the Western Classical Tradition and the second piece being in a style of your own choosing. You may have noticed that the overall duration for Option A is *less* than for AS, but don't be fooled into thinking that this means *less work*. Remember that the bar is raised at A level so expectations are higher. Maybe the quantity of work will be a touch lower but the quality will need to be higher.

- If you choose **Option B**, 35% of your grade depends on your portfolio, and 25% on your performance. Here, you will be required to submit three pieces totalling 8–10 minutes. Again, the first piece needs to reflect the Western Classical Tradition while the third piece can be in a style of your choice. The second piece should 'reflect the musical characteristics of a different area of study', so you could, for example, select from any number of twentieth century styles, including Impressionism, Neo-Classicism, serialism, nationalism or minimalism. More about this later.

I'm sure you're now eager to get cracking on your first composition but first of all I strongly advise that you read the following section carefully, which tells you how your compositions will be marked.

How will my composition portfolio be assessed?

Your portfolios will be assessed externally by an examiner.

The examiner will assess your compositions using specific assessment criteria. For AS, the criteria are set out in Appendix B (pp. 26–27) of the specification. For A level, they are included in Appendix B (pp. 35–36) of the specification.

Start composing early, don't leave it all to the last minute

> The specifications for your Music AS/A Level can be found on the Eduqas website at www.eduqas.co.uk/qualifications/music/as-a-level/ Don't leave it up to your teacher to explain what you have to do – go and read up for yourself so that you're completely clear.

First, note that your main aim should be to 'create and develop musical ideas with technical and expressive control and coherence.' In other words, your composition should contain:

1. A strong, distinctive musical idea
2. This idea will then be used (or developed) in different ways throughout the piece
3. Your piece should demonstrate a clear understanding of a specific style and technique
4. It should also demonstrate 'expressive control'
5. All elements should be shaped to create a piece that makes musical sense.

We'll come back to these five elements later.

Secondly, note that your compositions will be marked according to the following three categories:

1. Creating musical ideas
2. Developing musical ideas
3. Technical and expressive control of musical elements

Your aim should be to gain marks in the top two bands (i.e. 3 and 4).

For reference, here's a quick guide to the top band criteria at AS:

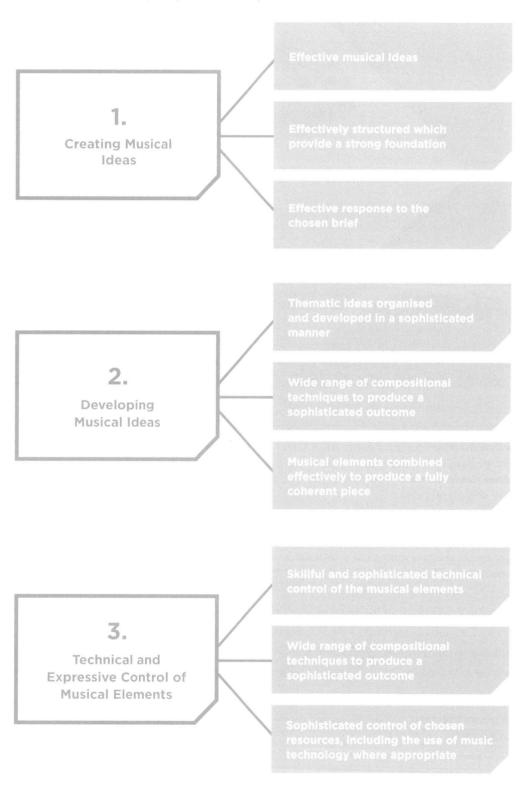

1.
Creating Musical Ideas

Effective musical ideas

Effectively structured which provide a strong foundation

Effective response to the chosen brief

2.
Developing Musical Ideas

Thematic ideas organised and developed in a sophisticated manner

Wide range of compositional techniques to produce a sophisticated outcome

Musical elements combined effectively to produce a fully coherent piece

3.
Technical and Expressive Control of Musical Elements

Skilful and sophisticated technical control of the musical elements

Wide range of compositional techniques to produce a sophisticated outcome

Sophisticated control of chosen resources, including the use of music technology where appropriate

The following is a quick guide to the top box criteria at A level:

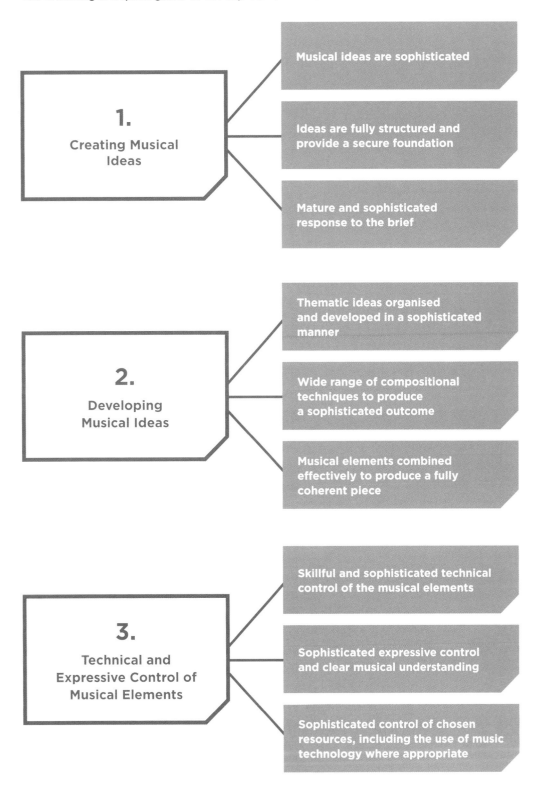

1.
Creating Musical Ideas

- Musical ideas are sophisticated
- Ideas are fully structured and provide a secure foundation
- Mature and sophisticated response to the brief

2.
Developing Musical Ideas

- Thematic ideas organised and developed in a sophisticated manner
- Wide range of compositional techniques to produce a sophisticated outcome
- Musical elements combined effectively to produce a fully coherent piece

3.
Technical and Expressive Control of Musical Elements

- Skillful and sophisticated technical control of the musical elements
- Sophisticated expressive control and clear musical understanding
- Sophisticated control of chosen resources, including the use of music technology where appropriate

For AS level, the key word is **effective**. When working on your composition, keep asking the following questions:

- Are my musical ideas **effective**?
- Are they developed in an **effective** way?
- Is my use of technique **convincing** and musical expression communicated **convincingly**?

For A level, the keyword is **sophisticated**. It's difficult to know exactly what *musical sophistication* means, but we can be fairly certain that the examiner will looking for evidence of more **musical substance, depth** and **complexity** than at AS level.

When working on your composition, keep asking the following questions:

- Are my musical ideas **sophisticated** enough?
- Are they developed **sophisticatedly**?
- Am I using technique at an advanced level and communicating the musical expression in a **sophisticated** and **nuanced** manner?

Composing to a brief

Whether you're working on a piece which reflects the Western Classical Tradition (WCT) or a composition in your own style, you will need to work with a clear brief in mind.

Working with a brief is all part of a professional composer's life. For your WCT composition you will be given a choice of briefs.

Perhaps your brief will be to write for a mixed choir, such as in number 1 in the following table

The following table provides examples of briefs followed by some tips and suggestions:

Brief	Tips
1. Set the following words to music for a Christmas concert: "Gloria in excelsis deo..." You may wish to add additional words to the specified text.	■ Choose your forces (unaccompanied SATB choir, SATB & organ, TTBB & piano...) ■ Choose your style (**Renaissance**, **Baroque**, **Classical**, **Romantic**...) ■ Choose your composer for inspiration (Palestrina, Vivaldi, Mozart, Brahms...) Choose your form – use the text as your guide, e.g. 'Glória in excélsis Deo et in terra pax homínibus bonæ voluntátis. Laudámus te, benedícimus te, adorámus te, glorificámus te...'
2. Compose an instrumental piece demonstrating aspects of imitation for a chamber concert. You may compose for a solo instrument, with or without accompaniment, or for a small ensemble.	■ Choose your forces (Harpsichord, Flute & Harp, String Quartet...) ■ Choose your style (Baroque, Classical, Romantic...) ■ Choose your form (**Fugue**, **Minuet and Trio**, **Sonata Form**...) ■ Analyse the use of imitation in specific compositions ■ Try to understand how imitation is used, then have a go at creating similar **textures**.
3. Compose a piece in **rondo** form for a local classical radio station. You may compose for any appropriate combination of instruments or voices.	Turn to the example on page 28, under 'Structure and the Western Classical Tradition'.
4. Compose incidental music for a 19th century play in a local theatre. This is an instrumental composition for inclusion in a play, and not a vocal piece for a musical or opera. The director has asked for 2-3 minutes of music before Act 1 'to set the scene' and has asked you to listen to Grieg's *Julens Vuggesang* ('Yuletide Cradle-Song').	■ Decide on the play for which you are writing (e.g. Henrik Ibsen's *A Doll's House*) ■ Find out about the play – its background and plot. You would want to create an atmosphere that suggests 'innocence' on the surface but something more disquieting underneath... ■ You should **not** make an arrangement of Grieg's song, or use his **melody** in any way – and remember that this is an instrumental piece! ■ Play through the chords in Grieg's song and experiment with similar chords.

Getting started on your composition

This section outlines a number of ideas that are applicable to composition at both AS and A level.

The table below provides a snapshot of the kind of creative process your composition should aim to follow. Your starting point should be a strong, 'ear-catching' musical idea which you then seek to develop in an **effective** or **sophisticated** way throughout the piece. Alongside the development of musical ideas, your piece should also try to bring into play a number of technical and expressive elements. These should work *together* to ensure a satisfying and convincing finished composition:

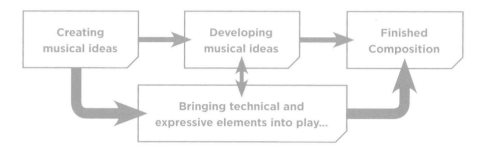

Easier said than done, perhaps? Let's start by applying some of these requirements to specific examples.

Finding the musical idea

Your piece will need a strong musical idea (or set of musical ideas) – strong enough to sustain a composition lasting around three minutes. Examiners will be searching for distinctive, memorable and imaginative ideas. These can be **melodic** (a vivid, memorable theme), **harmonic** (a sophisticated series of chords), **rhythmic** (funky, syncopated patterns on percussion, for example), **textural** (colourful combinations of instruments and sounds) or any combination of these elements.

Remember that your first musical idea may not be your best. Always write down (or record) your ideas and get into the habit of keeping sketches of your work. The more ideas you have in front of you, the more you will be able to select from. Many famous composers have used sketchbooks to notate their ideas, and often only reach the 'final' version after trying out dozens of different versions beforehand.

Sit down with a keyboard, piano, guitar or whatever instrument you prefer, and just play around with melodic, harmonic and rhythmic ideas until you strike upon something that you think has **potential for development**. Your starting point can be a piece of music that you admire, or something non-musical, such as an image, a picture, a photograph or scene from a film, or the lyrics to a pop song.

In fact, **images** can often be really helpful. Throughout the ages composers have been inspired by them. Haydn's String Quartet Op. 76, No. 4 was nicknamed 'Sunrise' due to the fact that the rising theme right at the beginning of the piece evokes the sun rising. Whether Haydn was actually inspired by a specific sunrise is beside the point: the idea got him started on the piece and laid the foundations for the rest of the **movement**.

More abstract ideas can also provide inspiration for your free composition. Take the image on the facing page, for example:

You could use this image of a mountain in a variety of different ways. You could use the overall outline of the mountain as a basis for your piece, as shown in the table, which reflects the image from left to right.

In this scenario the piece is planned for orchestra:

Form	A	B	C	B'	A'
Length	0–0.20	0.20–1.00	1.00–2.00	2.00–2.30	2.30–3.00
Notes	Introduction – quiet opening, with shimmering chords in woodwinds, celesta and harp	Main melody introduced, gradually, first quite low in trombones then higher in trumpets, reflecting the rocky landscape – NB. Keep the 'complete' version of the theme until the next section!	The music rises higher and higher before reaching a plateau – full, loud chords are now heard and the theme is played in its full version	Gradually the music fades back and the theme becomes more fragmentary; the orchestration becomes thinner – maybe this time with snippets of the theme heard in horns and bassoons	The coda reflects the opening shimmering chords of the intro, but now they're lower and heard instead in the violas, cellos and double basses

An overall plan of your piece at an early stage can help you to think about the following:

- How to divide the musical material between different instruments so everyone gets a shout
- How to pace and introduce your ideas – your main musical idea need not appear in bar 1, or even bar 6, but it should definitely be by around twenty or thirty seconds into the piece.

Composition is a little bit like a jigsaw. All the pieces need to be constructed first before putting them together to create the final shape. However, it's important you have a clear idea what the final shape is going to be from the beginning!

Going back to the image of the mountain, you can also use it as the basic shape for your main **melody**. Place the image on a music stand and look at the outline of the mountain, then start to **improvise** a melody. Does it sound a little bit like the following tune?

Play this theme on a piano or any other instrument. Can you see how the melodic line reflects the mountain's shape? Can you create something similar? Have a look on the internet for similar images of the natural world as sources of inspiration.

Developing the musical idea

Of course, there's no use creating a great musical idea if all you're planning on doing is repeating it over and over with little or no variation. What you do with the idea is just as important as the idea itself. Take Beethoven's famous four-note theme from the opening of his Fifth Symphony. The theme itself is striking, powerful and highly memorable, of course, but what Beethoven does with it is *just* as important. Look at the score. Already in the opening twenty bars he shifts the theme up and down the orchestra, dividing it between various instruments in a kind of 'call and response' pattern. He moves it around, combines it with different chords and chord patterns. He uses it to take the music through a series of different chords and keys. All this creates drama, tension and excitement. Beethoven's ability to **develop** the opening theme is what creates this excitement.

Musical ideas should only act as starting points. Again, try to develop them by sketching out different versions. Play your ideas in different keys. See how they might work when slowed down or sped up. What about register? How will the idea sound on a low instrument such as a double bass? What if you then introduce it later on flute or piccolo?

Structure and the Western Classical Tradition

Armed with a main theme and a clear idea of the piece's overall structure, as shown above, you're now in a strong position to flesh out the composition. If you're writing for orchestra, it is simplest to start in short score (i.e. treble line for the melodic material and treble and bass for the accompaniment). You can always write in which instruments should be playing on the short score. Only when the piece is finished should you start to orchestrate it fully.

While a 'free' composition allows you the freedom to compose to a brief set by yourself, it is perhaps more difficult to think up ideas when your composition reflects the Western Classical Tradition (WCT). Here is a ten-week planner which should get your WCT piece finished in plenty of time.

Weekly planner for a composition in the Western Classical Tradition

It is important not to leave your composition to the last minute before the deadline: too many students hand in work which is insufficiently developed and polished because they have begun their composing a week before the deadline. Here, therefore, is a structure for planning your time week by week, working with an example composition template of a **rondo** by Haydn:

Week	Aims and Objectives
Week 1	Complete the template exercise on Haydn's 'Rondo' (see below) and try to listen to other rondo **movements**, along with a score if possible. Try to analyse what's going on in the music's overall structure and the way in which the **tonality** is organised.
Week 2	Expand your knowledge of other forms (such as **Sonata Form** and **Theme and Variations**) by listening to a range of compositions which use these forms, again with a score. Make more notes. Use weeks 1 and 2 to brush up on chords, **cadences**, keys and their relationships.
Week 3	From the listening completed in weeks 1 and 2, choose a piece that you think will work as a template for your own WCT piece. Set it out in very much the same way as for the Haydn 'Rondo' you completed in week 1. Start with a basic structural 'skeleton'.
Week 4	Now gradually fill the template with more information, observing the tonal plan of the piece, melodic development, different types of **texture**, and so on. You will now need to get more familiar with the WCT style you've decided to adopt (**Baroque**, **Classical** or **Romantic**).
Week 5	You're halfway through so it's time to get cracking. Spend this week on the main theme and try to complete the opening 16 bars or so of your piece.
Week 6	Now work on the next section – from bars 16–32. Always consult your template, taking care to follow key **modulations**, tonal organisation and so on. Your template will get you from A to B, so use it.
Week 7	You should by now have arrived at the 'middle' part of your composition, so aim to complete maybe the first half of this section, from bars 32–48.
Week 8	Now aim to complete the second half of the middle section: say bars 48–64. Keep consulting the template!
Week 9	If you are using **ternary** or Sonata Form, there's a good chance that you will now have reached the return (or **recapitulation**) of the 'A' section, so push ahead and try to complete the first 16 bars of the final section: bars 64–80.
Week 10	You're almost there! Complete the last sixteen or so bars, which will take you to around bar 96. Check through your final version, making any tweaks and edits as necessary. Play it through or play it back on Sibelius, to make sure it sounds as effective as possible.

> You can use this planner in your composition log. Turn to page 34 for tips on completing your log.

In order for this planner to work you will need to become familiar with TWO important aspects of the Western Classical Tradition: 1) Structure and 2) Style.

Let's start with structure. First of all, as described above, you will need to create a template, i.e. a grid, that will 'abstract' a lot of information from a given composition. Below is a specific example. Following brief 3) from the table on page 25, our WCT composition will be in the **Classical** style, using rondo form. Our template will be a rondo **movement** by Haydn from his Piano Sonata in D major, Op. 50. First, you should play it on the piano or listen to a recording of it, following the score at the same time.

The opening 8 bars of Haydn's Rondo are as follows:

The template for the opening phrase extracts the main melodic and harmonic information. We hear the main theme in the right hand while the left hand provides light accompaniment. The opening theme rises by an octave from its opening notes to the last note of the phrase, and during this time modulates from the **tonic** key of D major to the **dominant** key of A major:

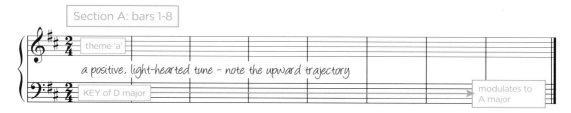

The second half of the opening section followed by the beginning of the 'B' section is as shown (remember that the Rondo form alternates A sections with B, C and so on, creating an ABACADA form):

As with the first eight bars, keep filling in the template with basic information about the music's tonal plan, **modulation**, melodic development, and so on. Your template should look something like this:

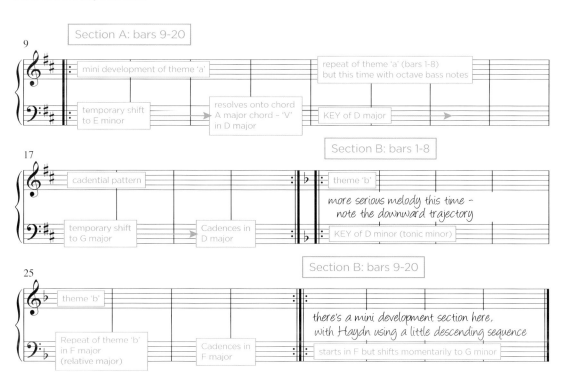

Now try completing the entire Rondo, using the opening 32 bars as your guide.

Armed with the information contained in your template, you are now in a strong position to compose a WCT piece that, at the very least, will obey the formal and harmonic principles of a rondo form in **Classical** music. Of course, you needn't slavishly follow Haydn's ground plan. Why not change one or two of the **modulations** and key centres? (For example, your Section B could be in B minor rather than D minor.)

If you are following the ten-week planner, you should now have arrived at week 5.

Style and the Western Classical Tradition

The structure of your composition is now in place, but what about style?

Style is a more difficult element to grasp, especially if you're not massively familiar with the WCT style you're adopting. The point about any WCT style is that it's a *language*, and, like any language, the more you speak it the easier it becomes. So, if you've decided on the Classical style, play as many pieces of Classical music as you can, and listen to as many pieces as possible, with a musical score to hand if you have it. Only by becoming familiar with the language of Classical music will composing using this style become easier. Remember: the more you put in, the more you'll get out.

Analysis of the style in question can help. We've already done a little bit of this in setting out the Rondo template, but let's look in more detail at how Classical music works.

Here's the opening ten bars of a Sonatina by composer Anton Diabelli (1781–1858), who is perhaps best-known today for the famous theme and set of thirty-three **variations** that Beethoven wrote, based on one of Diabelli's waltzes. An extension of this extract is available to download from the Rhinegold Education website, go to www.rhinegoldeducation.co.uk/product/wjec-as-and-a-level-music-study-guide/ and choose the 'Extras' tab.

First of all, let's look at the theme. Diabelli presents the theme in bars 1–2. It comprises two ideas: two repeated notes (G-G) followed by a little 'turn' figure (A-G-F#-G) in bar 1, then a minim which resolves down by step (B to A) in bar 2.

Note the way in which Diabelli repeats and varies this opening idea in the first nine bars. Bars 3–4 repeat the theme, this time with the bar 1 figure shifted down a step (starting on F♯ rather than G) and the bar 2 idea is changed into a **rhythmic** figure on a G major **triad** (G-B-D). Diabelli repeats the opening theme in exactly the same way in bars 5–6 (it's just an octave higher) and then again in bar 7 uses the bar 1 figure to end on D.

Alongside the different variations and repetitions of this theme, Diabelli also takes the music away from the **tonic** of G major to the **dominant** key of D major. Both the theme and chords therefore work in tandem: they serve to obey the overall tonal plan and direction of the music.

Let's now look at what happens harmonically in the opening, underneath the theme and its variations.

Can you work out the **harmony** for bars 1–4? It's a fairly standard sequence in a lot of **Classical** music, and one that you can certainly use. It goes: G-A minor-D7-G, or I-ii-V7-I.

Diabelli wants to establish the tonic key of G major here, so his opening gambit is to stick to a tried and tested pattern that will do this. He then uses the repetition of the theme in bars 5–6 to create a **modulation** to D major via 'chord ii' again, but this time with the sharpened third (C♯) in the bass. Rather than a chord of A minor, as heard in bar 2, we now have a chord of A major, which is also the dominant (chord V) of D major – this is where Diabelli wants the music to head towards at this point. At bar 8, the modulation to D major is secure, so Diabelli now plays out another **cadence** to secure the new key. The **melody** in the right hand in bars 8–10 is now in straight crotchets and outlines I (D major) and V7 (A major) under a tonic 'D' pedal.

What other aspects can we pick up from this opening? Diabelli makes use of another common idea: the **Alberti Bass** figure in the left hand, where a chord is 'broken up' and spread out across the entire bar. There are countless examples of Alberti Bass-type figures in Classical music. See if you can find other examples by trawling through Mozart's piano sonatas.

Here is the opening ten bars of my own take on Diabelli's sonatina:

Note that my own theme is different to Diabelli's but is used in a similar way: it's a two-bar theme, repeated with slight variation in bars 3–4 then repeated exactly in bars 5–6. The **modulation**, this time from **tonic** G major to **dominant** D major, occurs at bar 8, via a similar C-to-C♯ shift that Diabelli used. The opening chord sequence is similar, also using I-ii-V-I (but with a mini I-V-I added in bar 2). Like Diabelli, the melodic figure in bars 8–10 is there to establish the new key of D. A complete **pastiche** version of the Diabelli sonatina can be found online at the Rhinegold Education website. Go to www.rhinegoldeducation.co.uk/product/wjec-as-and-a-level-music-study-guide/ and choose the 'Extras' tab. Can you produce something similar?

A Level: advice for candidates thinking about Option B

If you are thinking about taking Option B, you will need to compose three pieces. The first should reflect the WCT style, as discussed above.

The second should 'reflect the musical characteristics of a different area of study' so my advice is that you choose a twentieth-century style for this piece, and then compose a final piece in your own style. For more advice on composing in a twentieth-century style, we recommend a book co-written by the author of this chapter, Pwyll ap Sion, with Iwan Llewelyn-Jones: *Composing Contemporary Music: A Student's Guide* (CAA, Aberystwyth, 2011), which gives advice on how to compose in a number of different styles (such as **Impressionism**, minimalism, rock and pop, and film music).

Completing your composition log

Along with your compositions, you must hand in composition logs. The logs are meant to show the compositional process you have taken for each piece you compose. Keep them specific to the piece in question, and make sure you fill them in as you go along, rather than trying to remember everything you did at the last minute before you hand in your portfolio.

You need not write a complete essay for every log entry, but at the same time you should aim to write more than just a sentence or two.

Here are some suggestions:

Log entry 1	■ Briefly describe your sources of inspiration, such as:
	  ■ a specific composer and piece of music
	  ■ an image
	  ■ a set of words
	■ Your initial musical idea – how did this idea come about? Did you sketch or record a lot of different versions?
	■ Planning – provide a plan of the piece; did you develop the structure?

Log entry 2	Here you might explain **how** you have developed the musical ideas in your piece, concentrating especially on the middle part.
Log entry 3	Finishing off – here you could talk about the **final** section of the piece and reflect on how the composition fits in with what you had in mind when you started planning it.

Component 3

Introduction

Component 3 is the written exam. At both AS and A Level it is worth 40% of your whole mark.

At AS Level, the exam will last 1 hour and 30 minutes (not including any extra time you might be entitled to) and is divided into two parts:

1. **Area of Study A: The Western Classical Tradition** – this is a compulsory area of study and focuses on the development of the symphony from 1750-1830. You will choose **one** set work from a choice of two for detailed analysis.

2. **Area of Study B, C or D** – You will choose only **one** of these areas of study, they are Rock & Pop, Musical Theatre and Jazz.

At A Level the exam will last 2 hours and 15 minutes (not including any extra time you might be entitled to) and is divided into three parts:

1. **Area of Study A: The Western Classical Tradition** – this is a compulsory area of study and focuses on the development of the symphony from 1750-1900. You will choose one set work for detailed analysis, and one for general study.

2. **Area of Study B, C or D** – You will choose only **one** of these areas of study, they are Rock & Pop, Musical Theatre and Jazz.

3. **Area of Study E or F** – You will choose only **one** of these areas of study, they are based on periods of musical history: Into the Twentieth Century, and Into the Twenty-first Century. Each area of study includes **two** set works.

So you **must** read and study the first chapter of this section, and further sections will depend on your and your teacher's choices.

Do not forget that detailed notes on set works can be found on the Eduqas website: Go to www.eduqas.co.uk/qualifications/music/as-a-level/ and choose 'Digital Resources' to find them.

In terms of listening practice, where possible links to works referenced have been given for recordings on YouTube. If not possible, advice has been given on where to find recordings. This is not a history exam, it's about listening to and analysing music, so you must listen to as much as possible.

At the end of each chapter there are practice questions which you are strongly advised to complete in preparation for the exam. You will find the answers from page 284.

Remember also that green words are those which you can find definitions for in the glossary from page 302.

The Western Classical Tradition

THE DEVELOPMENT OF THE SYMPHONY

This is a compulsory area of study which accounts for 40% of the Component 3 written exam at both AS and A Level. For this part of the course you will study the development of the symphony, both generally and through close analysis of set works.

What is the Western Classical tradition?

This tradition is generally understood to encompass the music of the Baroque, Classical and Romantic eras – and in a broader context, even perhaps beyond, from the Medieval era to the 2000s.

For the purpose of this examination, you are expected to know and understand the musical conventions and language of the time associated with the development of the symphony, throughout the Classical and early Romantic era for AS Level, and throughout both the Classical and Romantic eras for A Level.

Course Requirements

AS Level	A Level
Component 3: worth 40% of the full 88 marks for the written exam	**Component 3:** worth 40% of the full 100 marks for the written exam
Listening and Appraising exam Approx. 1 hour, 30 minutes	**Listening and Appraising exam** Approx. 2 hours, 15 minutes
Set work knowledge: Two movements of the symphony which has been selected for detailed study by your college or school.	**Set work knowledge:** Detailed study of four movements of the symphony selected for study by your college or school, plus a general knowledge of the second symphony.
General knowledge: The development of the symphony through the Classical era to the early Romantic era (1750-1830).	**General knowledge:** The development of the symphony through the Classical and Romantic eras (1750-1900).

Set works

Your teacher will choose which of these two set works you will focus on most, but for A Level you must have some knowledge of both of them:

Symphony No. 104 in D major, '*London*' by Haydn: **movements** 1 and 2 for AS, all four movements (i.e. the entire symphony) for A Level

OR

Symphony No. 4 in A major, '*Italian*' by Mendelssohn: movements 1 and 2 for AS, all four movements (i.e. the entire symphony) for A Level

This chapter will focus on the development of the symphony, with some hints and tips for study, including some example questions for your consideration.

What will the questions be like?

In the **AS Level** exam, there will be **four** questions in this section:

- An aural perception question, based on an unprepared extract of a symphony, with reference to a score. This will test your theoretical musical understanding of the elements.
- An aural perception question on an unprepared extract of a symphony with a skeleton score. This will include musical dictation, and associated questions e.g., on keys, chords, **cadences** and musical devices.
- A comparison question of two (unprepared) symphonic extracts. This will test your overall musical understanding of the periods set for study i.e. the development of the symphony.
- An analysis question on the set work which has been selected for study by your centre (i.e. either the Haydn or the Mendelssohn).

In the **A Level** exam, there will be **three** questions in this section:

- An aural perception question on an unprepared extract of a symphony with a skeleton score. This will include musical dictation, and associated questions e.g., on keys, chords, cadences, and location of errors.
- A detailed analysis question on the set work which has been selected for study by your centre (i.e. either the Haydn or the Mendelssohn).
- An essay-based question which assesses the knowledge of the development of the symphony 1750-1900, in relation to **both** set symphonies, to other relevant works and to the wider social, cultural and historical context.

At both AS and A level, you will be allowed to take clean, unannotated copies of your chosen set work into the exam with you.

What exactly do I need to focus on?

- An understanding of the musical characteristics of the Western Classical tradition and how musical elements were used
- An understanding of how the symphonic genre and the orchestra developed, through examples from different composers from the **Classical** and **Romantic** periods (1750-1830 for AS, 1750-1900 for A level)
- An in-depth knowledge of the chosen set work (and for A level, a general understanding of the second set work).

So, let's start by considering what you need to know in terms of understanding the musical language of the Western Classical tradition. Your teacher will introduce and explain the music theory concepts related to this during the course of your study. Some of them (such as key signatures, **cadences**, or recognition of musical devices and **textures**) you may well already know and understand. What you will be required to do is recognise how composers have used these elements in the set works (and other symphonies during the Classical and Romantic eras) – and be able to recognise such elements and devices when listening to the music.

The musical elements – what you need to know...

Structure	In the Classical era, the emphasis was on proportion and balance. **Sonata form** became the most important structure, used to organise the music within **movements** (particularly first-movements) and in single pieces such as instrumental **overtures**. Romantic music enjoyed further exploration and freedom, with some symphony movements being particularly lengthy and written in a modified and extended structure. Such works sometimes relied on such devices as **motto themes**, recurring themes, and *idée fixe*. Closer links with the arts resulted in music which relied on an accompanying program to explain the content.
	AS: sonata form; slow movement forms; **minuet and trio**; **scherzo**
	Additionally at A level: **sonata rondo**, variation forms, **cyclic forms**, **programmatic** forms
Tonality	In the Classical era, the major tonalities were more widely used, and the minor keys used for contrast; one important change was the shift towards keys in the **subdominant** direction (i.e. centering around 'flatwards' keys). Romantic harmonies were more adventurous and **chromatic**, looking back in some ways to the work of J.S.Bach, but also pushing **tonality** to its limits with increasingly **dissonant** content.
	AS and A level: related keys and their function within the structure
Texture	In the Classical era, the **textures** became lighter and generally less complex, with much emphasis on **melody**-dominated **homophony**. Romantic music was often presented in textures which were more dense in terms of the orchestral resources, exploring the wider range of timbres and tone-colours.
	AS: **monophony**, **homophony**, **polyphony**, imitation, **counterpoint** and more complex combinations of musical lines
	Additionally at A level: **fugue**

Melody / thematic development	In the **Classical** era, melodies tended to be shorter and simpler, with more balanced phrases (punctuated by **cadences**). **Romantic** themes were extremely lyrical and song-like.
	AS and A level: phrase structure, devices such as sequence, figuration, ornamentation, **augmentation** and diminution of thematic material, expansion/fragmentation of the theme, how themes are combined, **transposition** of themes, re-harmonisation and re-**orchestration** of themes, and so on.
Sonority	**AS and A level:** variety and contrasts of tone-colours, timbres, techniques
Harmony	In the Classical era, the **harmony** is more clearly defined, i.e. functional harmony. Keys are used to delineate sections in a composition, but are also an important element used to add colour and suggest emotion in the music. Romantic music used more complex chords, the harmonic function of which was sometimes ambiguous, and not so reliant on cadential definition.
	AS: typical progressions, **cadences**, chord inversions, **dominant** secondary/**diminished 7ths**, **cycle of fifths**, **chromaticism**, **modulation** and tonicisation
	Additionally at A level: Neapolitan chords, augmented 6th chords
Tempo/rhythm	Classical music employs a great deal of **rhythmic** figuration and repetition; the music of the Romantic era implied greater interpretive freedom with the use of **rubato** and changing time signatures.
	AS and A level: use of **accents**, simple and compound times, rhythmic devices such as dotted rhythms, **syncopation**, **hemiola**, divisions of the beat such as triplets, and so on.
Dynamics	**AS and A level:** all expressive directions and terminology become relevant, as a much greater range of expression is evident in the Classical and Romantic periods.
Instrumentation	In the Classical era, the orchestra increased in size and range of instruments as new developments were taking place. Eventually the harpsichord **continuo** fell out of use, and the woodwind section assumed greater importance in the orchestra. The Romantic orchestra expanded to mighty proportions in some cases, and continued developments in instrument-making enabled more flexibility, particularly with the brass instruments, which often dominated the **texture**. This was the era of the **virtuoso** performer.
Mood	There was more contrast found within Classical and Romantic works. Increasingly, composers were also known for incorporating nationalistic influences in their music.

An introduction to some classical structures

Remember that all of these were subject to modifications when used by composers.

Binary Form

This structure is in two sections – section A and section B, both of which are repeated:

Section A :‖	Section B :‖

In some pieces, these sections were equal in length.
In others, B was extended

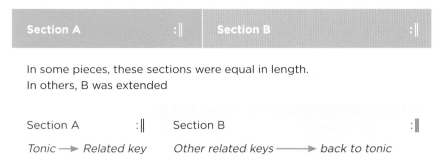

Section A :‖   Section B :‖

Tonic → *Related key*   *Other related keys* → *back to tonic*

Ternary Form

This structure is in three sections – section A, section B, then section A again (ABA). Section B may present contrasted (or slightly developed) material, section A may be altered on its return (if so, labelled A1).

Section A	Section B	Section A(1)
Tonic/main theme	*Related keys/ contrasting material*	*Tonic/main theme (maybe with changes)*

A **ternary** piece may also have an introduction and /or a coda.

Note: If the second A section is exactly the same as the first, the composer sometimes did not write the music out again. Instead, the instruction *da capo* would be found at the end of section B – this simply means 'repeat from the beginning'. The performers would then repeat section A, and at the end of the section the word *fine* would be found, which indicated the 'end' of the piece. This was known as **da capo form**. (Many operatic arias written between 1650-1750 were organised in this way).

Rondo Form

This is a structure with a recurring section A, separated by contrasting sections called 'episodes' (ABACA).

Section A	Section B	Section A	Section C	Section A
Tonic/ main theme	*Episode 1/ contrast*	*Tonic/ main theme*	*Episode 2/ contrast*	*Tonic/ main theme*

Sonata Form

Even some of the compositions of the **Baroque** era showed signs of what was eventually to become recognised and accepted as **sonata form**: for example, some of Bach's **movements** in binary form move to the **dominant** or relative major at the end of the first section, with the second section sometimes much longer than the first and modulatory. There can be little doubt than sonata form had gradually emerged from the binary form of the Baroque.

The general plan of sonata form (often to be found in first movements of sonatas, concertos, chamber music, some one-movement **overtures** and of course symphonies) is:

Sonata form – basic outline plan								
Exposition			**Development**		**Recapitulation**			
The **Exposition** **exposes** and presents the main thematic material.			The **Development** **develops** and explores the thematic material. New material may also be introduced.		The **Recapitulation** **recapitulates** and 'reminds' us of the original thematic material.			
First Subject S1	Transition passage (Bridge passage)	Second Subject S2	Exploring new keys while manipulating the thematic material (Usually ends with dominant preparation of the home key, ready for the return of I in the Recapitulation section)		**First Subject S1**	Transition passage (Bridge) now altered to stay in **Home key**	Second Subject S2	
Home Key (Tonic Key)	Changing key	Related key			**Home Key** (Tonic Key)		Now in the **Home Key**	

A (slow) INTRODUCTION at the beginning, or a CODA at the end is
often added to this structure

There are many cases where this form is adapted slightly, in which case it becomes referred to as 'modified sonata form'. (This may involve something like the composer omitting the development section, and just including a link between the exposition and the recapitulation). Sonata form is sometimes referred to as 'first-movement' form as it is widely used to organise the material in the opening movements of symphonies, concertos, sonatas and string quartets.

Sonata-rondo form

Sonata Rondo form is really what it says – a combination of sonata and the older rondo form.

Sonata-rondo form: basic outline plan		
Exposition	**Central section**	**Recapitulation**
The **Exposition exposes** and presents the main thematic material.	The central section may: ■ **develop** and/or explore the previous thematic material; ■ introduce new material; ■ do both of the above	The **Recapitulation recapitulates** and 'reminds' us of the original thematic material.

A	B	A	C	A	B	A
S1 (i.e. the recurring rondo theme)	S2	**S1 (i.e. the recurring rondo theme)**	Exploring new keys while manipulating the thematic material	**S1 (i.e. the recurring rondo theme)**		**S1 (i.e. the recurring rondo theme)**
Home Key (Tonic Key)	Related key	**Home Key** (Tonic Key)	(Usually ends with **dominant** preparation of the home key, ready for the return of I in the Recapitulation section)	**Home Key** (Tonic Key)	**Now also in the Home / tonic key**	**May be shortened.** **Home Key** (Tonic Key) May be followed by a coda, perhaps also making reference to the main theme.
Transition passage (Bridge passage) Changing key				Transition passage – now altered to stay in the tonic		

Sonata–rondo form is often found in the final **movement** of multi-movement works such as symphonies, concertos, sonatas, and string quartets.

Minuet and Trio Form

A minuet was a graceful French dance in $\frac{3}{4}$ time. Composers often composed these in pairs, and the second minuet became known as the 'trio' because it was often scored for just three instruments. The overall plan of this structure is **ternary** (i.e. minuet – trio – minuet), though each of the sections is in itself a binary or ternary design:

Section A – Minuet	Section B – Trio	Section A
‖: a :‖: b (a) :‖	‖: c :‖: d (c) :‖	‖ a ‖ b (a) ‖
Main theme – tonic key	*Contrasting material – new key*	*Main theme – tonic key, no repeats*

The minuet and trio was commonly found as **movement** 3 in symphonies of the **Classical** era. It was Haydn who stamped his personality on the minuet more than anyone else. Although the trio was not limited to just 3 instruments at that time, there was usually a clear change in instrumentation to provide a lighter contrast to the minuet.

Note: Beethoven gradually displaced the minuet with the **scherzo** (though the term had been in existence for some time). The word, loosely translated, means 'joke', and it became established as a lively movement in fast $\frac{3}{4}$ time (conducted as one beat in a bar), still usually found as the third movement in a multi-movement work such as a symphony, usually with a contrasting trio section.

Theme and Variation

Another form where the content is clearly indicated in the title – the composer presents the initial theme, and then develops, contrasts and manipulates the idea in a variety of ways.

Theme – this itself may be in **binary** or **ternary** form	Variation 1	Variation 2	Variation 3	Variation 4	and so on…

Development of the Orchestra, 1750–1900

You need to understand the gradual evolution of the Classical and Romantic orchestras.

The **Baroque** orchestra consisted of at least 4 part strings (2 violins, viola and bass line or basso played by cello and double bass) with a **continuo** to provide the harmonic support. Wind parts were considered to be optional.

At the start of the 18th Century, it was possible to see a new format emerging, and by the end of the century, the standard **Classical** orchestra was recognised as 4-part strings, 2 flutes, 2 oboes, 2 clarinets, 2 bassoons (playing independently and not doubling the bass), 2 or 4 horns, 2 trumpets and timpani. Some composers used larger and more unusual combinations of instruments; outside court circles, they had to use what was available to them: a system of **patronage** was the means whereby support was given to composers by the wealthy, royalty or the church. Composers basically worked on commission, to fulfill the demands required of them by their respective patrons.

> Make sure that you understand the characteristics of the early 'natural' brass instruments, the role of the continuo, and how families of instruments were used.

By the early 19th Century, technical developments facilitated improvements in tone and **pitch** range, and eventually the keyboard continuo fell into decline and violinist-conductors led the orchestra. Some **Romantic** composers expanded the orchestra to gigantic proportions.

Development of the symphony, 1750–1830 (AS), 1750–1900 (A Level)

The Age of Enlightenment, an intellectual movement of the 18th Century, affected all walks of life, including music: patronage for the arts was in decline, the rise of the middle classes ensured an increased interest in music and learning, and new, emerging audiences were keen for public concerts.

In France and Germany in the early 18th Century, a new style emerged out of the **Baroque** era. It became known as the **Rococo** period, an artistic movement that affected architecture, literature, theatre, and music. In music, the period generally refers to 1720–1770. Whether this is referred to as the 'late Baroque' or 'early Classical' is of no consequence. It relates to the lighter, simpler and more elegant style of composition which began to become popular: a clearer distinction between the **melody** and the accompaniment, a reliance on more basic harmonies which emphasised the **tonic** and **dominant**, **textures** which were less dependent on **polyphonic** procedures, and simpler, periodic musical phrases – often highly ornamented. In France the new style was called *'style galante'* with composers such as Jean Phillipe Rameau and François Couperin. Later composers such as C.P.E Bach, Domenico Scarlatti and Christoph Willibald Gluck wrote works that cut down on the overuse of ornamentation and decoration, which paved the way for the Classical era.

Other important terms:

- **Empfindsamer Stil** (*'tender/sensitive style'*) which was Germanic in origin. This was akin to the *'style galante'*, though it did not embrace the lavish ornamentation and was recognised by the use of **appoggiaturas**, 'sigh' figures and harmonic and melodic **chromaticism**, often associated with **adagio movements**. Composers included C.P.E. Bach, along with (among others) Carl Friedrich Abel, Carl Heinrich Graun and Johann Joachim Quantz.

The rococo style is very distinctive, in architecture and art as well as in music

- **Sturm und Drang** ('*storm and stress*') was initially a literary movement, also derived from Germany. This emerged slighter later, and was popular in the 1770s, characterised in music through extreme contrasts in register and **dynamics**, instability of key, and exciting orchestral effects – features which were commensurate with **Classical** features of the time. In a number of ways 'Sturm und Drang' was a precursor of **Romanticism**. For example, Haydn wrote some works which could be regarded as being in this style: in his Symphony No.44 (acknowledged as being typical of his Sturm und Drang period) the tense character in the last **movement** is achieved through the fast tempo, contrast between the full orchestra (albeit limited to just horns, oboes and strings at the time) and the more stark, disjunct **contrapuntal** passages, the **staccato** unison idea and use of **tremolando** in strings.

Classical composers embraced the style galante, empfindamer stil and Sturm und Drang, ultimately weaving them together to create a style perfectly balanced in form and emotional content. Around 1750, the style was still being perfected; by 1770 certain characteristics started to become common, and these are features you need to know in terms of understanding the development of the symphony during the Classical and Romantic eras.

What is a Symphony?

The generally accepted understanding is that a symphony is an extended composition for orchestra.

The word sinfonia had been in use prior to this, and had been associated with a number of different types of composition, but it usually referred to the orchestral pieces of music used in an Italian opera – for example, as an **overture**, interlude or postlude. As we have already noted, there were many changes taking place around 1750: the growth of the Italian opera **overture** into an orchestral work in three **movements** by such composers as Scarlatti led to the composition of similar works that were not intended for use in the theatre.

1750–1830 (Classical and early Romantic)

Society was changing and this affected the arts and, of course, music. There was a growth in public concerts intended for instrumental music, and composers had the opportunity to target the new concert-going audiences, and were not just beholden to their patrons; the symphony emerged as a new and important type of instrumental work.

Though they were initially in three movements, a four movement plan for the symphony soon became common:

- A **first movement** which was usually in **sonata form** (sometimes called sonata-**allegro**)
- A **second movement** which was slow, and perhaps in a form such as theme and variation
- A **third movement**, mostly a **minuet and trio**
- A **final movement**, perhaps a rondo (or sonata-rondo).

Works of this kind began to be written not only in Italy, but also in Vienna and Mannheim.

Mannheim

Around 1750, the court orchestra in Mannheim began to establish a musical reputation throughout Europe for its orchestral concerts, under the baton of the Czech composer Johann Stamitz (1717-1757).

He increasingly favoured the 4-movement plan and the audiences of the time delighted in some of the novel styling and unpredictable treatment of ideas:

- Strong thematic material
- Energised **rhythmic** drive
- Simple **tutti textures**
- Sudden loud and soft **accents**
- Sudden crescendos and diminuendos
- The Mannheim crescendo (a crescendo for the entire orchestra)
- The Mannheim climax (usually followed the Mannheim crescendo, and the instruments except the strings dropped out one by one)
- The Mannheim Rocket (a rising passage based on an arpeggio, together with a crescendo)
- The Mannheim Roller (a loud extended passage with an ascending **melody** over an **ostinato** bass)
- The Mannheim sigh (a pair of slurred notes with increased emphasis on the first)
- Mannheim birds (instrumental sounds which imitated birds in the solo passages)
- The Grand Pause (a sudden rest for everybody, before an energetic re-start).

In terms of the **orchestration**, Stamitz's symphonic works of the 1750s were written for strings, 2 horns and 2 oboes (sometimes replaced by flutes or clarinets). At times, he included the occasional solo lines for horns and oboes. He contributed to the development of sonata form, mostly in first movements but sometimes also in the finales – and occasionally in slow movements (if he did not use an overall ABA structure).

EXAMPLE WORK:

Johann Stamitz: Symphony in D major, Opus 3 No.2 (1750-1754)

Scored for: 2 horns, 2 flutes, 2 oboes, 2 bassoons, strings and **continuo**. Available on IMSLP – the online Petrucci Music Library, which can be found at imslp.org

Movement 1: Presto (**Allegro**) D major
Stamitz sometimes used a modified concerto form for the first movements and this is evident here as this includes 3 sections with no repeats (like the 3 tuttis of the older concerto form) – section 1 modulates to the **dominant**, followed by a 'solo' interlude with new material, concluding with section 3 back in the **tonic** key. The harmonic content and melodic phrasing is simple (with regular 4-bar patterns), and the opening pedal D is typical of the old opera symphony, where this device was used to create suspense before the opera started. The handling of figuration is rapid with familiar patterning of ideas and strongly marked **rhythms**. Texturally the music is quite freely handled.

Movement 2: (Andantino) G major
This is for strings and continuo only and is organised into a binary structure, with its characteristic two repeated sections. Note the distinctive rhythmical features here which provide interest.

Movement 3: (Menuetto – Trio) D major-G major
Both sections are in binary form; note the use of solo instruments in the trio.

Movement 4: (Prestissimo) D major
This is organised in extended binary form, scored for the full orchestra, illustrating textural variety and contrast in the working. As with movement 1, note the contrasts in **dynamics** and expression.

Other composers also important in ushering in the **Classical** symphonic style were: Matthias Georg Monn, (1717-1750), who dropped the continuo in his later works and extended the contributory role of the woodwinds; Carl Ditters von Dittersdorf (1739-1759), whose symphonies are in some respects similar to Haydn's in their use of humour, folk-like material and asymmetrical phrases, and Georg Christoph Wagenseil (1715-1777), notable for his skilful construction of thematic material.

Your studies of early symphonies must also include two of the sons of J.S. Bach.

J.C. Bach (1735-1782) initially worked in the realm of opera, but his symphonies are among the most impressive part of his output and he was well respected by later composers. C.P.E. Bach (1714-1788) wrote symphonies in the new German style, and it is possible to note the more refined and intricate working in his orchestral music which still did not demonstrate a clear handling of functional form and harmonic work.

ADDITIONAL LISTENING

Tip: Look for the scores to these works at imslp.org

- C.P.E. Bach: Symphony in E minor (1756) www.youtube.com/watch?v=3mmvr5OIXBc
- Wagenseil: Symphony in D major, WV 368, Symphony in D no 374
  www.youtube.com/watch?v=BJFu1Z_o-9k
- J.C.Bach: Symphony in B♭ major (1774) www.youtube.com/watch?v=GyR-dXq2Yls

1750-1830 (The Classical to Early Romantic Era)

Who were the main symphonic composers during this time?

- Franz Joseph Haydn (1732-1809)
- Wolfgang Amadeus Mozart (1756-1791)
- Ludwig van Beethoven (1770-1827)
- Franz Schubert (1797-1828)
- Felix Mendelssohn (1809-1947)

Haydn and Mozart were the first to perfect the symphonic style and they were influenced by each other. Haydn is fondly remembered as the 'Father of the Symphony', and his work in this genre shaped the symphony as we recognise it today. His most famous symphonies were composed at the end of his life, after Mozart had died; it is interesting to note that these works bear the influence of the younger composer. Mozart began his symphonic career by composing symphonies in the manner of Haydn; soon his individuality and personal genius shone through and his final works are orchestral masterpieces of note. Beethoven expanded his earlier models to produce expanded and more dramatic works, with Schubert and Mendelssohn in much the same position though increasingly starting to infuse the content with musical features characteristic of the Romantic era.

Haydn

Haydn composed over a hundred symphonies, and it is his works that offer the most extensive development of the genre from 1760-1780 (and after). His position and duties at Esterhazy are well documented, and also his opinion that he was 'forced to become original'. He experimented with musical form, and did much to establish the conventional structure as we understand it; however, many of the movements he wrote were a mixture of several forms.

Background notes on the Classical era, Haydn's musical style and a detailed analysis of Haydn's London Symphony are available on the Eduqas website: www.eduqas.co.uk/qualifications/music/as-a-level

For extended research, an analysis of the first two movements of the 'Drum Roll' symphony is also available on the WJEC website – as part of the AS Level specification for Wales: http://resources.wjec.co.uk/Pages/ResourceByArgs.aspx?subId=21&lvlId=1

Joseph Haydn (his first name, Franz, is not usually used)

Much of Haydn's early symphonic work relied on the generally accepted idioms of the time, though it was more akin to the Viennese 'charm' than the excitement of the Mannheim style: he employed concertante parts in the manner of the old concerto, yet utilised rounded binary form; he occasionally included slow introductions to his works. Among the first he wrote when he was initially hired by Prince Esterhazy were *Le Matin*, *Le Midi* and *Le Soir* – all three had four **movements** and included minuets.

In the 1760s his works were more substantial and he wrote more symphonies in minor keys; the following three are all associated with his early 'Sturm und Drang' period.

HAYDN EXAMPLE WORKS:

Symphony No.26 (c. 1768) 'Lamentatione'

D minor: scored for 2 oboes, 2 horns, 2 bassoons, timps, strings (no independent part for bass) and continuo (harpsichord).

This symphony is associated with the composer's 'Sturm und Drang' period and was interesting in a number of ways.

Movement 1: Allegro assai con spirito $\frac{4}{4}$. **Sonata Form**; D minor ⟶ D major

Movement 2: Adagio (chorale) $\frac{2}{4}$. Extended binary form, F major.

Movement 3: Menuet (F major/D minor) e Trio (D major) $\frac{3}{4}$. Both sections are in binary form.

Symphony No.49 (1768) 'La Passione'

F minor: scored for 2 oboes, 2 horns, bassoon, strings and continuo.

The four movements follow the old sonata da chiesa pattern: slow, fast slow (minuet), fast. This was the last time Haydn organised the movements this way in a symphony.

Movement 1: Adagio, $\frac{3}{4}$ – F minor

Movement 2: Allegro di molto, $\frac{4}{4}$ – F minor

Movement 3: Menuet e Trio, $\frac{3}{4}$ – F minor/F major

Movement 4: Presto, $\frac{2}{2}$ – F major

Symphony No.44 (1772) Trauer-Symphonie

E minor: scored for 2 oboes, bassoon, 2 horns (in E and G), continuo (harpsichord) and strings.

Movement 1: Allegro con brio, $\frac{4}{4}$ (sonata form)

Movement 2: Menuetto (E minor, which is a double canon): Allegretto (E major), $\frac{3}{4}$.

Movement 3: Adagio, $\frac{2}{4}$. E major, with the strings muted.

Movement 4: Presto, $\frac{2}{2}$. Sonata form; is quite contrapuntal in nature and is in E minor.

Note: Because all the movements have the same tonic, the work is described as homotonal.

Haydn's six 'Paris' symphonies (written 1785-1786) consolidated his style in this genre:

- Three of the works began with a slow introduction (a feature which began to appear more frequently, seemingly to add a serious tone for opening)
- In terms of the organisation, there was evidence of refinement and control in terms of defined structures, as Haydn was increasingly concerned with planning the tonal organisation and achieving shape and character:
  - sonata form was used for the opening movements (which often demonstrated striking character)
  - slow movements still demonstrated binary form characteristics (though sometimes the working was more free and presented, without repeats, with colourful use of the orchestra in the alternation of tutti and solo groups)
  - variation form was also used in some slow movements (including double variation)
  - all were in four movements and included minuets and trios as the third movement in the plan
  - finales were often rounded binary (though Haydn did not always stick to this)
  - within sonata form, monothematic movements were frequently evident
  - thematic contrasts were overshadowed by relentless rhythmic momentum, intense harmonic progressions and driving modulations
  - preparation for the modulation to the dominant was a feature.

The 'London' symphonies

Haydn's crowning glory in terms of his symphonic output, however, were the twelve so-called 'London' Symphonies (written 1791-1795). These are sometimes referred to as the 'Salomon' symphonies after Joseph Salomon, the man who brought Haydn to London and commissioned these works. They offer nothing new and are probably no more advanced in terms of the compositional style, but they are the works undoubtedly held as the standard in Classical symphonies. They were composed for the orchestra arranged by Salomon which consisted of about 40 performers in total. The music was scored for 2 flutes, 2 oboes, 2 clarinets, 2 bassoons, 2 horns, 2 trumpets, timpani, and strings, apparently with Haydn still choosing to direct from the harpsichord in some performances.

Noteworthy features of the 'London' symphonies (which included symphonies Nos. 93-104):

- Some of these symphonies have become known by their names e.g. 'Surprise', 'Military', 'Clock' (because of the pizzicato strings and bassoon ticking idea in movement 2), 'Drum Roll' and 'London'

- **Structure**: Haydn consolidated strong forms which were to influence later composers: apart from No. 95, all begin with a slow introduction, which generally exhibited extensive musical invention, some introducing motifs to be used in the movement itself; first movements were in sonata form and exhibited total control, tonal order and thematic development, or employed 'monothematic' techniques (such as in movement 1 of the 'Clock'). All these symphonies were in four movements. Haydn often used sonata–rondo form in the finales (such as in the 'Clock'); he was also fond of variation structure (e.g. double variation in movement 2 of the 'Drum Roll')

- **Tonality**: All were in a major key (No. 95 started in C minor, but ended in C major) – however, note his fondness for a tonic minor introduction, followed by the exposition in the tonic major key

- **Harmony**: Mostly diatonic and functional and using progression of chords which was occasionally slow (each chord lasted for longer which gave the music a sense of direction); chromatic inflection was built into the functional system; a highly sophisticated technique became apparent, with sudden modulations, use of suspensions, diminished, augmented and Neapolitan chords, and devices such as extended sequences based on secondary dominant chords (as seen in the slow movement of the 'London')

- **Melody**: Themes were co-ordinated within the tonal plan: note the use of scalic movement, arpeggios in the figuration, and a graceful style; he also included rustic themes (for example in the trio of the 'Clock')

- **Texture**: Reliance on homophonic presentation, but contrapuntal textures were also employed (for example fugue in the finale of the 'Clock')

- **Instruments**: Instruments are used with originality (for example the opening drum roll, and the use of horn at the start of the finale in Symphony No. 103; the 'Military' symphony, when S1 is introduced by just flutes and oboes, the use of divisi violas and clarinets in movement 2, and the incorporation of Turkish instruments – triangle, cymbals and bass drum). Sometimes Haydn wrote out the repeats to include changes of instrumentation (Symphony No. 102, movement 2) which added further contrast and interest.

The 'London' symphony is one of your set work options for this component. For detailed notes and analysis of this work, go to the Eduqas website: http://resources.eduqas.co.uk/Pages/ResourceSingle.aspx?rlid=687

Mozart

Mozart was a prolific composer whose musical style was influenced by a great variety of music which he encountered on his travels as a young boy.

Though perhaps he was less adventurous than Haydn in the experimentation with musical structure, he was to achieve a personal musical style that was distinguished by formal perfection, melodic character and imaginative control of **harmony** and **texture**. He wrote 41 numbered symphonies between 1764 and 1788, though additional similar compositions have been described as 'unnumbered' symphonies. Early experimentation with writing for orchestra is seen in the various divertimenti and serenades which bear evidence of rather slim thematic material, a light approach to texture and mechanical figuration.

In the late 1770s and early 1780s, Mozart wrote:

- Symphony in D 'Paris' K.297 (1778)
- Symphony in B♭ K.319 (1779)
- Symphony in C K.338 (1780)
- Symphony in D 'Haffner' K.385 (1782)
- Symphony in C 'Linz' K.425 (1783)
- Symphony in D 'Prague' K.504 (1786)

Wolfgang Amadeus Mozart

Some of these were in three **movements**, with the movements following without a break – just like the Italian **overture**.

EXAMPLE WORK:

'Prague' Symphony: Symphony No.38

D major: scored for double woodwind, 2 horns, 2 trumpets and strings.

This is in three movements, all in **sonata form**, though (unusually for the time) it has no minuet. In Prague where the work was first performed in 1757 audiences were accustomed to three movement symphonies (fast-slow-fast), which followed the style of the Italian opera overtures. This work depends more on the arrangement and development of motifs than on the organic development of thematic material.

Movement 1: **Adagio** introduction, followed by **Allegro** in $\frac{4}{4}$ time, D major. (Mozart only does this in two other symphonies). This is quite an original structure, bearing some resemblance to **ritornello** structure, and with S2 being a version of S1; the **development** also includes **contrapuntal** working of motifs.

Movement 2: Andante in G major, $\frac{6}{8}$ time. This includes contrasting moods and interesting harmonic and textural moments.

Movement 3: Finale – presto, $\frac{2}{4}$ time in D major. This is a lively and boisterous movement which features the flute. It is in two sections, both of which are repeated.

Mozart's last 3 symphonies, nos. 39-41, were all completed in 1788 in the space of about three months. These seemed to have been influenced by Haydn's 'Paris' symphonies as they had the same large dimensions.

- Symphony No.39 in E♭ major, K.543
- Symphony No.40 in G minor, K.550
- Symphony No.41 in C major – 'Jupiter', K.551

These symphonies are scored for slight variations on the standard **Classical** orchestra – all include just one flute, no.39 uses a pair of clarinets in place of the oboes, and there are no trumpets or timps in the G minor symphony. **Sonata form** is used in most **movements**, generally embodying the expected structural characteristics, and there was an increasing tendency to assign weight to the finale.

There is a tremendous amount of thematic material presented in the movements, and melodies are more lyrical than those of Haydn – at times the thematic development was even more lyrical than the initial ideas. The use of **rhythm** was often interesting (e.g. the cross-**accented hemiola** rhythm within the 3-bar phrases in the Minuet of the G minor symphony). He was less adventurous than Haydn in his choice of keys, though each Mozart symphony begins with a clear declaration of the **tonality**; the harmonies are more chromatic than those found in Haydn, and sound richer and fuller because Mozart fills out the inner parts of the **texture**. Texturally, it is interesting to observe the complexity of some passages, particularly the amount of **contrapuntal** working in the G minor symphony, and of course the fugal textures which provide substance to the texture rather than controlling the structure. For example, the finale of the 'Jupiter' presents no fewer than five subjects, which are combined in different ways (including inversion and **stretto**) with a coda that includes invertible five-part **counterpoint** 'without parallel in the symphonic literature' (New Grove).

LISTEN

Listen to these symphonies, following the scores, available at imslp.org

Try notating some of the melodies without looking at the score (for example the opening theme of the G minor symphony). As you listen, make observations on the way in which the musical elements have been used by the composer: the style of the melody, the use of the instruments, the rhythmic devices, the harmonic content and the textures.

Beethoven

In the symphonic genre, Beethoven found established forms which he was more than happy to use.

He expanded the structures, but did not change them, and in doing so he paved the way for the **Romantic** movement. He concerned himself with the creation of germinal motives which offered opportunities for fuller development, and substituted the minuet with the **scherzo** as the 3rd movement, which offered a difference in mood, pace and rhythm.

Beethoven's compositional style has been recognised as falling into three periods of development. The first lasts until about 1802, and includes the first symphony:

EXAMPLE WORK:

Symphony No.1, Op.21 (1765)

C major: standard Classical orchestration

This work is **Classical** in spirit and shows the influence of Haydn, though it includes interesting features in terms of the structure (particularly in the extended codas for **movements** 1, 2 and 4). Prominence is given to the woodwind instruments and **dynamic** shading is subtle (note the frequent use of sforzandi).

Movement 1: Adagio molto introduction – this actually begins in F, moves to G in bar 4, and hovers around C before C is finally established in the **allegro** con brio, which is in **sonata form**. S1 is military in character; S2 is quite operatic with instrumental dialogue between the flute and oboe. The **development** section is explorative in terms of the **harmony**, moving to remote tonal centres, and musically building to a turbulent section mid-movement.

Movement 2: Andante cantabile con moto, $\frac{3}{8}$ – F major (**subdominant**). **Contrapuntal** writing is in evidence here as Beethoven looks back to the formal dance-style of the 18th Century, and the movement begins with a **fugal** idea. The entire orchestra is used, and the movement is also in sonata form.

Movement 3: Is in the character of a **scherzo**, (entitled a minuet, though labelled 'Allegro molto e vivace'. $\frac{2}{4}$, C major. It uses the musical scales and **triads** from the first movement as motivic material.

Movement 4: Adagio – allegro molto e vivace, $\frac{2}{4}$ (C major). Sonata form. Note the musical humour here as this opens with the violins attempting to play a scalic idea, progressing one note further with each attempt; the two dramatic pauses towards the end are resolved in a simple march.

Beethoven's second style period includes symphonies numbers 2–8, though the second symphony was transitional in terms of Beethoven's symphonic development. Numbers 4, 7 and 8 are written for the standard Classical orchestra and display craftsmanship, worthy of consideration in terms of their structural, harmonic and textural content.

The middle period works exhibited more in the way of expansion and development:

■ There was extended use of forms, and a tendency to mix forms (i.e. sonata–rondo); the development sections assume more importance as the material is manipulated through textural variety, **polyphonic** devices and extensive **modulation**, and the coda becomes a further opportunity for thematic

Ludwig van Beethoven

development and expansion. In some works, there was less division between the two subject groups in the **exposition**, and he favoured short initial motifs that were capable of later development. Beethoven seemed intentionally to blur the dividing lines between sections in the attempt to unify the ideas.

> D.J. Grout says of Beethoven 'This capacity to organise a large amount of contrasting material into a unified musical whole is one of the chief marks of Beethoven's greatness.'

- The music in these works held a very dramatic and personal quality, which demonstrated an assured style of composition and included **rhythmic syncopation** and **dynamic** outbursts. He brought earlier forms and style to fruition with a new spirit, and introduced subject groups, using short melodies or motifs with an ability to prioritise the development of one idea (for example in the 5th symphony).

- Beethoven often slowed down the rate of harmonic change, thus giving individual chords increased meaning and establishing a strong sense of key: complex chords were more effective in many ways – generally simple in application, but feeling intense, and including remote and unusual **modulations** in the content.

- A recognised feature of Beethoven's work here was the energetic rhythmic drive and insistence of the ideas. Original patterns went on for longer, and the content manipulation of the themes was interesting.

- Minuets were eventually recognised and labelled as **scherzos**, with trios that were a world away from the grace and eloquence of Haydn.

- Texturally, it is possible to note the increased feeling of breadth and vastness achieved by the wide harmonic spacing and often leisurely style of the melodies. The use of **counterpoint** was evident.

- The size of the orchestra was also increased in some symphonic works of this period.

BEETHOVEN SYMPHONIES IN FOCUS:

Symphony No.3 (1803/4) *'Eroica'*

E♭ major: scored for 2 flutes, 2 oboes, 2 clarinets, 2 bassoons, 3 horns (E♭, C and F), 2 trumpets (in E♭ and C), timps and strings.

This has been considered to be something of a revolutionary work, as it broke new ground. It is long and complex.

Movement 1: Allegro con brio, $\frac{3}{4}$, in **sonata form**. The **triadic** nature of the simple opening statement, initially played by the cellos, offered opportunity for later variation and development. In total, 5 other themes are presented in the exposition, and a new theme is also introduced in the **development** section (which later returns in the coda). The extension of the coda is a main structural feature, with its unexpected harmonies and contrasting dynamics. Each idea seems to unfold out of the previous, showing his ability to organise a large amount of material into a unified musical whole.

Movement 2: Entitled 'Funeral March' in C minor (the **submediant** minor), including **fugato** treatment of the material. This starts with a basic three part song form which extends into a very long movement, including episodes in major keys. The double-basses clearly suggest the sound of drums.

Movement 3: **Allegro** vivace – a sprightly **scherzo** (one in a bar), full of **rhythmic** vitality, with a trio featuring the three horns (one more than in any of his other symphonies, except the 9th where there are 4). Another long movement (probably twice as long as any comparable third movement by Haydn). This movement is interesting because of the variety of **dynamics** and use of **syncopation**.

Movement 4: Allegro molto, a **theme and variations**. The theme is based on his own ballet music from *Prometheus*, though this is not heard until the 3rd variation. The amount of development here is impressive and imaginative, and the working contains fugally developed episodes and coda. Note the surprising change of tempo towards the end of the movement, when the winds embark on a variation of the theme. In the last presto, the horns again feature to present a hunting version of the theme.

Symphony No.5, Op.67 (1804-1808)

C minor: in addition to the standard Classical orchestration, the orchestra includes piccolo, contrabassoon and 3 trombones in movement 4.

Written during the time of the Napoleonic wars, this symphony has often been linked with Beethoven's famous comment 'I will grapple with Fate; it shall not overcome me'. In this work, Beethoven achieves a rhythmic and thematic **cyclical** relationship between the movements.

Movement 1: Allegro con brio in **sonata form**. Dominated by the well-known opening four-note motif (also identified in the other movements). Unison horns announce S2. The **exposition** is repeated (a typically Classical convention).

Movement 2: Andante, and in A♭ major – the **subdominant** of the relative major key of E♭ major. A welcome contrast to the dramatic opening. This movement is a set of variations, with two themes (double variation form).

Movement 3: An allegro scherzo, in **ternary** form plus coda. As expected, the trio is in C major and includes **contrapuntal textures**. Note the dynamic contrasts and writing for instruments.

This movement links directly to movement 4, with a coda that also functions as a transition to introduce movement 4.

Movement 4: Allegro, in a variant of sonata form. The use of the orchestra is noteworthy here, with addition of the 3 trombones, piccolo and contra-bassoon. Straightforward harmonic work clarifies the vague nature of the preceding material. Furthermore, a version of the horn theme from movement 2 is revisited. The majestic march theme returns, finally concluding in C major.

Symphony No.6, Op.68 (1808) Sinfonia *'Pastorale'*
In five movements with subtitles for each movement.

**F major: scoring is light, mainly for double woodwind, horns and strings.
Note the addition of piccolo in movement 4 and 2 trombones in 4 and 5.**

Beethoven considered this 'more the expression of feeling than painting', and parts are certainly programmatic in nature. The title and programmatic elements are still secondary in terms of the symphonic working. The composer himself warned that the descriptions were not to be taken literally.

Movement 1: *'Awakening of joyful feeling on arrival in the country'*
Fast, and in **sonata form**, this begins with a drone bass (open 5th) representing folk music or a rustic dance; this simple opening theme also offers much potential for development procedures later; indeed S1 is built up of motifs which are all important. The mood is relaxed, with harmonies sustained over bars at times. Towards the end of the movement, clarinet and bassoon anticipate the village band of the 'peasants' merrymaking' in movement 3.

Movement 2: *'Scene by the brook'*
Slow. This is in $\frac{12}{8}$, B♭ major (**subdominant**), and again in sonata form. Note the recurring silences in the first theme. In the coda, the flute, oboe and clarinet imitate bird calls.

Movement 3: *'Peasants' merrymaking'*
Scherzo and trio. This includes a reliance on dance-like melodies as the music portrays the scene with delightful touches of solo instrumental colour (particularly winds and horn). The movement ends abruptly as the peasants notice that a storm is about to break.

Movement 4: *'Storm'*
This is entirely programmatic, in F minor and based on a variety of figures. With lower strings depicting dark clouds, 2nd violins suggest raindrops before the storm breaks, with more agitated figuration in winds and thunderclaps in timps. The simple oboe **melody** at the end of this movement brings an end to the storm and an ascending scale on flute leads into the finale.

Movement 5: *'Song of thanksgiving after the storm'*
Once again, Beethoven is adventurous with the form which is sonata-rondo (back in the **tonic** key); in $\frac{6}{8}$ time and includes much use of variation.

In 1824, the 9th symphony was completed and this fell securely into Beethoven's third style period. It was on a grander scale than anything previously; each movement was longer, and the tonal content more varied.

Symphony No.9, Op.125, (1823/4) *'Choral'*

D minor: scored for the largest orchestra Beethoven ever used. To the standard Classical orchestration, he added a further 2 horns (4 in total), 3 trombones in movements 2 and 4. In movement 4, additionally – piccolo, contrabassoon, bass drum, triangle and cymbals, plus SATB soloists and choir. Gigantic proportions in comparison to anything heard previously.

Movement 1: A dramatic **allegro** – and interesting interpretation of **sonata form** that intrigues from the open pianissimo section through to the final coda. At first, it feels as if the key is A major by implications of the bare 5th; D minor is not firmly established until bar 17. The main theme is presented in both major and minor versions. The pace of harmonic change is generally slow, and this adds solemnity to the content. The **development** includes a triple **fugue** and the thematic material is presented in a variety of ways, with great variety in the figuration, and lots of motivic ideas evident. The structure is not as clearly defined as in previous works (even tonally), with no distinction between sections. As in the third symphony, the coda is like another complete development section and includes use of the chromatic 4th.

Movement 2: This is the **scherzo**, labelled molto vivace. Written in triple time, but with **accents** that make it feel like quadruple time. Note (as in the 8th symphony) the tuning of the timps an octave apart. It is a substantial movement in terms of the proportions, the central section (i.e. the trio) is somewhat similar to the same section in his 2nd symphony. The scherzo section itself conforms to the principles of sonata form within the overall **ternary** structure. The trio introduces the trombones for the first time in the movement.

Movement 3: An **adagio** movement, loosely in double variation form. **Romantic** in spirit, with main harmonic changes noted only in the modulatory sections.

Movement 4: Allegro/andante/allegro. The decision to include vocal resources in this movement posed problems for Beethoven. He needed to decide how to conclude this symphony, and his solution was to quote from the previous three movements. It transpires as a huge rondo-finale, probably the most intricate movement he ever wrote. The inclusion of a chorus in the last movement, with the 'Ode to Joy' theme, was innovative. The movement begins with quotes from the previous movements before incorporating the choral idea. The overall structure is unusual:

1. Begins with a violent and **dissonant** passage
2. Lower strings are given a number of 'quasi-operatic' passages (suggesting the human voice) offering brief reminders of material from the three preceding movements
3. Solo baritone delivering similar phrases, gradually with the chorus being included in the **texture**
4. Orchestral **exposition** of the main theme in four 'stanzas'
5. Reminder of the opening dissonant passage
6. Bass **recitative**
7. Orchestral/choral section –'Joy' theme including an instrumental section which is a double fugue
8. New theme for chorus and orchestra
9. Double fugue utilising both themes
10. Complex and extended coda section.

It must be remembered that Beethoven bridged two eras of music. He was respected by every subsequent composer – and the character of his music was the stuff of the early nineteenth century. He was always indebted to the instrumental forms of the **Classical** period, and extended their ideals to the limit, and even beyond as he inspired the spirit of **Romanticism**. The way that Beethoven inspired others may be seen in the way he developed his thematic material, through his dramatic and emotional style seen in the way he used contrasting **dynamics** and effects, his use of harmonic **dissonance** and adventurous **modulations**, and the powering force of his relentless **rhythmic** ideas (the use of **accents**, **syncopation** and so on), and musical figuration.

Early Romantic composers

How to follow in the steps of Beethoven? Not an easy task, by any means – and increasingly it seemed that composers were avoiding the issue.

Composers began to react against the existing formal conventions, and began to write in alternative genres to that of the symphony, as they became increasingly interested in and influenced by literature. The Romantic movement began in the late-eighteenth century as a literary movement in Germany, when writers were captivated by medieval romance, adventure, pictorial images of nature, by folk-lore and the mystical – and this was to spread throughout Europe. Some composers started to write what became known as symphonic **tone-poems** instead of symphonies. Melodies became more expressive, harmonies more colourful and the writing for orchestra increasingly sonorous, with exploitation of the timbral qualities of instruments, and experimentation in terms of rhythm and **texture**, dynamics and expression.

Some important features of the time were:

- further decline of the old patronage system,
- the increasing popularity of commercial opera and public concerts
- music education and a more accessible approach to music for the middle classes
- the popularity of exceptionally gifted **virtuoso** performers (such as Liszt)
- appearance of the music critic and music journalist, particularly noted through the introduction of magazines and newspapers.

For the purpose of AS study, the main composers of the early Romantic era included Schubert and Mendelssohn.

Mendelssohn

Between 1830-1833, Mendelssohn composed three symphonies of importance:

- Symphony No.3 in A minor, Op.56 – '*Scotch*'
- *Symphony No.4 in A major, Op.90 – '*Italian*'
- Symphony No.5 in D minor, Op. 107 – '*Reformation*'.

*This is one of your set work options for this section of the exam.
For detailed notes and analysis of this symphony, go to the Eduqas website:
http://resources.eduqas.co.uk/Pages/ResourceSingle.aspx?rIid=687

Felix Mendelssohn   Franz Schubert

As you can see, all these symphonies had titles and some kind of **programmatic** meaning, but they did not have a programme as such. Mendelssohn continued to compose within conventional classical forms and styles, described by D.J. Grout as 'Classical by disposition, but with a special gift for **Romantic** scene-painting.'

Schubert

Schubert was influenced by Haydn, Mozart and Beethoven. He is remembered as a 'lyrical' composer, evident in his many songs, and also in his symphonies, as the thematic content always delights. In terms of structure, he was perhaps rather over-dependent on repetition, and the developmental passages sometimes disappoint. In the realm of **harmony**, he was more adventurous, fond of moving to the key a major 3rd below the **tonic**, and he enjoyed the contrast between tonic major and tonic minor. There are two symphonies of note by Schubert:

Symphony No.8 (1822), known as the '*Unfinished*'. It is in B minor and has only two **movements**; he started a third movement, but it never amounted to a great deal. Despite that, it remains a well-known and frequently performed work, with some interesting use of harmonies and imaginative exploration of the material. Schubert never actually heard it performed as it was not premiered until 43 years after its composition.

The first performance of Symphony No.9 (1828) was not given until 11 years after Schubert's death. This work is known as the '*Great*', is in C major and is unusually long for the period. It includes colourful writing for the orchestra, some interesting structural features and a profusion of melodies to interest the listener. In both these works, the trombone became an essential part of the scoring.

A LEVEL EXTENSION
1830–1900 (the Romantic period)

For A Level, you must study everything which has come before in this chapter, and also the Romantic period, from 1830-1900, as covered from here to the end of the chapter.

During this time, no one composer led the way in terms of style. It was a period of change and emancipation which allowed for further musical and artistic creativity. Nationalism became important as composers used elements of folk music to express their cultural background. Compositions became longer, musical resources and the orchestra were expanded, and composers experimented with instrumental sonorities and effects; there was also continued exploration in harmony which involved the extended use of chromaticism and dissonance.

Who were the main symphonic composers during this time?

- Hector Berlioz (1803-1869) – French
- Robert Schumann (1810-1856) – German
- Franz Lizst (1811-1886) – Hungarian
- Anton Bruckner (1824-1896) – Austrian
- Johannes Brahms (1833-1897) – German
- Peter Ilyich Tchaikovsky (1840-1893) – Russian
- Antonín Dvořák (1841-1904) – Czech
- Gustav Mahler (1860-1911) – Austrian
- Richard Strauss (1864-1949) – German

The compositional style of the German composer Richard Wagner (1813-1833) as seen in his music-dramas undeniably had a profound effect on other composers; he wrote in a symphonic way, but did not write symphonic works.

What new terms or forms do I need to know for this period?

- The symphonic poem, or tone-poem is an orchestral work, symphonic in style, but in one continuous form with different sections illustrating an additional programme which is linked to an idea or extra musical source. The term was first used by Liszt about his thirteen one-movement pieces in this genre.

- Cyclic form is when the composer uses the theme from the opening movement elsewhere, and at the end of the piece, or in the 'finale', which tended to shift the emphasis from the opening to the end of a work.

- The idée fixe was a term initially coined by Berlioz, and refers to a recurring theme which represented a particular idea, or person. The concept is the same in the use of thematic transformation (Liszt) and leitmotif (Wagner).

Berlioz

Here we find a composer who was ready to challenge the symphonic form – and he succeeded in doing so. His writing for the orchestra was experimental, really interesting and forward-looking for his time.

In 1829, he composed the original 'Episode in the Life of an Artist' (*Symphonie Fantastique*). It was in five **movements**, the intentions of which were each clearly explained in the accompanying text; the piece was autobiographical, as the composer wrote of his unhappy relationship with Harriet Smithson, an actress. The music still held to the symphonic principles held by Haydn (perhaps modified by Beethoven) and most of the movements can be appreciated in **Romantic** style without the programme. Nevertheless, this was a new departure in symphonic terms and is notable particularly for his use of the **idée fixe** and in terms of orchestral colour, sudden contrasts, harmonic effect, use of **syncopation**, lyricism in the slow movement and

Hector Berlioz

writing for percussion. Four tuned timpani were used in the slow movement to produce chords, and tubular bells were employed in the finale.

Symphonie Fantastique (1829)

Movement 1: *Reveries, Passions*
This begins with a long, slow introduction which is almost as long as the fast section which follows. Violins introduce the idée fixe which recurs throughout the work, and the treatment of the theme is imaginative. The **development** presents a new theme for oboe (heard with the idée fixe in **counterpoint**). Different visual ideas emerge – for example, there is a march-like passage, and a religious style passage evident in the inclusion of slow chords which represent an organ playing.

Movement 2: *A Ball*
This illustrates the composer's understanding of orchestral **sonority** and lyricism. Unusually, harps are included in the score which presents a waltz-like theme; the **texture** is string-based with the occasional wind chord to provide added colour, including a clarinet solo which reminds us of the idée fixe.

Movement 3: *Scenes in the Country*
This includes two **scherzos**. The first one begins with the duet between the cor anglais and off-stage oboe, painting the picture of two shepherds calling out to each other across the valley. Then, a unison **melody** paints the picture of solitary main figure, and wind instruments later imitate bird calls.

Movement 4: *March to the Scaffold*
The opening is interesting as each note is given to a different instrument, and the **orchestration** is expanded to include extra bassoons, trombones, tubas, cymbal and bass drum. The opening bars present a two-note motif for timps and **divisi** double basses, creating a menacing chord; other features of interest include ideas in the upper register of the bassoons, and the various counterparts presented in the first thematic section. The 2nd thematic section is presented as a march, characterised by dotted **rhythms**, brass and explosive percussion effects.

Movement 5: *Dream of a Witches' Sabbath*
There are two contrasting themes (one violent, the other solemn) which eventually combine in **contrapuntal** fashion. This shows the influence of Beethoven (particularly the 9th symphony). The grotesque transformation of the **idée fixe**, inventively painted by the orchestra e.g. the 8-part upper strings at the start, the lower strings suggesting darker meaning, the inclusion of the Gregorian chant (the Dies Irae), the ringing of the bells, chaotic responses from woodwind, a **fugal** presentation of the witches' theme and aggressive syncopated interjections from brass. Note the use of *col legno* which eventually brings the woodwind trills on every main note along with effective **dynamic** contrasts.

In earlier symphonic works by Haydn and Beethoven, the initial theme grew and developed, increasing in depth and meaning; with Berlioz the meaning was evident from the outset, as the theme has programmatic significance. Unity between all **movements** was achieved in this way. Effective orchestral work was realised through the program rather than through key or inventive development of the initial ideas; the theme 'transformed' and the meaning explained in the programme. For example, consider the way that the theme of the last movement is distorted to represent the character of the witches.

FURTHER LISTENING

- *Harold in Italy*, 1834 (said to be based on Byron's 'Childe Harold') included a solo viola part and a theme that is meant to represent the main character, Harold. It is in four movements, without a programme, but each with a title which explains the idea behind the musical content)

- *Romeo and Juliet,* 1839/40 (This is a large scale choral symphony, with original use of form).

Berlioz's use of the orchestra broke new ground. He portrayed his total understanding of the medium by achieving effects of orchestral colouring previously unrealised (e.g. 8 pairs of kettledrums to produce chords in the Dies Irae of his *Requiem*). He mixed the timbres, and employed same-type instruments for effects, delighted in the clarity of solo sound as well as mass orchestral power, and enjoyed antiphonal, doubling and unison writing for instruments. He wrote his *Treatise of Modern Instrumentation and Orchestration* in 1844.

Schumann

Schumann injected his piano compositions with symphonic grandeur, but did not really achieve similar success in his symphonic works, of which there are four. Probably the best known symphonies are Symphony No.1 in B♭ (1841) and Symphony No.4 in D minor (1841, but revised in 1851).

He kept quite close to traditional practice, though 4 horns and trombones were employed. Structurally, all the movements of the D minor are to be performed as one continuous whole, i.e. without a break between movements. He also connected the **movements** with the same themes, clearly concerned with the overall unity of the piece (in the manner of Berlioz). Stylistically, there was at times a lack of effective orchestral colour, but moments of harmonic richness and exciting progressions; harmonies sometimes moved more quickly and more intricately, though figuration was perhaps less imaginative. He seemed to manage smaller forms with more success than the larger structures.

Robert Schumann

Liszt

Liszt was a brilliant **virtuoso** pianist. As a composer, he admittedly wrote much that was 'flashy'; however, we must also appreciate his compositions that are explorative and pushed the boundaries, at times demonstrating harmonic and **rhythmic** originality.

He became the conductor of the orchestra at Weimar in 1848 and then produced a number of important symphonic works: two **programme** symphonies, and 12 shorter '**symphonic poems**'. He was said to be the first person to use the term **programme music** and he used what he called 'metamorphosis' or 'transformation' of themes (the same concept as the **leitmotif** of Wagner and the **idée fixe** of Berlioz). This was a device he used to extend the initial material in different ways and associate the listener with the main idea or character in the program. Stylistically, his use of the orchestra was more important than thematic development as such, and within his work he often chose to slow down the rate of harmonic change to give a broader effect – using more chromatic content than Beethoven, often giving the effect of remote **modulation** (consider his use of 2nd inversion chords) – and concentrating on the quality of a single chord, allowing the feeling of key to grow from a single starting point.

Franz Liszt

EXAMPLE WORK:

Faust Symphony

This work is scored for double woodwind (plus piccolo); a large brass section comprising 4 French horns, 3 trumpets, 3 trombones and tuba; timps and various percussion; organ, harp and strings; tenor soloist and male (TTB) choir. It premiered in 1857, was dedicated to Berlioz and conducted by Liszt.

Liszt was influenced by literature and it seemed perhaps unsurprising that he was tempted to compose music on the legend of Faust as presented by Goethe. The piece contains three **movements**: 'Faust' (in **sonata form**), 'Gretchen' (3-part form) and 'Mephistopheles' (a **scherzo** in 3 part form followed by an extra **development** section and a coda.). Themes are transformed according to the program.

In the first movement, the opening idea includes all the notes of the chromatic scale. The second idea in the woodwind undergoes a series of transformations in the work and he combines his thematic ideas skillfully. In 'Gretchen' he uses solo groups of instruments within some **contrapuntal textures**; **orchestration** is delicate, with interesting use of woodwind and strings and much use of sequence. In the third movement, more transformations of the Faust theme are in evidence, with ideas sometimes scattered through the different instruments, and a quite remarkable distorted **fugue** created out of the themes. Three years after completing the orchestral score, Liszt composed an additional section for a more solemn ending, scored for tenor solo and male voice chorus.

FURTHER LISTENING
Listen also to the 'Dante' symphony (first performed in 1857).

Liszt's **symphonic poems** were written between 1848 and 1858. Each of the 12 symphonic poems had titles which indicated the subject matter (though not the inner structure – which remained symphonic), though the relationship between the title and the content varies. Liszt used the programme to explain to the audience how his ideas were combined in different movements. Some were originally intended as **overtures** (e.g. *Tasso. Lamento e Trionfo; Orpheus; Prometheus; Hamlet)* with perhaps the most famous of these being *Les Préludes*, which was originally intended as an overture for a choral work but eventually re-titled after a poem by Lamartine. The music came first, followed by the suggestion of ideas explained in the programme as Liszt later offered an interpretation of his music. The work is in four parts which reflect different moods. What is particularly interesting is the manner in which the composer 'transforms' the themes to produce an extended structure.

Bruckner

Bruckner composed nine symphonies and was influenced by Beethoven and Wagner, though he wrote lyrically, like Schubert, and melodically he was typically Romantic in nature. He continued to organise his works into four movements and expanded the dimensions to monumental proportions, though he still used an orchestra of double woodwind, 2 trumpets, 4 horns, 3 trombones, tuba, timps and strings.

His use of **harmony** is often chromatic and Wagnerian. Structurally, his symphonic works lacked the intensity of structure witnessed in the **Classical** works, with '**cyclic**' style finales that recall material from the previous **movements**, and his structural methods were described as unorthodox by some as he used melodic variation and transformation of themes to extend the ideas. However, his symphonies all follow the conventional four-movement plan and none are explicitly programmatic. He was fond of a 'modified' **sonata form** and presented a number of thematic groups in the construction; he employed chorale-like themes, and in the slow movements, often utilised ABA¹B¹A² lied form, and included **scherzos** as third movements.

FURTHER LISTENING

- **Symphony No.4 in E♭ major, 1874 revised 1888**
- **Symphony No.7 in E major, 1881-3 revised 1885.**

Brahms

Brahms took many years to pen his first symphony, ever-aware of the need to follow in Beethoven's footsteps. In his disciplined and traditional use of forms, he used Classical techniques of motivic development and counterpoint, yet infused the Romantic spirit with his colourful, rich (and sometimes dark) use of harmony, a Schubertian sense of lyricism, complex rhythmic combinations (for example use of polyrhythms), and colourful and rich contrasts of orchestral sonority.

Johannes Brahms

In all, he eventually composed four symphonies, and all are worthy of your attention. He is described as 'conservative' in his musical style – but don't be misled. There is much of depth and interest in a Brahms symphony, and he filled the symphonic structures with interest, working hard to make the musical figuration functional.

Overall, the symphonies are scored for double woodwind plus contrabassoon, 2 trumpets, 4 horns, 3 trombones, timps and strings (there is a violin solo at the end of movement 2 in the first symphony).

Background notes on Brahms' musical style, and a detailed analysis of the finale of his first symphony is available on the WJEC website, as this movement is one of the choices of set works for A level music (specification for Wales): http://resources.wjec.co.uk/Pages/ResourceByArgs.aspx?subId=21&lvlId=1

EXAMPLE WORK:

Symphony No.1 in C minor, Op.68 (1876)

Movement 1: Sostenuto-**allegro**. An extended introduction contains the germinal seeds from which later thematic ideas grow. The movement is in **sonata form** though the **development** section introduces new thematic material; the **recapitulation** follows a reasonably predictable path though with some surprises, and the final bars hark back to the introduction. The movement ends peacefully in C major.

Movement 2: Andante sostenuto. This is in E major, and brings a beautiful theme for the oboe, later to be developed by other instruments. Brahms combines some unusual but effective solo colours here e.g. the combination of the solo violin and 1st horn in the re-statement of the **melody**.

Movement 3: Allegretto. **Ternary form**, in A♭ major (**subdominant** of the relative key of E♭ major). The first clarinet theme is made up of two 5-bar phrases, the second of which is an inversion of the first, followed by a secondary theme scored for woodwind. This movement includes a number of changes in mood which builds up before the opening theme returns; however, the movement ends with another reference to the middle section.

Movement 4: Note the use of **cyclic** devices (i.e. the horn-call of the introduction). This is a substantial movement which shows originality: detailed notes on it are available online (see note above).

Other points of interest:

- The first movement of Symphony No.2 in D major is in sonata form and is based on the melody formerly composed for his *Wiegenlied* (i.e. Brahms' Lullaby); movement 2, the **adagio** movement, is in B major (the **submediant** of the **tonic** or major version of the related minor) and is in sonata form. The transformation of motives is interesting. Movement 3 is a **scherzo** in G major (**subdominant**), and the substantial sonata form finale is also worthy of note.

- In Symphony No.3 in F major, listen out for the **motto theme** which is used to unify the work: F–A/A♭–F (meant to signify 'Frei aber Froh' – 'free but happy'). The first movement is in sonata form, the second in modified sonata form and in the **dominant** major (C major). The choice of the dominant minor for movement 3 is presented with reduced **orchestration** and yet another complex sonata form movement is used for the finale.

- The four movements of Symphony No.4 in E minor present some unique features in terms of organisation and development. The first movement is in sonata form with no repeat of the **exposition**; the andante is in the tonic major (which begins and ends with hints of the Phrygian **mode**) and modified sonata form (with no development section). The scherzo is a C major movement in a sonata form with a shortened recapitulation section and little reference to S2 in the development and coda, while the finale is a rare example of a symphonic **passacaglia** which emerges as a set of thirty variations based on a theme by J.S. Bach.

Dvořák

Dvořák's symphonies were quite traditional in concept, yet different from his Germanic counterparts. He was influenced by Brahms, though his music is in some ways more reflective of nationalist ideas. His melodies were infiltrated with dance rhythms of the Bohemian folk dances, and his work shows the influence of folk music, control of structural elements and orchestral colour. In all, he composed nine symphonies, of which the last two are particularly noteworthy.

Antonín Dvořák

Symphony No.8, Op.88, (1889) in G major: the first rather unconventional **movement** presents lots of thematic ideas, the 2nd movement is said to be based on an earlier piano solo by the composer, the 3rd movement is a delicately styled waltz, and the finale is a **theme and variations** movement which starts with a trumpet fanfare and goes on to include rondo-like features within the structure.

EXAMPLE WORK:

Symphony No.9 *'From the New World'* 1893

E minor: scored for 2 flutes, 2 oboes, cor anglais, 2 clarinets, 2 bassoons, 4 horns, 2 trumpets, 3 trombones, tuba, strings and percussion (timps, triangle in movement 3, cymbals in movement 4)

Dvořák was working in America from 1892-5. He was greatly influenced by the native American music and the spirituals, and he wanted to reflect this in the piece. The thematic material includes folk-like elements and syncopated rhythms, presented through a colourful orchestral palette and **dynamic** contrasts, supported by harmonies that varied from effectively simplistic with **modal** flavourings to richly chromatic substance.

Movement 1: An **adagio** introduction precedes sonata-**allegro** form, though the **recapitulation** brings back the themes in unexpected keys, closing with an explosive coda based on the 3rd theme.

Movement 2: Largo in the key of D♭ major. This is in **ternary form**, influenced by Longfellow's *Hiawatha*. (The slow theme was later adapted into the spiritual-like song '*Goin' Home*'.)

Movement 3: **Scherzo** and trio in E minor. The *Hiawatha* influence continues as this movement portrays the 'wedding feast'; apparently inspired by an American-Indian warrior's dance. The trio bears all the characteristics of his homeland with a theme which is actually styled in the manner of a Czech folk-song.

Movement 4: Allegro con fuoco in E minor (again in sonata-allegro form) demonstrates the **cyclic** structure as the music brings back themes from the earlier movements. Ends in E major.

Tchaikovsky

Tchaikovsky was a composer perhaps most famous for his ballet music and concert overtures. His symphonies essentially followed the German Romantic tradition, and were a kind of mix between the symphony and the symphonic poem; however, he rather struggled with sonata form and did not follow it strictly. Perhaps this was because it did not fit in with the Russian style of writing, which was to deal with things in smaller sections which either repeated or proceeded immediately from one idea to the next. He did not really seem to care for programme music. His work sometimes displayed Wagnerian intensity, and like Brahms he used traditional devices and presented normal phases of stylistic development.

Peter Ilyich Tchaikovsky

In this genre, he composed six numbered symphonies and a programmatic symphony entitled *Manfred* (which was inspired by Byron's poem of the same name). His main orchestral works are his last three symphonies. These were scored for double woodwind (plus piccolo), 4 horns (including the new valve-horn), 2 trumpets, 3 trombones and tuba, timps (3 in symphony no.5) (plus bass drum, cymbals, triangle in symphony no.4, and tam-tam in no.6) and strings.

Symphony No.4, is in F minor (Op.36, 1877). Note the horn 'Fate' motif and $\frac{9}{8}$ time in **movement** 1, a very long movement organised according to a complete series of 3rds (i.e. F–A♭–B–D–F) which emphasise the **rhythm** and textural elements between the rhythm of the 'Fate' motif and the gentler waltz idea; a charming slow movement in B♭ minor (**subdominant** minor); **pizzicato** string writing in movement 3, and the Russian folk-song included in movement 4 along with reminders of the earlier Fate motif.

Symphony No.6 is in B minor ('Pathétique', 1893). Sonata form is evident in movement 1, though unconventionally, the music is in E minor to start – note the contrasts of moods,

divisi writing for instruments and the way that Tchaikovsky transforms and develops ideas; **movement** 2 is influenced by Russian folk music and uses the dance structures of the minuet/**scherzo** (with central trio) but is in $\frac{5}{4}$ time; movement 3 is a march in $\frac{4}{4}$ ($\frac{12}{8}$), and the finale is a very sad '**adagio**' movement, which recalls ideas from the opening movement. This symphony was first performed only weeks before the composer died. He had said that the symphony had a programme which would remain a mystery – some have suggested that perhaps it was simply a reflection of his own personal situation.

In terms of his style, note:

- Colourful though essentially simple **orchestration** in the manner of Berlioz which used same-**sonority** instruments for a block of sound rather than a mixture, and with vivid solo passages

- Extremely tuneful content, often with thematic material that was already complete, therefore not opening itself up for further development in the manner of the conventional **sonata form** plan. His work tended to be organised in contrasting sections, with all elements working together to result in a coherent and unified whole.

Mahler

Mahler wrote nine symphonies, and like Bruckner, they were of gigantic proportions. He demonstrated the ability to write sensitively for the orchestra. He provided detailed programmes with the first four symphonies, but these were later withheld. In four of his symphonies he also uses voices.

Gustav Mahler

He was influenced by Beethoven and Wagner and despite the inclusion of operatic and programmatic elements in his work, he kept to the tradition of a symphony being in distinct movements, the last of the line of the German symphonists since Haydn. However, he was preoccupied with poetry, song and philosophy and that influenced his ideas; he was a composer of songs, and lyrical skills are found in his symphonic writing, such as use of folk song in the scherzo, and incorporation of some of this early song material in the later symphonic works where a song theme or text was sometimes used as a structural device. He depended on many programmatic elements, but retained the **Classical** concept of a symphony as a work in several movements governed by the requirements of the musical organisation.

He adopted a similar stance to Bruckner in the slow movements, and like many of the other **Romantic** symphonic composers, the weight of interest is found in the finales of his works, where he referred to earlier themes – even using similar themes across symphonies ('**cyclic**' practice). He embraced the exploration of new keys and sometimes did not return to the **tonic** home key at all (ending the symphony in a different key to what it began). The works are very long and structurally complex.

Only the first four of Mahler's symphonies fall into the period up to 1900 as required by the A level specification. It is worth considering the orchestration in each one as the requirements are so great.

- Symphony No.1 in D major (1887-8). Scored for a large orchestra of about 100 musicians, though not all are used in every **movement**. In its final form, there are four movements and extended proportions are also evident in terms of the musical structure.

- Symphony No.2, in C minor/E♭ major, (1897) *'Resurrection'*. Again scored for extremely large orchestra, including voices. The work has 5 movements, and lasts between 80-90 minutes. Movement 1 is long and detailed, 2 is in the style of a slow waltz (or Austrian folk-song), 3 and 4 adapt ideas from his song-cycle *Das Knaben Wunderhorn*, and the finale presents an orchestral depiction of the day of Resurrection, followed by an impressive setting of a Resurrection ode (by the German poet Klopstock).

- Symphony No.3 in D minor/F major (1893-6). The scoring requirements are again immense – and the work has 6 movements in all: the first is colossal and the remaining 5 shorter, though each presenting interesting moments in terms of mood (2 and 5), **rhythm** (3), scoring and **cyclic** techniques (4).

- Symphony No.4 in G major (1899-1900). This is a shorter though popular four-movement work scored for a smaller orchestra without trombones or tuba. Again, there is a variety of percussion instruments, and there is a part for soprano in the finale. The entire work is built around a song, *"Das himmlische Leben"*, originally written in 1892.

Mahler's preoccupations with the balance of fulfillment and pleasure against grief and anguish is found in many of his works, and as D.J. Grout states: 'In his symphonies he attempted – not always with success – to join sophistication with simplicity, to juxtapose the most lofty, wide-ranging cosmic conceptions and struggles with lyricism, Austrian folk-song, nature painting, popular dance-rhythms, chorale themes, marches, elements of parody, the spooky and the grotesque.'

Richard Strauss

Like Mahler, Strauss was also a well-known conductor and perhaps the most famous of the German 'post' **Romantic** composers. In his symphonic compositions, he preferred the symphonic **tone-poem**, the Romantic ideal, and was influenced by Berlioz and Liszt. His tone-poems are similar to the model used by Liszt.

Of particular significance are the early **symphonic poems**, including: *Don Juan* (1888), *Tod und Verklärung* (1889), *Till Eulenspiegel* (1895), *Also Sprach Zarathustra* (1896 – the opening theme of which became famous after its use in the 1968 film *2001: A Space Odyssey*), *Don Quixote* (1897), and *Ein Heldenleben* (1898).

Richard Strauss

EXAMPLE WORKS:

Till Eulenspiegel

A popular work based on an old German story, this was about a peasant folk-hero and prankster called Till Eulenspiegel. It is a programmatic **tone-poem** scored for a large orchestra, expanding on the triple woodwind usual at the end of the century and employing quadruple woodwind instruments; it builds to 8 horns and 6 trumpets by the end of the piece, 3 trombones and tuba, 5 timps and various percussion (including a rattle) and strings. Further explanatory information states 'Till Eulenspiegel's Merry Pranks, After the Old Rogue's Tale, set in Rondo Form for Large Orchestra.'

The music which describes the main character is convincing and consists of two themes. The work has a prologue and epilogue, perhaps consistent with folk-lore. Rondo form is evident though not in the classical sense, as its use is very free; it is described so because of the continuing recurrence of the two main themes.

Ein Heldenleben

It has been suggested that this work is probably autobiographical in nature, and it contains more than 30 quotations from his earlier works. In terms of the scoring there are 3 flutes (plus piccolo), 3 oboes (plus cor anglais), 4 clarinets (including E♭, soprano and bass), 3 bassoons (plus contrabassoon); 8 horns, 5 trumpets (plus 3 off-stage at one point), 3 trombones, tenor tuba and tuba; timpani and various percussion including tam-tam; strings, 2 harps and a solo violin part.

The piece is through-composed, with 6 main divisions that were once given titles, though may not always be indicated today. The work displays elements of **sonata-rondo** form, and is reliant on **leitmotifs**.

Strauss' works show the influence of Wagner, both in his use of **harmony** and in the way he harnessed the power of Wagner's opera-orchestra for the concert hall. He was also influenced by Berlioz and Liszt. Like Mahler, he embraced gigantic forces in terms of the **orchestration**, but as a composer he was also influenced by Mozart, and was still able to demonstrate the delicate **textures** akin to chamber music, including a stylistic figuration which is still relatively Classical in spirit. His music is constructed according to symphonic conception, at times using well defined forms (such as the rondo in *Till Eulenspiegel* or the variations in *Don Quixote*). He also used 'transformation of themes', sometimes combining his ideas in a **polyphonic** manner again in the style of Wagner.

AS Level Component 3 Practice Paper

Area of Study A: Western Classical Tradition

In the exam, you will be given **four** questions for this part of the paper. The first two will be divided into around 6 to 8 parts (a-f or perhaps a-h), and worth **13 marks** and **10 marks** respectively. Both of these will require you to listen to extracts of unprepared works and answer short questions about them or fill in missing elements from the score.

The third question is an essay question, you will hear two extracts of unprepared works and be required to compare them: they are likely to be from different eras of the period of study. This question will be worth **10 marks** and will require you to use your more general knowledge about the genre.

Finally you will have a choice between two questions, depending on which is your chosen work for study from the two set works. For this part of the paper you are allowed to have an unannotated copy of the score for your chosen work. Again you will be asked a number of short questions, adding up to a total of **15 marks**.

Here we have given you one example paper. Sample assessment papers are also available to download from the Eduqas website, and you should practise answering these as much as possible

Listen to an extract from a symphony by Haydn

Listen to the music at this link, from the start of the video until 40 seconds in: www.youtube.com/watch?v=JESXMWrwzVQ

1. A piano reduction is printed below. The extract will be played **twice** with a **1 minute** pause between each playing and a **5 minute** silence after the final playing for you to complete your answer.

   You now have 30 seconds to read the questions.   [13]

(a)   State the full name (e.g. F minor) of the key in which the extract begins.   [1]

....

(b)   State the full name (e.g. F minor) of the key in which the extract ends .   [1]

....

(c)   Name the two treble instruments playing the theme throughout this extract.   [2]

1. ....

2. ....

(d)   Identify the type of melodic movement heard in bars 1 and 2.   [1]

....

(e)   (i) Identify the cadence heard in bars 6–8 ....   [1]

(ii) Identify the harmonic device heard in bars 17-18 ....   [1]

(f)   Indicate whether the statements below are **true** or **false.**   [3]

Musical Statements	True or False
The dynamic at the start of the piece is *pianissimo*	
The tempo of the extract is *Andante*	
The ornament used in bar 9 is an acciaccatura.	

(g)   Name the chord used in bar 6.   [1]

....

(h)   Identify the following intervals (e.g. minor 3rd), as indicated on the score.   [2]

(i) Between the two notes, bar 12^1 – 12^2 in the bass clef ....

(ii) Between the two notes, bar 12 in the treble clef ....

TIPS

■ As you can see, these questions relate to your overall musical and theoretical understanding. Make sure that you have completed plenty of practice questions and tasks to understand the requirements and the terminology.

■ Don't rush – but don't panic! Work out the chords of the key on the side of the score if it helps.

■ Don't write your answers while the music is playing – jot the answer in pencil, and carry on listening and following the score carefully.

■ Use the time in between the playing to write your answers.

Listen to an extract from Symphony No.28 by Haydn

Listen to the music at this link: www.youtube.com/watch?v=I0BU4Rrmt_M –
The extract begins at 5 minutes and 7 seconds.

2. An outline of the score is printed below. The extract will be played **5 times** with a **1 minute** pause between each playing and a **2 minute** silence after the final playing for you to complete your answer.

You now have 30 seconds to read the questions.

[10]

(a)   State the full name of the key (e.g. F♯ minor) in bar 7.   [1]

....

(b)   Name the key and cadence in bars 29-30.   [2]

    (i) Key ....

    (ii) Cadence ....

(c)   Write in the correct note lengths for the given pitch/note-names in bar 15.   [2]

....

....

(d)   Complete the violin part in bars 19-21. The note lengths have been given to you.   [3]

....

....

....

(e)   Give the bar and beat number of a dominant 7th chord in bars 1-18.   [1]

....

(f)   Give the bar number of a harmonic suspension in the extract.   [1]

....

TIPS

- You may have some time to look over the score after the previous questions and before this extract starts. Use the time wisely: establish the key, work out the chords and make notes in pencil.

- As with the previous question, always keep your focus. For example, don't go writing in the answer for what the key or cadence is (even if you get excited that you know the answer!) Make a quick note, then write in your answer during the time allowed between playings of the extract.

- It is especially important that you prepare yourself for the rhythmic or melodic dictation part of the question. **Remember**, this is one part of the question which **must** be completed as you listen. Work to improve your dictation skills on a regular basis so that you can write notation efficiently and quickly.

- Look out for patterns, and repetition of ideas.

Listen to the music at these two links: www.youtube.com/watch?v=2jsOLXNWhZI and www.youtube.com/watch?v=_X9UEYDeTEO

3. You will now hear 90 seconds of music from each of the openings of two movements from two different symphonies. The first was composed in 1772 (early Classical era), the second was composed in 1822 (early Romantic era).

Compare the stylistic features of each era which can be heard in the extracts.   **[10]**

In your answer you must refer to:
- *Dynamics*
- *Orchestration*
- *Tonality/Harmony*
- *Any other features you consider relevant*

....

....

....

....

....

....

....

....

....

....

....

....

....

....

....

....

....

....

....

....

....

Set work

4. You must either answer the question on the Haydn, or the question on the Mendelssohn.
You will need an unannotated score.   **[15]**

Either HAYDN's 'London' Symphony (movements 1 and 2),

or MENDELSSOHN's 'Italian' Symphony (movements 1 and 2)

HAYDN's 'London' Symphony

(a)   The 2nd movement of this symphony is in a: [1]

      Binary structure   **Rondo structure**   **Tripartite structure**

(b)   The texture at the start of the movement is: [1]

      Contrapuntal   **Fugal**   **Homophonic**   **Unison**

(c)   Which woodwind instruments are used to a lesser extent in this movement?   [1]

    ....

(d)   State 2 ways in which the opening phrase 'a' is changed in bars 17-32.   [2]

      1. ....

      2. ....

(e)   This symphony was first performed in: [1]

      1785   **1795**   **1805**   **1815**

(f)   Identify the section which begins in bar 38.   [1]

    ....

(g)   Describe Haydn's use of harmony and tonality in bars 38–56.   [5]

    ....

    ....

    ....

    ....

    ....

(h)   Explain some ways in which Haydn develops the thematic material in
    bars 98–112.   [3]

    ....

    ....

    ....

MENDELSSOHN's 'Italian' Symphony

(a)   The 2nd movement of this symphony is in: [1]

   An extended binary structure

   An overall arch structure

   Sonata form structure

(b)   The texture at the very start of the movement is: [1]

   Contrapuntal   Fugal   Homophonic   Monophonic

(c)   Name two places where the opening motif is heard later in the movement.   [2]

   1. ....

   2. ....

(d)   This symphony was first performed in: [1]

   1803   1813   1823   1833

(e)   State the key of the movement.   [1]

   ....

(f)   Describe Mendelssohn's use of harmony and tonality in bars 45–56.   [5]

   ....

   ....

   ....

   ....

   ....

(g)   (i) Identify the section which begins in bar 57.   [1]

   ....

   (ii) Compare this material with its first appearance in the movement.   [3]

   ....

   ....

   ....

A Level Component 3 Practice Paper

Area of Study A: Western Classical Tradition

In the exam, you will be given **three** questions for this part of the paper.

The first will be divided into around 3 to 4 parts and worth **10 marks**. You will listen to an unprepared extract, for which you will be given a score and asked to fill in or correct notes.

The second will be on your set work, you choose between two questions, depending on which work you have studied. You must answer a few short and one longer question on this work, and you will be allowed to refer to an unannotated score. This is worth **15 marks**.

The third question is an essay question which tests your general knowledge of this topic. This is also worth **15 marks**.

Here we have given you one example paper. Sample assessment papers are also available to download from the Eduqas website, and you should practise answering these as much as possible.

Listen to part of a symphony by Mendelssohn ('Scottish', movement 3)

Listen to the music at this link: www.youtube.com/watch?v=xkRiX4r6TxE

1. Most of the melody is printed below. The extract will be played **5 times** with a **1 minute** pause between each playing. There will be a **2 minute** silence at the end for you to complete your answer. [10]

   You have 30 seconds to read the questions.

(a) There are two errors in the music, one in pitch and one in rhythm. Circle the notes that are incorrect and above each write what you actually hear in the music. [4]

(b) Describe the chord used in bar 6. [1]

   ....

(c) Write in the missing **pitch and rhythm** in bars 8-10. [5]

2. You now have **1 hour** to answer on

Either HAYDN's 'London' Symphony

or MENDELSSOHN's 'Italian' Symphony   [15]

HAYDN's 'London' Symphony

You will need an unannotated score of Symphony No.4 by Haydn.
The following questions are on movement 3.

(a)   Name in full (e.g. C minor) the **keys and cadences** in the following bars.   [4]

Bars	Key	Cadence
$3^3 - 4$		
$19^3 - 20$		

(b)   Explain the overall structure of the movement. You must identify the
main sections and include bar numbers.   [6]

....

....

....

....

....

....

(c)   Analyse the musical content of bars 53–64. You must comment on the melody,
harmony, texture, writing for instruments and any other features of interest.   [5]

....

....

....

....

....

MENDELSSOHN's 'Italian' Symphony

You will need an unannotated score of Mendelssohn's 'Italian' symphony.
The following questions are on movement 3.

(a)   Name in full (e.g. C minor) the **keys and cadences** in the following bars.   [4]

Bars	Key	Cadence
7^3-8^1		
45^3-46^1		

(b)   Explain the overall structure of the movement. You must identify the main
        sections and include bar numbers.   [6]

....

....

....

....

....

....

(c)   Analyse the musical content of bars 93-108. You must comment on the melody,
        harmony, texture, writing for instruments and any other features of interest.   [5]

....

....

....

....

....

3. This will be the final essay question which assesses knowledge of the development of the
   symphony and understanding of the symphony in the wider cultural and historical context.
   Much of the content of this chapter has been directed towards supporting your knowledge
   and understanding in this aspect. Examples of this question are available in the sample
   assessment materials on the Eduqas website: http://tinyurl.com/glfyqwo

TIPS

- The questions will demand a response which will include detail from both set works
  and other relevant symphonies from the Classical and Romantic eras.

- You need a broad understanding of the main developments of the genre from
  Mannheim to the later programmatic forms and how musical elements were utilised.

- Make sure you reinforce your learning in class by listening to a variety of appropriate
  works from across both periods.

- Develop your essay writing skills by completing regular written observations when
  listening to extracts from symphonies, and doing all practice essays set by your
  teacher. Using bullet points is not sufficient at this level.

- Explain your observations as fully as time allows in the examination, and support
  with reference to the music of the era. Ensure that you use accurate terminology and
  appropriate musical vocabulary.

- Make sure that you answer the question set! Identify carefully what has been asked,
  and plan your response before diving into a hurried response which fails to answer
  the question.

Rock and Pop

FROM 1960 ONWARDS

Rock and Pop is one of the optional Areas of Study (AoS). The AoS covers the development and stylistic features of rock and pop music from a variety of genres, between 1960 and 1990 for AS level, and between 1960 and 2000 for A level.

There are no set composers or bands for this area of study, instead you will work through a number of decades and genres within Rock and Pop music: 3 decades and 4 genres for AS Level, and 4 decades and 5 genres for A Level.

Course Requirements

What do I have to study at AS level?

For AS level, you will study **four** rock and pop genres over a period from 1960-1990:

- **Pop**
- **Rock**
- **Soul**
- **Funk**

Well-known and characteristic works that encapsulate these styles are examined in this section, although many of the features identified are generally common to rock and pop music as a whole.

What do I have to study at A level?

At A level, the time-span is slightly extended to cover music written from 1990 up to and including the year 2000, and you will study an extra genre **in addition to the four listed above**:

- **Folk**

How is this Area of Study assessed?

Music from this AoS will appear in Section 1 of the Component 3 'Appraising Music' exam paper.

At AS level, you will be required to answer three questions on AoS B:

- Two questions, one on each of two unprepared extracts
- A question assessing understanding of the wider context of the area of study.

These questions are collectively worth **40 marks**.

At A level you will be required to answer two questions on AoS B:

- One question on an unprepared musical extract
- A comparison question based on two unprepared extracts assessing wider understanding of the area of study.

These questions are collectively worth **30 marks**.

An introduction to Rock and Pop since 1960

In the 1960s, there were unparalleled changes in rock and pop music. The move to write music with more artistic intent towards the end of the 1960s led to a plethora of new styles in the 1970s and 1980s.

Advances and developments in music technology led to the increasing use of synthesisers, samplers and recording effects, along with more polished recordings and artistic freedom and the evolution of further styles, the development of those already in existence and the creation and amalgamation of sub-genres. In the 1990s, there was even more reliance on technology, but some artists and bands chose to simplify things, taking a step backwards and becoming more independent in their approach to songwriting and releasing music.

Rock Music: The Electric Guitar

A pivotal moment in the development of rock music was the invention of the electric guitar. The original intention, to make the acoustic guitar more audible when playing in big bands, now pales in comparison with the flexibility of its use across the genre. The electric guitar was initially hollow-bodied like an acoustic guitar. It was Leo Fender who created the first commercially-successful solid-body electric guitar.

NEW INSTRUMENTS, NEW SOUNDS:
The Fender Stratocaster

- The Stratocaster was first introduced in 1954, and was made famous by artists such as Buddy Holly and Jimi Hendrix.
- The solid body design of the Stratocaster meant that the guitar was less likely to cause feedback when played with heavy amplification
- It was the first guitar to feature a spring tension tremolo system which slackens and tightens the strings and enables the guitarist to bend the pitch of a note
- It also had three separate pickups with a selector switch, so guitarists could change the tone of the instrument during performance.

The Rock and Roll Revolution

In the 1950s, rapid changes in youth culture had occurred throughout Britain and the U.S.A., with the explosion of Rock and Roll music.

While the 1950s are outside the dates in the specification, it is beneficial to spend a moment considering the impact this had and the way this influenced Rock and Pop music as we headed into the 1960s.

Rock and Roll shares many features with Blues:

- 12 bar blues chord progressions
- Stop chorus
- Blues scale and blue notes
- Shuffle rhythms

Chuck Berry: *Johnny B. Goode,* 1958

- 'Johnny B. Goode' is loosely biographical and is said to relate to Berry himself
- The song begins with an overdriven guitar solo based on the blues scale and accompanied by two stop chords
- The song's 12 bar blues start to become apparent as the rhythm section introduce a walking bass pattern based on chord IV
- There is a strong backbeat emphasis and the repeated vocal patterns in the chorus are syncopated
- The melody in chorus is structured like a blues 3 line lyric (AAB).

Rock and Roll's cultural revolution was equivalent to its musical impact. In the 1950s, Britain and the U.S.A. were moving beyond their 'post-war' years. Teenagers were rebelling, had more spending power and were looking for a musical style to call their own.

Rockabilly was an early form of rock and roll that fused country and blues music and was made famous by Carl Perkins and Elvis Presley. Presley ended up a rock and roll icon who quickly moved away from his Rockabilly roots, and whose attitude, clothing and hairstyle were emulated by a generation. Bill Haley's 'Rock Around the Clock', released in 1954, is often credited as marking the start of the new rock and roll style. Artists such as Chuck Berry and Bo Diddley pioneered this new, guitar-led style with reduced instrumentation and shorter, snappier song structures than had been seen in jazz and big band music.

A LEVEL EXTENSION
The Influence of Country

Country music had its origins in the southern states of the U.S.A. and evolved from folk traditions. However, it shares more parallels with pop than it does with folk; country artists were often heavily promoted by recording labels.

This led to commercial success and country artists finding their way into the mainstream music industry. For the most part, folk music tends to lack this commercial success. Country songs often feature polished recordings, with a focus on capturing the true sound of the acoustic instruments; a booming industry developed in Nashville, Tennessee in order to do this.

Tammy Wynette: *D.I.V.O.R.C.E.*, 1968

- 'D.I.V.O.R.C.E.' begins with a 'rocking' bass line that alternates between the root and fifth of each chord
- The introduction features a slide/bottleneck guitar lead, while the rhythm section emphasises the backbeat of the music with a snare hit and guitar chord on beats 2 and 4
- The chordal accompaniment is provided by a fingerpicked guitar.

New Styles in Britain and the 'British Invasion'

In 1960s Britain, pop artists such as Cliff Richard and Adam Faith were releasing music to great success amongst older generations, and Lonnie Donegan was recording Skiffle music; this sound formed the basis of the Beatles' early recordings.

Skiffle music featured everyday items used as instruments, such as washboards and home made basses along with a strummed instrument such as a guitar or banjo. John Lennon's first band, his 'Quarrymen' performed in a Skiffle style.

The Beatles

Formed in Liverpool, The Beatles were signed to EMI after performances at the Cavern Club, and a brief spell performing in Germany. After their moderately successful release 'Love Me Do', increasingly popular 'Please Please Me' and hit 'From Me to You', they were under pressure to recreate the success in their fourth single. 'She Loves You', with its repeated vocal hook refrain, achieved the fastest sales of any UK record up to that time.

The Beatles and The Rolling Stones sparked a British musical revolution and gained huge amounts of commercial success at home and abroad. The music was new and emulated the R&B music coming out of the U.S.A. This music quickly became known as **British Beat or Merseybeat**, reflecting its Liverpool origins. It was a little bit controversial and appealed to a young audience. The success of the bands and music in the U.S.A. is often referred

The Beatles were nicknamed 'The Fab Four'

to as the 'British Invasion'. The music was clearly British in style, with simple, catchy and memorable melodies that were performed with British accents.

The Beatles later became more experimental in their use of technology, and their image also changed along with an increase in political awareness that came through their music. This was linked to the freedom of expression generally apparent throughout popular culture in the later 1960s.

The Beatles: *Sergeant Pepper's Lonely Hearts Club Band,* 1967

- 'Sergeant Pepper' was a huge turning point for the Beatles, and both a commercial and critical success
- Concept albums became increasingly common in the late 1960s and 1970s, with all songs often sharing one continuous musical narrative or thematic link
- 'Sergeant Pepper' is set as a fictional performance by Sergeant Pepper's band
- One of the key tracks on the album was 'Strawberry Fields Forever', which was reportedly inspired by Lennon's memories of playing in the garden of Strawberry Field, a Salvation Army children's' home in Liverpool
- It begins with a simple chord progression played on the flute setting on a Mellotron
- At the end of the Mellotron phrase, a portamento is used to shift the pitch of the notes from the chord of D major to A♭.

NEW INSTRUMENTS, NEW SOUNDS:
The Mellotron

- The Mellotron is an early sampler that was invented in the 1960s
- It has been used by artists as diverse as The Beatles, Pink Floyd and Oasis, and is based upon individual strips of tape that are triggered by a keyboard
- Each piece of tape represents a different pitch.

NEW INSTRUMENTS, NEW SOUNDS:
The Electric Piano

- An electric piano functions like an acoustic piano, but instead of hitting strings, the hammers hit small metal reeds or wires called tines
- Vibrations on the tines are then captured using pickups and amplified
- The Fender Rhodes is one of the most famous electric pianos.

In the late 1960s The Beatles, in particular George Harrison, began to look to other styles of music and musical cultures for inspiration. Harrison took up lessons with Ravi Shankar, a sitar master. The Beatles, and subsequently The Rolling Stones incorporated elements of Indian Classical Music into their songs.

Instruments such as the sitar and tanpura were often used, along with scalic influences from Indian Rāga. Repeated rhythmic patterns reminiscent of the Tāla patterns found in Indian Classical music formed an influential part of the psychedelic rock movement in the 60s and 70s.

A tanpura

The Beatles: *Lucy in the Sky with Diamonds,* 1967

- Although often regarded as a thinly-veiled reference to the drug L.S.D., Lennon and McCartney maintained that 'Lucy in the Sky with Diamonds' was actually in response to Julian Lennon coming home from nursery school with a picture he had drawn showing 'Lucy – in the sky with diamonds'

- The majority of the song is written in triple metre with a contrasting chorus pattern in simple quadruple time

- The descending organ pattern introduces the piece, punctuated with short descending bass guitar notes to outline the chord progression at the beginning of each bar

- In the pre-chorus, a drone is played by a tanpura

- The song contains a modulation in each new section. The introduction and verses are in A major. The music then moves to the apparently unrelated key of B♭ major in the pre-chorus and G major in the chorus.

The Rolling Stones

The Rolling Stones were contemporaries of The Beatles and were famous for having an edgier, grittier sound. They were successful in Britain and the U.S.A. as part of the 'British Invasion'. The Rolling Stones were instrumental in embedding stylistic features from blues music into rock, while also creating a style that was rich in rhythm and blues, and soul.

Mick Jagger of The Rolling Stones during a gig in The Hague, 1976

The Rolling Stones: *(I Can't Get No) Satisfaction*, 1965

- *(I Can't Get No) Satisfaction* opens with Keith Richards' heavily distorted electric guitar riff
- Distortion creates an overdriven or fuzzy sound and was initially created by turning amplifiers up too loud
- Nowadays, artists can also use a distortion pedal or an amplifier setting
- Richards had reportedly intended the guitar track to be a rough guide track, over which the intention was to record a horn section
- However, their manager released the track without the planned horn overdubs and The Rolling Stones achieved their first international number one.

The Who

The Who also gained significant success in the 1960s, and were known for their heavy guitar sound along with Pete Townshend's use of **feedback**, power chords and his 'windmill' guitar-technique. They were also well known for destroying their instruments on stage during live performances. The Who influenced 'mod' culture with followers wearing parkas and smart suits, and riding scooters, and are still cited as influential by punk rock bands. The Who also released two rock operas: *Tommy* in 1969 and *Quadrophenia* in 1973, both of which were later made into films.

Pete Townshend of The Who leaps into the air during a gig in Toronto, 1980

The Who: *My Generation*, 1965

- Pete Townshend has stated that '*My Generation* was all about trying to find a place in society, while giving a nod to mod counter-culture and the angst of being a teenager'
- The vocal phrases follow a call and response structure, with Roger Daltrey shouting a line and the response coming in close **harmony** at the end of each phrase.
- The vocal phrases focus on both dotted **rhythms** and **syncopation**, with a quaver at the beginning of Daltrey's phrase emphasising the weak beats.

Other famous 1960s rock bands included The Kinks, The Small Faces, The Animals and The Spencer Davis Group. All played a part in defining the British musical style that became so successful.

A LEVEL EXTENSION
Music for Protest – Politics and Civil Unrest

The 1960s were also a time of protest, with unrest over Vietnam and the Cold War. Artists used music to make political points and raise the issues associated with black civil rights. Bob Dylan spearheaded this kind of 'protest song' and wrote a number of songs with strong political messages.

Dylan's music had its origins in folk music, featuring a narrative and a focus on story-telling. The term 'folk' was initially used to represent any style of music that does this and tended to be performed on the instruments available at the time by people who were community members rather than trained musicians. In the 1960s, the term was increasingly used to refer to popular music with a sense of social conscience. Folk material was adapted and performed by more skilled and talented performers for recording and broadcast, and a popular style of music quickly evolved from its original roots.

Bob Dylan: *These Times They Are a-Changin'*, 1963

- This song chronicles the social unrest in the U.S.A. in the 1960s and became an anthem for the American civil rights and anti-war movements
- It is in strophic form, with a single repeated section
- The song negates some of the traditional features of a popular song, being in triple metre and consisting of a six-line stanza as opposed to the more conventional four lines
- Dylan uses an irregular phrase structure, by making the first and third lines of each stanza five bars long, as opposed to four.

(A) Come mothers and fathers, throughout the land **(5 bars)**
     And don't criticise what you can't understand **(4 bars)**

(A) Your sons and your daughters are beyond your command **(5 bars)**
     Your old road is rapidly agein'. **(4 bars)**

(B) Please get out of the new one, if you can't lend your hand **(4 bars)**
     For the times they are a-changin'. **(4 bars)**

Bob Dylan: *Like A Rolling Stone*, 1965

- Despite his initial folk-focus and use of acoustic instruments, in 1965 Dylan's style began to develop into something more electric
- *Like a Rolling Stone* attracted criticism as Dylan was accompanied by rock musicians and sported a Fender Stratocaster on stage when it was performed for the first time
- This caused controversy amongst his die-hard fans who saw this as a betrayal of the style of music that had made him famous and that they saw as 'typically Dylan'.

Dylan also had an influence on other artists; his music helped to politicise a large segment of rock culture, and inspired The Beatles to use their popularity as an opportunity to speak to their ever captive youthful audience about issues that 'mattered'. Lennon and McCartney's music increasingly became a medium for addressing issues and events affecting a generation, and the writers of the songs became increasingly politically aware.

Dylan's influence extended beyond simply his words and music – Jimi Hendrix once said of Dylan that he was one of the people who proved to him that it was possible to be an artist – 'not the words or his guitar, but as a way to get myself together'.

Hendrix pushed the instrument to its limits in flamboyant stage shows during which he demonstrated his talent by using extended and technically complex techniques on the electric guitar, playing the instrument behind his back and sometimes even with his teeth. The roots of his music were in **R&B** but his focus on technique, along with the sounds of psychedelic rock meant that he was able to use all of the instrument to create sounds and showcase his ability. This, along with his use of effects such as **wah wah**, distortion and the **tremolo** arm demonstrated his virtuosic ability.

Meanwhile, in the U.S.A.

Early 1960s Soul music has its origins in Rhythm and Blues and Gospel. Soul was R&B with a pop edge; initially uncontroversial, it was designed to achieve commercial success. Soul music is characterised by the use of catchy vocal hooks, **improvisation** in tightly controlled solos, **blue notes** and **pentatonic** scales along with an upbeat, danceable tempo and 3-minute songs based around simple structures.

Motown was a Detroit record company formed by Berry Gordy in 1959. Detroit was known as '**Mo**tor-**town**' due to the city's car manufacturing industries. The label spearheaded the idea of a 'hit factory' approach, where studios were running most hours of most days and Gordy had a strict handle on quality control, ensuring that only the best songs were released. This ensured that Motown records were always top of the charts. Motown also played a crucial role in the racial integration of popular music. It was an African-American owned record label but had significant success across the whole record-buying public.

Motown generally avoided complex arrangements and encouraged its producers and engineers to 'KISS' (keep it simple, stupid). The style is characterised by melodic bass lines, a **backbeat** emphasis and call-and-response singing style. Like soul music in general, Motown also used horn section riffs that were tightly rehearsed along with string sections to augment the ensembles. The same group of session musicians was used to record most tracks, to ensure a specific 'Motown-sound'.

Martha and the Vandellas: *Nowhere To Run,* 1967

- *Nowhere to Run* features a range of percussion layers and in this track the tambourine, handclaps and snare on the backbeat are layered to add weight and power to the arrangement
- The riff-based bass line patterns are designed to be catchy, and also emphasise the **root** notes of each chord with some fills to move between chords at the end of each bar. These often feature chromatic notes
- The horn section parts provide a syncopated countermelody, along with stabs and sustained notes
- The accompaniment in this track has been further augmented by the use of strings.

Stax were a rival record label based in Memphis. They produced soul music with a grittier sound than Motown, which quickly became known informally as 'Memphis Soul'. Stax featured several ethnically integrated bands and the label itself employed a racially integrated team of staff. This was unprecedented in a time of racial tension in Memphis and the American South.

Booker T and the MGs: *Green Onions*, 1962

- Booker T and the MGs were the Stax house band, and *Green Onions* started life as an extended jam based on the 12-bar blues
- It has no vocal line and is entirely instrumental, featuring the Hammond B3 organ playing the lead melody
- The entire track centres on the riff played by the instruments in the introduction
- The playing is groove-based, and the ensemble plays together tightly
- It is entirely based around the chordal ostinato of F major followed by A♭ and B♭
- Contrast occurs through textural change and solo parts played by the guitar and organ
- The texture is almost entirely homophonic, with movement and chords in the bass and guitar mirrored by the organ and the drum kit keeping a steady $\frac{4}{4}$ beat throughout.

NEW INSTRUMENTS, NEW SOUNDS:
The Hammond Organ

- The Hammond Organ was originally designed to save space and money compared to a traditional pipe organ
- Each drawbar on a Hammond Organ adds or removes harmonics ('pulling out all the stops'), making the sound brighter or duller
- There are a number of manuals (separate keyboards), along with foot pedal notes
- The Leslie Speaker was used with the Hammond Organ to give a rotary effect, created by spinning the speaker.

Philadelphia Soul became popular in the 1970s, with direct influence from Motown and Stax. The arrangements were more extravagant, with a focus on strings and horns along with increasingly expressive vocal lines. Philadelphia Soul was smoother and more refined in comparison to previous, grittier soul styles and formed a key influence on the early origins of Disco music.

Ike and Tina Turner: *River Deep, Mountain High,* 1966

- Phil Spector pioneered the 'Wall of Sound' production technique in the 1960s. This involved using an echo chamber (a very reverberant room)
- The reverb was then added to the final mix, which often included many guitar, horn and string layers and doubled basses
- There were also plenty of percussion layers, sometimes using overdubbed drum kits
- Spector regarded *River Deep, Mountain High* as the pinnacle of this production technique
- The texture of the song is so dense that you can barely make out the sound of specific instruments below the vocal and backing vocal parts.

Increasing Divisions in Rock Music

In the late 1960s and early 1970s, rock began to take a number of different directions, with a core of similar, basic features but divided into discrete sub-styles. It became increasingly common to divide up mainstream rock into soft and hard rock towards the late 1960s.

Soft rock tended to have its origins in folk rock and used more acoustic instruments; artists such as Fleetwood Mac had particular success. Other British soft rock artists included Cat Stevens, 10CC and Elton John.

Elton John: *Rocket Man,* 1972

- Elton John's music was particularly successful in the 1970s, and he gained a reputation as an excellent songwriter, along with his lyricist, Bernie Taupin
- They used to work separately, with Taupin first writing the lyrics and John sitting down to put them to music, and rarely worked in the same room while doing so
- In line with other artists in the late 1960s and early 1970s (e.g. David Bowie's *Space Oddity* and *Ashes to Ashes*), Elton John's *Rocket Man* is indicative of an underlying fascination with space and space travel
- This fascination with space travel as an 'everyday occupation' is apparent in the song's opening lyrics, 'She packed my bags last night, pre-flight. Zero hour: 9am. And I'm gonna be high as a kite by then'
- The song was reportedly inspired by Taupin's sighting of either a shooting star or distant aeroplane, and the lyrical themes ponder the everyday life of an astronaut outside their public perception as a hero.

Another successful 1970s pop band were ABBA. Their record sales figures are uncertain, but estimates range from 380 million to over 500 million records sold.

ABBA: *Dancing Queen,* 1976

- Dancing Queen was a worldwide hit, with a hook-laden melody and piano accompaniment incorporating disco features

- The track is organised in verse and chorus structure with an introduction and coda that repeats to fade

- The introduction features a sweeping glissando on the piano, along with a declamatory piano phrase in chords. The string and vocal parts play in sixths throughout the introduction, underscored by syncopated orchestral piano chords and octaves

- The entire introduction until 'you can dance' is based on a tonic pedal of A

- We then hear the second half of the chorus (although we do not know this yet)

- There is a brief instrumental interlude between the end of the chorus and the start of the next verse

- The track remains in A major throughout, but briefly moves to the dominant (E) in the second half of the chorus before moving through chords of C♯ and F♯m7

- There is use of a suspended 4th chord on E on the lines 'getting in the swing' and 'everything is fine'. This is when the third degree of the chord is replaced with the fourth. This often then resolves back down to the 3rd, as in a 4/3 suspension, but this is not always the case in popular music.

The development of **psychedelic rock** was linked to the beat generation and festival culture of the late 1960s and early 1970s, along with the rise of drug use. Artists such as The Doors and The Grateful Dead became famous; the music was often long and loosely structured with extensive groove-based playing and long, extended solos. Guitar effects such as flanger, phaser and wah wah were used and there was a focus on musical experimentation. A number of bands incorporated elements of psychedelia in their sounds; The Beatles, Pink Floyd and David Bowie to name but a few.

NEW INSTRUMENTS, NEW SOUNDS:
The Synthesiser

A MiniMoog from 1970

A Yamaha DX-7 (1983)

- The synthesiser is an electronic musical instrument that first came to prominence in the late 1960s
- Synthesisers imitate and recreate the sounds of other instruments, but can also create brand new sounds
- In the 1970s, synthesisers were commonly used in disco music and formed the basis of later electronic dance styles.

The Doors: *Light My Fire*, 1963

- The long, improvised solos in this track are typical of psychedelic rock
- The meandering, spiralling organ part that opens the track was played on a Vox Continental organ
- The song was originally over seven minutes long but was regularly requested for radio play, so a three-minute version was edited.
- This removed the majority of the long instrumental break in the middle of the song.

A parallel development to psychedelic rock was **progressive rock**. It was known for its long, meandering song structures with solos that often incorporated complex time signatures and changes between them, with a focus on the musicianship and virtuosity of the players. Many musicians had classical training and thus more technically complex melodic and harmonic writing that was sometimes based around modes became more common. Artists such as Genesis and Pink Floyd spearheaded the idea of a concept album and 'album-orientated rock'.

Genesis: *Supper's Ready,* 1972

- At over 23 minutes in length, and loosely structured in seven sections, 'Supper's Ready' is a good example of the long, extended structures that became increasingly common in Progressive Rock
- The opening heavily features the 12-string guitar, on which the strings are arranged in pairs to give a thicker, richer, chorus effect
- Themes and melodic ideas do return throughout the piece, and the song goes through a number of tonal, metrical and textural contrasts as it progresses
- Progressive rock music often uses modes, and in section 2, the harmonic language can be described as predominantly mixolydian.
- Despite the implication of A major, the music focuses on G natural rather than G♯
- In section 6 (particularly around 16 minutes), the drums play in $\frac{9}{8}$, and the organ solo enters playing a combination of $\frac{4}{4}$ and the irregular metre $\frac{7}{8}$, contrasting with the drum kit.

Heavy rock came about through a focus on riff-based guitar patterns based on pentatonic and blues scales. Again, the features associated with blues music make an appearance here, along with showcasing more complex guitar techniques such as tapping, pitch bends, hammer ons and pull offs.

Led Zeppelin: *Whole Lotta' Love,* 1969

- *Whole Lotta Love* was written in 1968 for the album 'Led Zeppelin 2', and built entirely around Jimmy Page's famous guitar riff, which is based on the pentatonic scale
- The track was later used as a theme tune for Top of the Pops on BBC TV
- It is structured in thirty-two bar popular song form (AABA structure), and in the opening riff, the lower notes function as a tonic pedal, reinforcing the tonality and home key
- The harmony remains relatively static throughout the verses except for some harmonic variation implied by the end of the phrase which gives a sense of chord V
- In the solo, there is a break featuring a Theremin; an early, motion-sensitive synthesiser that creates sound without any physical contact from the player
- The riff emphasises beats 1 and 2 of the bear, with palm muted root notes on the semiquaver offbeats.

Glam Rock

Glam Rock first became popular in the 1970s, and was characterised by extravagantly dressed male performers sporting make up and outrageous hairstyles. The pinnacle of the style featured artists such as Marc Bolan and T-Rex, Slade, Sweet and Roxy Music.

David Bowie was a key pioneer of the Glam Rock style, taking on a diverse range of influences. Initially, songs such as *Space Oddity* fed upon the public feelings around the space race of the late 1960s. Bowie later created the persona of Ziggy Stardust along with backing band The Spiders from Mars who feature in the 1972 song and album of the same name. The concept album tells the story of Ziggy Stardust who is a messenger for extra-terrestrial beings. Bowie went through later shifts in style for his albums 'Young Americans' and 'Station to Station'.

Noddy Holder, the lead singer of Slade, in his glam rock attire, 1973

David Bowie: *Heroes*, 1977

- Bowie's influence was such that his performance of *Heroes* in 1987 at the German Reichstag in West Berlin contributed to the later fall of the Berlin wall
- *Heroes* featured musicians Brian Eno and Robert Fripp (of King Crimson) on synthesiser and electric guitar
- The soaring guitar notes in the introduction were a result of Fripp moving towards and away from his amplifier, creating feedback, and changing the pitch in real time
- Eno then fed these through a synthesiser and changed parameters of the sound, also adding white noise.

Punk and New Wave

In the mid to late 1970s, **Punk Rock** burst onto the scene, characterised by short, fast and aggressive songs and focusing on a raw, live sound. Lyrics often courted controversy and intentionally tackled anti-establishment and political themes, although sometimes superficially for the sake of being infamous.

The punk subculture had close links to fashion; bands and punks were identifiable by their distinctive clothing of offensive t-shirts, leather jackets, spike bands, studded jewellery and safety pins.

The Sex Pistols in 1977

Malcolm McClaren put together the Sex Pistols in 1976. He had visited New York and had seen the New York Dolls perform. His intention was to create a band in London using the same punk 'look' and ideals. The Sex Pistols released songs and deliberately built up their notoriety by trying to shock, resulting in their music sometimes being banned by radio stations and TV networks.

Sex Pistols: *Anarchy in the UK,* 1977

- *Anarchy in the UK* is characterised by Johnny Rotten (John Lydon's) vocal, delivered using a limited pitch range and restricted range of rhythmic patterns that often mimicked an elaborate style of talking or speech rhythms
- In the verses and choruses, the guitar and bass chords continue with quaver power chords based around the first, fourth and fifth degrees of the scale, along with a descending power chord pattern in the introduction
- The guitar solo in the bridge is short and simple, focusing on a single repeated idea.

After the success of the first bands, later bands tended to take influence from other styles with more political and socially responsible considerations, and produced music that was more polished.

The Clash fused influences from a variety of styles, from reggae to country with more insightful and socially aware lyrics written by Joe Strummer. The Clash's politicised lyrics, musical experimentation and rebellious attitude had a far-reaching influence. This more polished sound later became known as **New Wave**, with bands such as The Stranglers and The Jam gaining much commercial success.

The Clash: *London Calling*, 1977

- In *London Calling*, Strummer's lyrics highlight the problems of rising unemployment, drug use and racial conflict in Britain
- The bass guitar plays arpeggio-based patterns in the opening of the track, which outline the chord progression
- The introductory drum beat and guitar chords all emphasise the four beats to the bar $\frac{4}{4}$ metre, but the drums then feature swung 16ths as Strummer begins to sing the verse
- Jones' guitar solo is played backwards; it was recorded and then the tape reversed to create the sustained, fading sounds audible in the instrumental break.

Many of New Wave's stylistic features are more common to popular music than they are to punk. Although embodying the original punk rock sound and ethos, New Wave tends to have a greater focus on complexity, melody and a glossier, more polished sound. Common features include electronic production, focus on style, fashion and the arts, and diverse musical influences along with the use of synthesisers and keyboards.

Blondie: *Heart of Glass*, 1979

- Blondie, fronted by Debbie Harry, combined stylistic influences from Punk and New Wave, Reggae, early Rap and were condemned by some critics in 1979 for using Disco influences in *Heart of Glass*
- Despite this, the song was a critical and commercial success
- Drummer Clem Burke later cited the stylistic origins of the track in an older song Blondie had been playing for years in a reggae style, fused with the sounds of Kraftwerk and a drum beat emulating *Stayin' Alive* by the Bee Gees (with Harry mirroring the falsetto effect famously used by the Bee Gees using the upper register of her own voice).

Disco

In the early 1970s, there was a move towards more complex arrangements and polished production in music taking influence from funk and soul. This style was spearheaded by bands such as the Bee Gees, and artists gained much commercial success as they produced glossy, catchy and polished music that was intended for dancing in clubs.

Disco based itself on an insistent four-to-the-floor kick drum pattern that mixed offbeat quaver and semiquaver open and closed hi-hat patterns with a handclap and snare backbeat emphasis on beats 2 and 4. Syncopation was common, with bass lines emphasising root notes in repeated quaver patterns, or having melodic interest similar to that in soul music. Choppy semiquaver riffs and chord patterns were often played on bright, wah wah and high-frequency heavy guitar parts that created a chordal accompaniment, along with syncopated piano block chords.

Technological developments such as the increased number of tracks available in multitrack recording, the Fender Rhodes and the Moog synthesiser, along with the changing role of the DJ, pushed disco forward towards the late-1970s. Disco vocal parts tended to be catchy and hook-laden, and horn sections, sustained strings and electric piano sounds were used to thicken the **texture** and create a dense accompaniment to the vocal and solo parts. Orchestral instruments such as the flute were increasingly used for solo melodies, and the lead guitar is often featured using an increasing array of guitar effects. Nile Rogers' disco guitar style became part of the 'gold standard', and this is showcased throughout the 1970s and later, in his work with artists as diverse as Chic and Daft Punk.

Disco was often seen as tacky and 'sold out' in style, with funk music seen as its grittier and underground cousin. Despite this, there were a number of artists who managed to create a more authentic disco sound; in particular bands such as Earth Wind and Fire, and Chic, who made careers as songwriters for disco and other styles.

NEW INSTRUMENTS, NEW SOUNDS:
Sequencers and Drum Machines

- A drum machine is an electronic instrument that stores, creates and replays drum sounds or patterns

- Modern drum machines are essentially sequencers that incorporate sample replay or synthesis technology

- The Roland TR-808 and TR-909 became particularly famous in Hip Hop and Electronic Dance music

- The Roland TB-303 is an example of a bass sequencer that became the sound of Acid House music in the 1990s.

A Roland TR-808 Drum Machine

Donna Summer: *I Feel Love,* 1977

- The use of sequencers and drum machines revolutionised the sound of late-1970s disco music. The work of Giorgio Moroder in producing music by Donna Summer was a key influence on this

- Almost all of the instruments on *I Feel Love* are electronic and synthesised

- It was a number 1 hit in the UK and is entirely based around the opening four-to-the-floor kick pattern and iconic synth bass part

- The track opens with a sustained synth pad which fades in with a phaser effect

- The electronic snare and handclap on beats 2 and 4, along with the offbeat quaver hi hat patterns form the basis of the rhythm track.

Earth Wind and Fire blended horn section riffs and stabs with energetic performances, taking influence from soul, funk, disco and pop. Their contemporaries, Kool and the Gang were at their most successful when performing their pop-influenced funk, with smash hits such as *Celebration* and *Ladies Night.*

The DJ's role became increasingly creative in the 1970s, as they were not only expected to pick tracks to judge the mood of the dance floor and keep people dancing, but also to remix and re-edit tracks, adding in longer **breaks** or cutting back the **texture**, or even soloing a single instrument. They used more complex effects such as **reverb**, delay and **EQ**.

By the mid-1970s, the stylistic features of disco shared a majority of similarities with those of popular music, and this continued until the mid-1980s.

Funk

At the end of the 1960s, the foundations had already been laid for **funk music**. Performances among funk artists such as James Brown and Stevie Wonder moved towards up-tempo, groove based music, with some significant overlap between **R&B**, soul and funk. Features of funk included the use of slap-bass, **improvisation** in solos and heavy use of **syncopation** in drum beats. Other features shared parallels with disco music.

James Brown's music was typified by his energetic stage presence, dancing and powerful vocals, along with his commitment to music of the highest quality and strictness as a bandleader. Other famous artists included George Clinton's Parliament and Funkadelic bands.

James Brown: *I Feel Good,* 1964

- *I Feel Good* uses a repeated question and answer lead vocal phrase that is similar to the AAB three-line lyric structure found in blues music
- The song makes use of extended chords and chromatic movement in the backing horn section parts, demonstrated in the example below
- The piece is up-tempo, as is often the case in funk music, at approximately 144bpm.

Stevie Wonder was born in America in 1950 and was signed to Motown when he was only 11 years old. His singles included *Signed Sealed Delivered*, *Superstition* and *Sir Duke*.

Stevie Wonder: *Superstition*, 1972

- *Superstition* was released as part of the album 'Talking Book' in 1972.
- It features the Hohner Clavinet with wah wah, producing a bright overall timbre
- *Superstition* is primarily based around pentatonic scale patterns on top of a repeated G♭ pedal in the bass
- Above this, the clavinet parts imply an extended E♭7♯9 chord
- In the bridge, there is a focus on the dominant 7th on 'when you believe...'. This adds to the tension created by the chromatic movement in the bass line and pushes the music back towards the tonic of G♭ in the break before the next verse.

Stevie Wonder playing a gig in Las Vegas in 2015

NEW INSTRUMENTS, NEW SOUNDS:
The Hohner Clavinet

- The Hohner Clavinet was created as an electronically amplified clavichord
- It was used predominantly in disco and funk music in the 1970s, and particularly by Stevie Wonder
- It gives a staccato sound that is similar to a harpsichord, but without its characteristic resonance.

Taking influence from reggae

Ska and **Rocksteady** were Jamaican music styles from the 1960s that had an influence on rock and pop music. Ska fused Jamaican Mento (a style of Jamaican folk music featuring acoustic instruments that is similar to calypso music) with American R&B and is characterised by off-beat rhythms, syncopation and horn section riffs and stabs.

Rocksteady was an early form of reggae music that incorporated stylistic features from American music, along with slower tempos than ska and a heavy bass guitar part playing a $\frac{4}{4}$ pattern. Guitar chops emphasised beats 2 and 4.

'Roots' reggae came about in the early 1970s. Bob Marley became Jamaica and reggae's greatest export, with his music generally featuring a slower tempo than ska, and characterised by offbeat guitar chops, offbeat quavers, simple chord sequences and songs written in verse and chorus form. Bass guitar patterns tended to be melodic and riff based, and an electric organ sound is often utilised, playing a shuffle or 'bubble' rhythm.

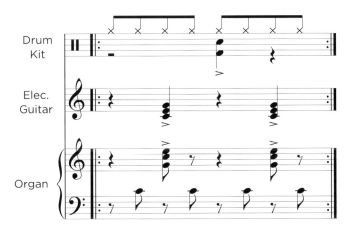

Dub reggae originated in Jamaica when DJs played reggae records on their sound systems: big PA systems around the island on which DJs remixed tracks on the spot, adding spot effects such as reverb and delay to single notes. They were often linked to studios on the island, and it was common for DJs to extend instrumental sections, removing the vocals and stripping back instruments so they could talk over the top of the music.

This became known as 'toasting' and was often used to announce how good their sound system and music choices were. This was an early influence on the rap and hip hop style of the late 1970s and early 1980s. A variety of other reggae styles gained success in the 1980s and 1990s, including dancehall reggae and reggae fusions.

The 1980s UK **2-tone** genre which initially centred on Coventry was a fusion of Jamaican ska and punk rock that was named after The Specials' Jerry Dammer's record label. The movement promoted racial unity and the music of The Specials drew public attention to the issues of racism and fighting. Another successful band in what became known as the **'ska revival'** were Madness, who had a great deal of commercial success and are often credited with bringing the 2-tone label into the mainstream.

The Specials: *Ghost Town*, 1980

- *Ghost Town* chronicles the desolate sense of living in a city where 'all the clubs are being closed down', based on what The Specials had observed happening in their hometown of Coventry

- It opens with a string of consecutive diminished chords that ascend by step as they increase in harmonic rhythm

- The bass line moves chromatically in the introduction

- The flute melody in the opening emphasises the 6th degree and the sharpened 7th degree of the harmonic minor scale, and plays on the augmented 2nd interval between them

- The chord progression in the verse heavily features a G7♭9 chord

- While the piece is predominantly in C minor (although with much chromatic interest), the bridge features an unusual modulation to F♯ major, which gives the music a sense of brightness and optimism

- Here the change to the major mode in the music reflects the lyrics, as we hear about 'the good old days before the ghost town'.

Synthesisers and New Romantics

The **New Romantic** movement developed in London nightclubs in the late 1970s and was epitomised by eccentric and flamboyant costumes and make-up with their origins in the historical Romantic era.

It was spearheaded by Steve Strange of Visage and harked back to the Glam Rock styles of David Bowie and Roxy Music. This gave rise to bands such as Spandau Ballet, with Duran Duran emerging from a similar scene in Birmingham. Many of these bands settled on **synth pop** as their musical style; defined by the use of synthesisers, drum machines and sequencers, it was popularised by Ultravox, The Human League and Gary Numan & Tubeway Army.

Ultravox were formed in 1974 and were led by John Foxx and later Midge Ure, taking influence from glam rock artists such as David Bowie. They were also influenced by bands such as Kraftwerk, who were already gaining acclaim for their ground-breaking use of synthesisers and equipment that was often designed by themselves, with tracks such as *Autobahn* and *The Model*.

Ultravox: *Hiroshima Mon Amour*, 1977

- *Hiroshima Mon Amour* is often regarded as one of the earliest examples of synth pop
- Given the very sparse texture, the main rhythmic interest comes from the electronic drum beat provided by the Roland CR-77 drum machine
- This is combined with arching melodic saxophone phrases
- Later Ultravox songs such as *Vienna* contrasted with the earlier sounds of *Hiroshima Mon Amour* with more textural layers and a more polished sound.

Human League: *Don't You Want Me*, 1981

- *Don't You Want Me* signalled the start of the Human League's more commercial, pop-orientated work
- The track features the Linn Drum Machine
- The vocal part is almost entirely syllabic, with the only hint of melisma at the end of the second line of the chorus ('Don't You Want Me... ohh')
- The track is written in verse and chorus structure, with the introduction and pre-chorus based around the key of A minor, and the verse and chorus in F major, with the modulation at the end of the pre-chorus focusing on stepwise movement between chords from A minor to E major
- The overall texture of the song is melody-dominated homophony, as is common in popular music. However, it incorporates offbeat countermelodies throughout the chorus
- The pre-chorus is an example of a modified ascending sequence. Each line moves up a step with a similar rhythmic pattern and melodic shape. *'Both be sorry'* is deliberately different, giving emphasis to the words and reflecting the meaning of the lyrics.

  'It's much too late to find

  You think you've changed your mind

  You'd better change it back or we will both be sorry'

Artists such as Orchestral Manoeuvres in the Dark, Depeche Mode, Eurythmics and Soft Cell subsequently began to enjoy success in the early 1980s with synth pop sounds.

Eurythmics: *Sweet Dreams*, 1983

- *Sweet Dreams* uses three layers of synths to create an interlocking ostinato pattern that outlines the chord sequence
- The layers are separated by panning; the synths are audibly separate in the left and right speakers or headphones
- This is accompanied by a four-to-the-floor kick pattern that continues throughout, but is developed in the vocal break after each verse pattern by the addition of the snare drum on beats 2 and 4
- A reverse piano sound is also used before the bridge
- Call and response is used between the main vocal and the backing vocals in the bridge ('hold your head up'). This is where two patterns alternate, with the backing vocals giving a reply to the main vocal
- Annie Lennox records the harmony parts over the top of the main vocal. This process is called overdubbing, and involves adding layers over the top of previously recorded instruments or parts.

The music moved away from its initial purely artistic intent and became more slick and commercial, and in the late 1980s, duos such as Erasure and Pet Shop Boys became highly successful, writing catchy pop-influenced synth pop.

Pet Shop Boys: *It's a Sin*, 1987

- *It's a Sin* is a quintessentially synth pop song that is influenced by disco
- It uses numerous synth layers with reverb and delay effects
- The chord progression which is used as a unifying hook repeats throughout the verse patterns and focuses on movement by a fifth
- The track opens with this chord progression and up to and including the chord of A♭, these chords form a circle of fifths
- Each chord moves down by a fifth (or up by a fourth)
- The chord progression is as follows:

Cm	Fm	B♭	E♭	A♭	Fm	G	G

Samples and Hip Hop

In the late 1970s, parallel developments were also occurring in the New York Bronx, taking influence from commercial disco sounds and 'toasting'. The culture was very much linked to block parties, breakdancing and a 'street' influence that featured rapped vocals, drum beats created through sample loops or drum machines and the use of DJ techniques such as scratching.

Initially, hip hop came from DJs using two turntables to extend the breaks in songs. This led to the idea of 'breakdancing' – filling these extended musical breaks with dancing.

Artists also used a technique called scratching, where a vinyl record is moved back and forward under the needle on a turntable and the cross-fader is used to fade the sound in and out. Hip hop later made use of samples and quotations from other songs.

NEW INSTRUMENTS, NEW SOUNDS:
The Sampler

- Samplers are used to take (or indeed record) a pre-existing bit of audio which they are then able to replay when triggered by a button or keyboard press
- One of the most important functions is to be able to edit, manipulate and add effects to the raw sample.

Sugarhill Gang: *Rappers' Delight,* 1979

- *Rappers Delight* is widely regarded as the first ever commercially successful hip hop song.
- The track was originally released as a 12" single, and is famous for its use of Bernard Edwards' bass part, which, along with Nile Roger's choppy guitar chords and the trademark string stabs, were interpolated from disco band Chic's 1979 hit *Good Times*
- Hip hop used a variety of influences, which included loops and musical quotations from earlier music. Disco was a common source of samples
- The Sugarhill Gang members then rapped over the repeated chord progression and bass line, introducing themselves and each other.

In the early 1980s, there were a number of stylistic collaborations with Aerosmith and Run DMC releasing *Walk This Way* in 1983, combining rock riffs with scratching and rapping. This paved the way for artists such as The Beastie Boys and Rage Against the Machine to produce new and more diverse music influenced by hip hop in the 1990s

Modern R&B

In the 1980s, artists such as Prince bridged stylistic boundaries, producing music that combined elements of rock, R&B, soul and funk. Prince's acrobatic vocal range spanned between F3 to A5, a range of over two octaves.

A LEVEL EXTENSION
The 1990s

In the 1990s, the term R&B started to be used to describe music of urban origin. It featured distinctive production including drum machines and jazz influences such as the saxophone and polished vocal parts.

These tracks tended to take influence from the hip hop music of the 1980s and 1990s, but were commercially successful and demonstrated increasingly polished production. It is common to hear artists using very **melismatic** vocal delivery, for example in music by Whitney Houston and Mariah Carey.

Increasing independence

In the late 1980s and early 1990s, smaller bands were increasingly unsatisfied with the deals they were negotiating with larger record labels. These often included losing the rights to their own songs and unfavourable margins when discussing their royalty payments. Indie music was used as an umbrella term to refer to 'independent' artists who were not tied to a major label, but also to refer to the style that developed, involving jangly broken chord-based guitar parts with light distortion, delay and chorus effects, and a DIY production ethic that focused primarily on the capture of the artists' live sound.

Rough Trade was a record shop based in London that set up an independent distribution network to sell and publicise artists' music. Record shops around the country signed up to this and it allowed bands such as The Smiths to have success without having to sign a contract with a large label. This, in turn, meant that they retained control of the rights to their songs. Johnny Marr's famous Smiths guitar sound is audible on *This Charming Man* (1984). Often described as 'jangly', it uses a lightly-distorted but treble-heavy arpeggio based guitar part with some chorus and delay.

In Manchester, Factory Records was set up to distribute the songs recorded by Joy Division. Tony Wilson also owned the Hacienda nightclub in Manchester city centre, which enabled him to publicise artists' music. Artists signed to Factory included Happy Mondays and New Order.

Nirvana: *Smells Like Teen Spirit*, 1991

- The development of Indie in the UK was mirrored in the late 1980s by a new heavier, guitar-based style from the U.S.A.
- Grunge had its origins in metal music with high-powered guitar riffs and power chords
- *Smells Like Teen Spirit* features contrast between its loud and distorted chorus with shouted vocals and its more intimately delivered and softer verse parts
- The ascending fourth idea in the lead guitar functions as an inverted **tonic** pedal, alternating between a C and a sustained F, in the song's key of F minor.

Back to Britain

Brit Pop had its origins in the Indie style, with Oasis often identified as a particularly successful Brit Pop band. The style itself saw 1960s British rock music as a 'gold standard' and wistfully looked back, while also putting a modern slant on the music. Other Brit Pop artists included Blur and Pulp.

Oasis: *Don't Look Back In Anger,* 1995

- *Don't Look Back In Anger* owes much to Lennon and McCartney of the Beatles. This is indicative of the respect towards and the influence of the band on Oasis
- Noel and Liam Gallagher have never hidden this, and if you listen to the opening piano chords in *Don't Look Back In Anger*, you cannot fail to hear the block chords in the opening of Lennon's *Imagine*
- There is a further nod to Lennon in the lyric 'I'm gonna' start a revolution from my bed', which is a throwback to Lennon's famous 'bed-in' peace protest in 1969
- The use of the ageing Mellotron at the end as the other instruments fade out is a further Beatles reference
- Gallagher's vocal part is doubletracked in the choruses, which has the effect of thickening the vocal performance and helping it to cut more effectively through the other instruments.

Folk, Celtic Music and Varied Influences

In Ireland there was a movement towards revitalising and repopularising Irish traditional music, with bands such as The Dubliners and The Pogues taking on aspects such as the use of tin whistle, fiddles and bodhran while fusing it with rock elements such as the Electric Guitar. This was later mirrored by artists such as Thin Lizzy and U2.

Thin Lizzy: *Whisky in the Jar,* 1973

- *Whisky in the Jar* is a traditional Irish song that makes lyrical references to the counties of Cork and Kerry
- It was originally performed by Irish folk band The Dubliners but was became a No. 1 single when covered by Thin Lizzy who had success in the charts in 1973
- The term 'Celtic music' is often used as an amalgamation of Irish, Scottish and other traditional styles of folk music associated with the historic Celtic languages
- Thin Lizzy were one of the first bands to take on board traditional Irish music as an influence on their rock style
- Eric Bell, the guitarist in Thin Lizzy, said that when creating the memorable guitar opening riff, he was trying to recreate the sounds of the Uilleann Pipes
- Metallica also covered the song in a heavier rock style in 1998.

In the 1990s, artists fused electric and acoustic instruments, and a new generation of artists began to break through to commercial success, partially through the summer folk festival culture. Artists such as Kate Rusby have had success with an authentic folk style in the mainstream, and pop artists such as The Corrs found a place in popular music using folk influences.

Electronic Dance

In the late 1980s and early 1990s, a number of different electronic dance styles developed. These owed much to the technological developments of digital multitrack recording, and increasingly the ability to use computers to mix and create music 'in the box'.

NEW INSTRUMENTS, NEW SOUNDS:
MIDI

- While not an instrument in its own right, MIDI (Musical Instrument Digital Interface) was revolutionary as a standard allowing electronic instruments to communicate with each other. Introduced in 1983, General MIDI became an industry standard in 1991.

In the early 1980s, artists such as Frankie Knuckles in Chicago were remixing disco music, creating their own song edits and adding instrumentation such as the Roland TR-808 and TB-303. This style became known as **house** music. **Garage** was a parallel development in New York that shared many features, namely influences from soul and disco music. **Acid house** was a later development that came from British rave scenes and used the Roland TB-303 sequencer to create basslines. **Trance** music was based on syncopated sawtooth synth lead patterns accompanied by arpeggios and big build ups and breakdowns. **Techno** tended to be faster, with synthesised arpeggios triggered by a sequencer and often in a minor key, with breakdowns and build ups foreshadowed by snare rolls. **Jungle** and **drum and bass** music used sampled drum breakbeats at a faster tempo, often featuring the 'Amen' break – a now-famous short extract from a drum solo.

Fatboy Slim: *Praise You,* 1999

- *Praise You* was released as the third single from Fatboy Slim's second album, 'You've Come A Long Way Baby'. It reached number one in the UK Singles Chart
- The vocal sample used is from Camille Yarbrough's 1975 song 'Take Yo' Praise'
- Fatboy Slim is very skilled at manipulating samples and there are a number of examples in the track where the original vocal sample is altered through technology based processes
- *Praise You* is in G major, and the main piano riff is based on the chords of F, C and G
- The bridge passages are based around D major (the dominant).

AS Level Component 3 Practice Paper

Area of Study B: Rock and Pop

In the exam, you will be given **three** questions for this part of the paper. The first two will be divided into between 5 and 7 parts (a-e or perhaps a-g), and each worth **15 marks**. Both of these will require you to listen to extracts of unprepared works and answer multiple choice or 'describe' questions about them. The third question is an essay question, beginning with the word 'Explain'. This question will be worth **10 marks** and will require you to use your more general knowledge about the genre. Here we have given you one example paper. Sample assessment papers are also available to download from the Eduqas website, and you should practise answering these as much as possible.

Listen to Elton John – *Philadelphia Freedom* (0'00" – 1'50")

1. You will hear an extract from a pop song, the lyrics of which are written below together with an outline of the structure.   [15]

Verse 1	Verse 2	Pre Chorus	Chorus
Lines 1-3	Lines 4-6	Lines 7-10	Lines 11-15

1.   *I used to be a rolling stone you know*

2.   *If a cause was right*

3.   *I'd leave to find the answer on the road*

4.   *I used to be a heart beating for someone*

5.   *But the times have changed*

6.   *The less I say the more my work gets done*

7.   *'Cause I live and breathe this Philadelphia freedom*

8.   *From the day that I was born I've waved the flag*

9.   *Philadelphia freedom took me knee high to a man, yeah*

10. *Gave me a piece of mama, daddy never had*

11. *Oh Philadelphia freedom, shine on me, I love you*

12. *Shine the light, through the eyes of the ones left behind*

13. *Shine the light, shine the light*

14. *Shine the light, won't you shine the light*

15. *Philadelphia freedom, I love-ve-ve you, yes I do*

(a)   Identify the year when this song would have been recorded.   [1]

1965   1970   1975   1980

(b)   Precisely identify the harmonic device used in the opening string parts.   [1]

....

(c)   Identify one feature of the flute part in the introduction.   [1]

....

(d)   Other than the electric guitar, identify the instrument that provides a chordal
       accompaniment in verse 1.   [1]

....

(e)   State the change in vocal production in the chorus compared to the previous
       sections.   [1]

....

(f)   Compare the writing for strings in verse 2 and the chorus.   [3]

....

....

....

(g)   Identify the two missing chords from the beginning of the chorus.   [2]

B♭		**B♭/D**	

(h)   Underline the word that best describes the overall texture of the chorus.   [1]

Homophony   Heterophony   Antiphony   Monophony

(i)   Describe two features of the bassline in this excerpt.   [2]

....

....

(j)   Compare the use of the drum kit in the introduction and verse 1.   [2]

....

....

Listen to Marvin Gaye and Tammi Terrell –
Ain't No Mountain High Enough **(0'58" – end)**

2. You will hear an extract from a pop song, the lyrics of which are written below. **[15]**

1.   *Oh baby there ain't no mountain high enough,*

2.   *Ain't no valley low enough,*

3.   *Ain't no river wide enough*

4.   *To keep me from getting to you babe*

5.   *Oh no darling*

6.   *No wind, no rain*

7.   *Or winters cold can stop me baby, na na baby*

8.   *'Cause you are my goal*

9.   *If you're ever in trouble;*

10.   *I'll be there on the double*

11.   *Just send for me, oh baby, ha*

12.   *My love is alive*

13.   *Way down in my heart*

14.   *Although we are miles apart*

15.   *If you ever need a helping hand,*

16.   *I'll be there on the double*

17.   *Just as fast as I can*

18.   *Don't you know that there*

19.   *Ain't no mountain high enough,*

20.   *Ain't no valley low enough,*

21.   *Ain't no river wide enough*

22.   *To keep me from getting to you, babe*

23.   *Don't you know that there*

24.   *Ain't no mountain high enough,*

25.   *Ain't no valley low enough,*

26.   *Ain't no river wide enough*

27.   *Ain't mountain high enough*

28.   *Ain't no valley low enough*

(a) (i) Identify the year when this song would have been recorded. [1]

1960   1966   1972   1978

   (ii) Give a reason for your choice. [1]

....

(b)   Identify the change in tonality before line 12.   [1]

....

(c)   Compare the vocal performances in the chorus and bridge (lines 1-11).   [4]

....

....

....

....

(d)   This piece uses a variety of instruments that may be viewed as unconventional for a pop record at the time of recording. Identify two instruments that may be regarded as such.   [2]

....

....

(e)   Describe how the music in lines 5-11 give a sense of build into line 12.   [2]

....

....

(f)   Name the specific type of chord on 'Ain't No Mountain...' in line 19.   [1]

Suspended 4th	
Major 7th	
Diminished 7th	
Neapolitan 6th	

(g)   Name the cadence at the end of line 22.   [1]

....

(h)   *Ain't No Mountain High Enough* is an example of a soul song.
Describe two features of the music that you consider typical of this style.   [2]

....

....

3. Explain how the electric guitar was a key influence in popular music in the 1960s and 1970s.

Support your answer with examples of the ways it has been used in some songs
you have studied throughout the course. **[10]**

You may refer to:

■ use of instruments

■ use of technology (e.g., type of instruments used, studio effects, recording techniques)

■ other features such as stylistic influences etc.

....

....

....

....

....

....

....

....

....

....

....

....

....

....

....

....

....

....

....

....

....

....

....

A Level Component 3 Practice Paper

Area of Study B: Rock and Pop

In the exam, you will be given **two** questions for this part of the paper. The first will be divided into several parts (perhaps a-d or a-e), and worth a total of **10 marks**. You will listen to an extract of an unprepared work and answer 'identify' or 'describe'-type questions about it. For the second question you will listen to **two** unprepared extracts, and again answer a number of 'identify' or 'describe' short-answer questions, followed by a **10 mark** comparison essay. In total, question 2 will be worth **20 marks** so that in total this section is worth **30**. Here we have given you one example paper. Sample assessment papers are also available to download from the Eduqas website, and you should practise answering these as much as possible.

Listen to Chicago – *Hard to Say I'm Sorry* (0'00" – 1'31")

1. You will hear part of *Hard to Say I'm Sorry* by Chicago. The lyrics, together with an outline of the structure of the extract, are printed below.   **[10]**

Introduction	Verse	Pre-Chorus	Chorus
	Lines 1 – 4	Lines 5 – 7	Lines 8 – 11

1.	*Everybody needs a little time away*
2.	*I heard her say, from each other*
3.	*Even lovers need a holiday*
4.	*Far away from each other*
5.	*Hold me now*
6.	*It's hard for me to say I'm sorry*
7.	*I just want you to stay*
8.	*And after all that you've been through*
9.	*I will make it up to you, I promise to*
10.	*And after all that's been said and done*
11.	*You're just a part of me I can't let go*

(a) Discuss the use of harmony in the introduction to this song.   **[2]**

....

....

(b)   Identify the four chord pattern in lines 5 and 6. The first has been completed for you.   [2]

vi			I

(c)   Identify the specific type of chord that is used at the end of line 11.   [1]

Diminished 7th	
Neapolitan 6th	
Suspended 4th	
Major 7th	

(d)   Compare the use of lead and backing vocals in the verse and chorus with reference to specific line numbers.   [3]

....

....

....

(e)   Compare the texture and instrumentation of the introduction and pre chorus.   [2]

....

....

2. You will hear two extracts of music. Answer questions (a-d) in relation to extract 1 only. Question (e) is a comparison of extract 2 with extract 1.   [10]

Opening	Introduction	Verse 1	Chorus	Link
		Lines 1-4	Lines 5-8	

The lyrics for **extract 1** are printed below.

Thin Lizzy – *Whisky in the Jar* (0'00" – 1'35")

1.   *As I was goin' over the Cork and Kerry mountains.*

2.   *I saw Captain Farrell and his money he was countin'.*

3.   *I first produced my pistol and then produced my rapier.*

4.   *I said stand o'er and deliver or the devil he may take ya.*

5.   *Musha ring dumb a do dumb a da.*

6.   *Whack for my daddy-o,*

7.   *Whack for my daddy-o.*

8.   *There's whiskey in the jar-o.*

(a)   Describe three memorable features of the opening passage.   [3]

....

....

....

(b)   Describe the texture in verse 1 (lines 1-4).   [2]

....

....

(c)   Complete the diagram below to give a harmonic structure for the verse.   [3]

I			

(d)   This track is influenced by traditional Irish folk music.
Identify two features of the music that demonstrate this influence.   [2]

....

....

(e)   Next, you will hear part of a different version of the same song.
Explain the stylistic differences in version 2 from version 1.
You may wish to mention matters such as form and structure, melody,
use of instruments or any other features you consider to be relevant.   [10]

The lyrics used are printed below.

The Dubliners – *Whisky in the Jar* (0'00" – 1'01")

1.   *As I was a goin' over the far famed Kerry mountains*

2.   *I met with captain Farrell and his money he was counting*

3.   *I first produced my pistol and I then produced my rapier*

4.   *Saying "Stand and deliver" for he were a bold deceiver*

5.   *Mush-a ring dumb-a do dumb-a da*

6.   *Wack fall the daddy-o, wack fall the daddy-o*

7.   *There's whiskey in the jar*

8.   *I counted out his money and it made a pretty penny*

9.   *I put it in me pocket and I took it home to Jenny*

10.   *She sighed and she swore that she never would deceive me*

11.   *But the devil take the women for they never can be easy*

12.   *Mush-a ring dumb-a do dumb-a da*

13.   *Wack fall the daddy-o, wack fall the daddy-o*

14.   *There's whiskey in the jar*

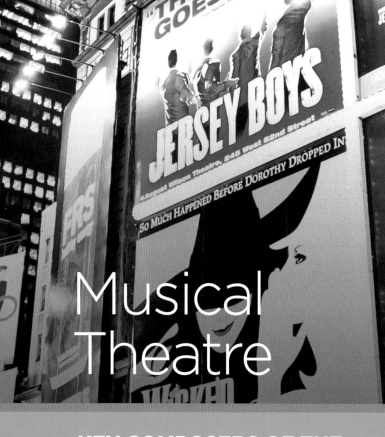

Musical Theatre

KEY COMPOSERS OF THE MUSICAL THEATRE GENRE

Musical Theatre is one of the optional Areas of Study (AoS). This area of study focuses on the work of **five** musical theatre composers at AS Level, and six at A Level: they are Richard Rodgers, Leonard Bernstein, Stephen Sondheim, Claude-Michel Schönberg, Andrew Lloyd Webber, and at A Level also Stephen Schwartz.

As well as a knowledge of key works by the suggested composers, it is a good idea to have a broad knowledge of the history and styles of musical theatre.

This guide will give a brief background to each of the listed composers, with suggested listening, as well as an indication of the types of question that will be set for the exam and how to answer them. There is a more in-depth look at one musical by each composer to help recognise features of their general writing style, and of musical theatre in general, plus a 'test yourself' section on each composer based upon songs from musicals not already featured. The answers to each set of 'test yourself' questions begin on page 292.

How does Musical Theatre fit into the Component 3 exam?

Music from this AoS will appear in Section 2 of the exam paper at AS and A Level.

At **AS Level** there will be **three** questions on AOS C:

■ **Question 4:** Short answer questions on an unprepared extract to be played from a musical theatre song. (15 marks)

■ **Question 5:** Short answer questions on an unprepared extract to be played from a different musical theatre song. (15 marks)

■ **Question 6:** A longer answer (short essay style) in response to a general question about musical theatre. (10 marks)

In total, therefore, at AS Level, AOS C accounts for **40** of the 88 marks available on the paper.

Please note: Unprepared extracts may be by composers other than the five or six studied in this chapter. When this is the case, you will not be expected to identify the composer, and you should bring your general musical theatre knowledge to bear in answering the questions.

At **A Level** there will be **two** questions on AOS C:

■ **Question 3:** Short answer questions on an unprepared extract to be played from a musical theatre song. (10 marks)

■ **Question 4:** Short answer questions on an unprepared extract to be played from one musical theatre song, followed by one longer-answer question in which you are played a second extract from a different musical theatre song and asked to compare it with the first. This is to assess your wider understanding of the area of study. (20 marks)

In total, therefore, at A Level, AOS C work accounts for **30** of the 100 marks available on the paper.

What do I have to study?

Throughout both AS and A Level, you will look at how a range of musical elements are used in musical theatre, including:

- **Structure** (e.g. **strophic** and 32 bar song form)
  Many composers favour the 32 bar song form, but the influence of more rock and pop genres has led to verse and chorus style songs

- **Tonality** (e.g. how it affects mood and atmosphere)
  You should consider how composers can change tonality within a song for effect (such as in 'Everything's Alright' from *Jesus Christ Superstar*)

- **Texture**
  Consider for example the **monophonic** opening of 'Oh What a Beautiful Mornin'' from *Oklahoma*, compared to the rousing **polyphonic** title number in the show's finale to Act 2

- **Sonority** (e.g. vocal and instrumental combinations such as duets and choruses, and vocal qualities such as falsetto, twang, speech-like and belt)
  Consider the use of falsetto in 'Gee Officer Krupke' compared to the 'belt' style voice of Anita in 'America' from *West Side Story*)

- **Melody** (e.g. range, syllabic, **melismatic**, **leitmotifs** and **thematic transformation**)
  Consider the **augmented** 4th leitmotif in *West Side Story*

- **Harmonic language** (e.g. major and minor 7ths, **dominant 7th**, **diminished 7th**, sus4 chord, added 6th, **blue notes**)
  Consider the use of jazz and blues notes in Sondheim's show *Follies* as he **pastiches** the style of the 1930s

- **Tempo**, **metre** and **rhythm** (e.g. dotted rhythms, **syncopation** and dance rhythms)
  Andrew Lloyd Webber uses a number of different time signatures in his musical *Cats*. Consider 'Skimbleshanks' for example, which is in $\frac{13}{8}$

- **Dynamics**
  A large range of **dynamics** can be used for dramatic effect (such as in Andrew Lloyd Webber's *Phantom of the Opera*)

- **The relationship between lyrics and music** (i.e. integration and how composers employ musical elements to underline a song's lyrics)

- **Music for different types of character** (e.g. comic, serious, lovers and chorus)
  Consider how the mood and **orchestration** is changed for characters, compare the quirky rhythms, small range and syncopation in Thenardier's song 'Master of the House' from *Les Miserables*, compared to Jean Valjean's 'Bring Him Home'

- **Types of song** (e.g. love, comedy, patter and show-stopper)
  Love duets are very common in musicals, they will normally involve both voices singing together and some **harmony** (Listen to 'People Will Say We're in Love' from *Oklahoma*, 'One Hand, One Heart' from *West Side Story*, and 'Seeing is Believing' from *Aspects of Love*)

- **The role of the orchestra** (e.g. accompaniment and **underscoring**)
  'If I Loved You' from *Carousel*, is a perfect example of a classic musical theatre scene, involving both dialogue and singing with orchestral accompaniment and underscoring throughout

- **Genres** (e.g. musical comedy such as *A Funny Thing Happened on the Way to the Forum* by Sondheim; through-sung such as *Miss Saigon* by Schönberg; or rock musicals such as *Jesus Christ Superstar* by Lloyd Webber.

Background and Context

Musical theatre is a diverse art form as it encompasses many different genres and styles of music.

However, all musicals contain spectacle, drama and music, including integrated musical numbers which propel the action of the story forward. The 1950s and early 1960s were considered the golden age of musical theatre, with **book musicals** establishing the importance of music and story as an integrated art form. Throughout the 1970s the rock musical grew in popularity. Often composers worked in partnership with the same lyricist over many years, for example Rodgers and Hammerstein or Andrew Lloyd Webber and Tim Rice. This highlights the importance of the relationship between lyrics and music. Other composers sometimes wrote both lyrics and music for their works: Stephen Sondheim and Stephen Schwartz both fall into this category.

Some useful technical terms:

- **Book musical**: A musical that contains dialogue scenes as well as songs (such as *West Side Story*)

- **Through-sung musical**: A musical that has no dialogue and is sung all the way through (such as *Les Miserables*)

- Pit band/orchestra: The name given to the musicians who accompany and **underscore** the singing and dialogue in a musical production

- **Overture**: A piece of music at the beginning of act one of a musical which can help set the mood of the show. Sometimes in earlier musicals this can be a selection of songs from the show (this is the case in Rodgers and Hammerstein musicals such as *South Pacific* and *Oklahoma*)

- Ballet: This is sometimes included in shows and very often represents a dream, sometimes representing a better life for the characters (this happens in *Oklahoma, Carousel, West Side Story*). The ballet usually contains musical material already heard and often provides some interesting musical variations

- Chorus: Can refer to a type of song for a group of people (a chorus). This tradition has continued from opera and operetta and can be an effective way to establish the idea of community and larger scenes in a musical. These pieces often include **harmony** (SATB) and/or unison passages (examples include 'Real Nice Clambake' from *Carousel* and 'Look down' from *Les Miserables*)

- Ensemble songs: Ensemble (group) songs can range from smaller ensembles, for example trio (such as 'You Can Drive a Person Crazy' from *Company*) to larger ensembles (such as 'Jet Song' from *West Side Story*)

- 32 bar song form: A form for song writing that became very popular in 1930s American popular song, consisting of two contrasting 8 bar sections, an A section and a B section arranged into an AABA format. This was a good way to create a memorable **melody** (such as 'The Surrey with the Fringe on Top' from *Oklahoma*)

- **Underscore**: Music that is written to play underneath a scene of dialogue; this could act as leitmotif to show what a character is really thinking, or be a continuation in a larger scene that includes singing (such as 'If I Loved You' from *Carousel*)

- **Vamp**: A section of music that is designed to be repeated until the singing is ready to start, often used when singing comes after underscored dialogue

- **Leitmotif**: An operatic device, used most famously by Wagner, where a musical theme or motif is assigned to a character, action, object or event and returns in the musical line whenever that thing is referenced.

Musical Theatre: Getting to know the genre

Your exam requires that you know all about musical theatre generally, and how different styles of the genre work. As with all areas of musical study, by far the best thing you can do to prepare for this part of your AS or A Level is to listen to and analyse as much of it as possible: works by the set composers for this area of study, but also others who are not listed, for example Cole Porter, John Kander, Jason Robert Brown or Adam Guettel.

TEST YOURSELF

To help you to get to know the music, try asking yourself these questions while listening to musical theatre tracks:

(a)   Identify the overall tonality of this song.   [1]

   The answer is likely to be either major or minor.

(b)   Identify the **time signature** at the opening of the extract.   [1]

   Is the time signature an unusual one? Watch out for $\frac{5}{4}$ and $\frac{7}{4}$ or possibly $\frac{12}{8}$.
   If not, it could just be a straightforward $\frac{3}{4}$ or $\frac{4}{4}$.

(c)   Tick **two** statements below which correctly describe the harmonic content
   of the extract.   [2]

Musical Statements	Tick
The key of the song ends a semitone higher than the opening key	
The key of the song ends a semitone lower than the opening key	
The melody contains augmented 4ths and flattened 7ths	
The melody is mainly stepwise and contains no chromatic movement	

   This question involves careful listening, don't forget you need to tick
   two statements, make sure you read the question accurately.

(d)   Comment on the use of rhythm in the extract.   [3]

   Watch out for some of these obvious answers: Dotted rhythms,
   syncopation, triplets, hemiola.

(e)   Suggest a suitable date of composition for this song.   [1]

   Make sure you know the main composers and when they were writing.
   The exam board would not expect an exact date but an approximate
   level of accuracy such as the correct decade.

(f)   Describe the use of harmony and tonality in this extract. Refer to line
   numbers in your answer.   [4]

   Harmony = types of chords used (7ths and so on) it could also refer to
   ***chromaticism**. Tonality = key (major or minor): does it change key?*

(g) Describe the writing for the accompanying instruments heard in the extract. [3]

Don't just list the instruments playing, what are they doing? Is there, for example, muted brass? Cello pizzicato? Try to **explain** *rather than* **state**, *for questions that have a larger mark allocation.*

(h) Explain how the writing for the accompanying instruments heard in the extract helps to add to the dramatic content of the song. Refer to line numbers in your answer. [4]

Referring to line numbers is really important! Remember all of the elements of music that may help answer this question, there are probably lots of 'right' answers, don't be scared, write down what you believe you can hear and justify it with the music and the line number.

(i) Describe the vocal writing in the first two lines of the extract. [3]

This could refer to the setting of the words: is it syllabic or melismatic? You should try to identify the music written for the voice here: is it stepwise, based upon one note, moving by larger intervals; does it have any relevance to the tonic note of the key? and so on.

This chapter will now provide a background to the life and musical styles of each of the set composers you have to study, and a focus on one of their key works. Remember that this is only an introduction, however: you must not rely on only one of their musicals to see you through this part of the exam paper. Listen to and analyse other works by each composer as well.

Richard Rodgers (1902-1979)

Richard Rodgers in 1948

Rodgers was an American composer who wrote music for 43 Broadway shows, and more than 900 songs.

His gift as a composer of **melody** has made many of his songs some of the most popular songs ever written for musical theatre. Many of them have become popular jazz standards, such as 'My Funny Valentine' and 'The Lady is a Tramp'. Rodgers' work can largely be split into two sections according to which of two lyricists he worked with: Lorenz Hart and Oscar Hammerstein II.

Richard Rodgers' musicals were written as **book musicals**, integrating dialogue and songs together, and many of them had successful film adaptations, such as *Pal Joey, The Sound of Music, South Pacific* and *The King and I).*

Work with Lorenz Hart:

- *A Connecticut Yankee* (1927)
- *On Your Toes* (1936)
- *Babes in Arms* (1937)
- *I Married an Angel* (1938)
- *The Boys from Syracuse* (1938)
- *Higher and Higher* (1940)
- *Pal Joey* (1940–41)
- *By Jupiter* (1942)

LISTEN

Listen to some of the most notable songs from his collaboration with Lorenz Hart:

'My Funny Valentine', 'The Lady is a Tramp', 'Bewitched, Bothered and Bewildered', 'I Could Write a Book', 'Johnny One Note', 'Where or When', 'I Wish I Were in Love Again', and 'There's a Small Hotel'.

DEVELOPMENT AND HISTORY OF MUSICAL THEATRE

In his musical *On Your Toes* in 1936, Rodgers included a ballet 'Slaughter on Tenth Avenue'. This was the first time classical dance had been used in an extended ballet scene in musical theatre.

Work with Oscar Hammerstein II

- *Oklahoma!* (1943)
- *Carousel* (1945)
- *State Fair* (1945) (film)
- *Allegro* (1947)
- *South Pacific* (1949)
- *The King and I* (1951)
- *Me and Juliet* (1953)
- *Pipe Dream* (1955)
- *Cinderella* (1957)
- *Flower Drum Song* (1958)
- *The Sound of Music* (1959)

Many of the musicals written by Rodgers and Hammerstein are among the most successful musicals ever written, with performances all over the world and academy award winning film adaptations. Their shows also remain a popular choice for many schools and amateur dramatic companies.

DEVELOPMENT AND HISTORY OF MUSICAL THEATRE

Lyricist Oscar Hammerstein II was a mentor to composer and lyricist Stephen Sondheim, and Sondheim also collaborated with Rodgers in 1965 with a musical called *Do I Hear a Waltz*, although this was not a big hit for either of them, lasting only 220 performances on Broadway.

EXAMPLE WORK:

Oklahoma! (1943)

Oklahoma! was the first musical written by Rodgers and Hammerstein and ran for a then record run of 2,212 performances on Broadway. It was later adapted into an academy award winning film in 1955, and the writers also won a Pulitzer prize a year later.

Singing 'The Surrey with the Fringe on Top'

The show is an example of a **book musical**. It contains **leitmotif** and recurring themes which help develop characters and integrate the story into the music.

As well as dialogue and song, the musical also contains a fifteen-minute ballet sequence depicting Laurey's dream-like state.

A brief plot synopsis

Set in the Oklahoma territory in the early 1900s, the musical tells the story of two pairs of lovers. Two cowboys, Curly and Will, try to capture the hearts of Laurey and Ado Annie. Both Laurey and Ado Annie have attention from other men, Jud (a farm hand) and Ali Hakim (a street pedlar). During Curly and Laurey's wedding, a drunken Jud tries to attack Curly with a knife. During the fight, Jud falls onto his own knife and dies. A judge finds Curly 'not guilty' of any wrongdoing and Laurey and Curley depart for their honeymoon.

Orchestration

The **orchestration** of the show is for a traditional orchestral setup. As this show is not at all jazz-influenced, there are no saxophones included.

There are parts for:

- Flute (doubling piccolo)
- Oboe (with optional English horn)
- Clarinets I-II (clarinet I doubles as bass clarinet)
- Bassoon

- Horns I-II
- Trumpets I-II
- Trombone
- Percussion
- Violins, A-B (**divisi**)
- Viola (divisi)
- Cello
- Double bass
- Guitar (doubling banjo)
- Harp

Musical numbers and analysis

Act One

- **'Overture'**

This is a bright energetic orchestral piece that includes the songs ('The Farmer and the Cowman', 'Pore Jud is Daid', 'Many a New Day', 'Out of my Dreams', 'People Will Say We're in Love' and 'Oklahoma'). It was common in this period of musical theatre to have an overture that played the tunes from the show, and it helped to popularise the songs. It is interesting to note that Rodgers and Hammerstein's next collaboration, *Carousel*, replaces the traditional overture with 'The Carousel Waltz', a completely original orchestral piece which contains no songs from the show.

- **'Oh, What a Beautiful Mornin''**

One of the most famous and recognisable songs from the show, this is a solo, sung by Curly, in $\frac{3}{4}$ time and a major key. The song begins **monophonically**, with voice alone singing the verse, then the orchestra joins in five bars before the main chorus. Notice in the verse that the writing is syllabic and the **melody** moves largely by step:

- **'The Surrey with the Fringe on Top'**

Written for Curly, Laurey and Aunt Eller, the **tonality** of this song is major and it is mostly in a bright $\frac{4}{4}$. The main part of the song is in 32 bar song format with the A section relying heavily on **tonic** and **dominant** harmonies. The song also uses a section of **underscored** dialogue within.

- **'Kansas City'**

A solo for Will Parker, with some interjections from Aunt Eller and chorus of cowboys. In a major key and $\frac{6}{8}$ time, the song begins in a **parlando** style: the instruction in Rodgers score states 'Starts speaking and gradually goes in to melody'. The song then moves into a dance sequence where Will demonstrates some different dance styles. Two step and **ragtime** are featured, and the music changes for this accordingly into $\frac{4}{4}$ time but maintains the main melody from the song.

■ **'I Cain't Say No'**

Another solo, this time for the comedic character Ado Annie. In a major key and a fast $\frac{2}{4}$, the accompaniment figure resembles a similar figure in the later 'Farmer and the Cowman' song. Ado Annie's character is conveyed through the use of **syncopation**, repeated notes and two note patterns as well as octave leaps.

■ **'Many a New Day'**

A solo song for Laurey and a group of 'singing girls'. The song is in a bright major key with an **allegretto** tempo in $\frac{4}{4}$. It is characterised by its playful quaver triplet figure which starts every other bar. The song modulates up a semitone and the girls sing the **melody** in three-part **harmony**.

■ **'It's a Scandal, It's an Outrage!'**

This song begins with spoken words from Ali Hakim and a vocal line sung largely on one note by a chorus of men over a four note **ostinato**. This song was omitted from the film adaptation.

■ **'People Will Say We're in Love'**

A duet for Curly and Laurey which is in a major key and uses major 7th chords. Each character sings their own verse, with no harmonies at this stage, perhaps a reflection of their relationship status at this point.

■ **'Pore Jud is Daid'**

A duet for Curly and Jud, this song is in a church or preacher style, with some sections of chanting on one note. There are some interesting uses of **chromaticism** and parallel chords, **underscoring**, and two-part harmony.

■ **'Lonely Room'**

A solo song for Jud which goes through a range of **dynamics** and is largely in a minor key. This song was omitted from the film adaptation.

■ **'Dream Sequence'**

This scene incorporates the song 'Out of my Dreams': a waltz tune in A♭ major. The ballet music then presents variations and motifs from the songs 'Oh, What a Beautiful Mornin'', 'Surrey with the Fringe on Top', 'Poor Jud is Daid', 'I Cain't Say No' and 'People Will Say We're in Love'.

Act Two

■ **'Entr'acte'**

An orchestral piece used to settle down the audience for the start of Act Two (many of the audience would have heard this from outside the auditorium and taken it as a cue to take their seats). The songs included are 'People Will Say We're in Love', 'Many a New Day' and 'The Surrey with the Fringe on Top'.

■ **'The Farmer and the Cowman'**

A rousing chorus number for the whole ensemble in F major and B♭ major and $\frac{2}{4}$ time, featuring solo and chorus lines and a dance section.

■ **'All Er Nothin''**

A duet for Will and Annie, major key, very light hearted, with a mixture of singing and speaking the lyrics.

■ **Reprise of 'People Will say We're in Love'**

A duet for Curly and Laurey, this time they sing in unison and break into **harmony** at the end.

■ **'Oklahoma'**

A big chorus number, led by Curly. In a major key and $\frac{2}{4}$ time, there are lots of scalic runs and arpeggiac figures in the **melody** and accompaniment, and eight-part harmony at times, the most advanced and texturally interesting piece for the full ensemble within the show.

■ **'Finale ultimo'**

After an encore of 'Oklahoma' the company sing 'Oh, What a Beautiful Mornin'' in unison as Curly and Laurey go off on their honeymoon in the surrey with the fringe on top.

TEST YOURSELF: RICHARD RODGERS

Listen to 'I'm in Love with a Wonderful Guy' from the musical *South Pacific* and answer the following questions. You should listen to the extract a maximum of three times.

(1)   Comment on the composer's use of tonality at the start of the extract and the section where the lyrics begin 'I'm as corny as Kansas in August'.   [2]

(2)   Choosing from the list below, state the form used from the lyrics 'I'm as corny as Kansas in August' until the end.   [1]

Strophic AABA (32 bar song form)   Verse/chorus   12 bar blues

Leonard Bernstein (1918-90)

Bernstein was an American composer, conductor, teacher and pianist who made a huge contribution to 20th Century music through his work.

In addition to writing many orchestral and chamber compositions, operas, song cycles and film music, Bernstein wrote music for some celebrated works of musical theatre.

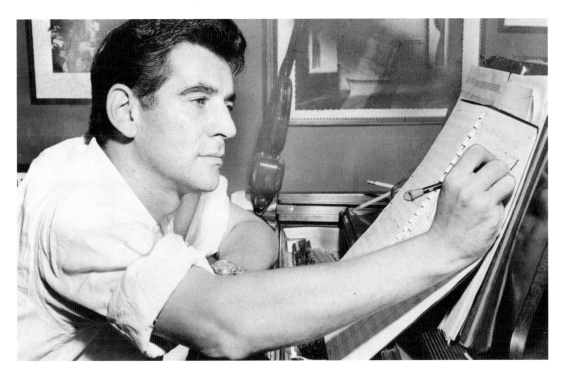

Leonard Bernstein in 1955

Bernstein's musicals:

- *On the Town* (1944)
- *Wonderful Town* (1953)
- *Candide* (1956)
- *West Side Story* (1957)
- *Mass* (a theatre piece for singers, players and dancers) (1971)

Listen to some of Bernstein's most notable musical theatre songs:

'Somewhere', 'Maria', 'Tonight', 'America', 'New York, New York', 'Lonely Town', 'Some Other Time', 'Wrong Note Rag'.

DEVELOPMENT AND HISTORY OF MUSICAL THEATRE

Bernstein's first musical, *On the town*, was inspired by his ballet score *Fancy Free* from 1944, which is also about three sailors in New York. The ballet was choreographed by Jerome Robbins, who also choreographed *West Side Story* in 1957.

EXAMPLE WORK:

West Side Story (1957)

West Side Story was composed by Leonard Bernstein with lyrics by Stephen Sondheim, book by Arthur Laurents and choreography by Jerome Robbins. It is a modern adaptation of Shakespeare's *Romeo and Juliet* story and is set in 1950's New York with the two families represented by two rival gangs, the Jets (Americans) and Sharks (Puerto Ricans).

George Chakiris as Bernardo, the leader of the Sharks, in a still from the 1961 film

This is another example of a **book musical**, and again it contains **leitmotif** and recurring themes which help develop characters and integrate the music with the story. The themes of love, death and racial tension are as relevant today as they were in in Shakespeare's time.

Musical Style

The music of *West Side Story* is immediately distinctive. Bernstein uses extra percussion in his pit orchestra, including congas and timbales, to help create a Puerto Rican sound, along with habanera **rhythms**. For the Jets' music he uses a young jazz style, imitating the popular music of the time: his use of vibraphone in the song 'Cool' is typical of the 'cool jazz' style of this period. The Jets' music is tied together by repeated use of a **tritone** (**augmented** 4th interval).

Orchestration

The **orchestration** of the show is for a traditional orchestral setup but with additional percussion, keyboard and guitar. Note that each reed player is required to play all of the instruments listed for their part, this is a common practice for reed players in musical theatre.

- Reed 1 (alto sax, bass clarinet, clarinet, flute, piccolo)
- Reed 2 (B♭ clarinet, bass clarinet, E♭ clarinet)
- Reed 3 (B♭ clarinet, baritone sax, bass clarinet, English horn, flute, oboe, piccolo, tenor sax)
- Reed 4 (bass clarinet, bass sax, clarinet, flute, piccolo, soprano sax)
- Reed 5 (bassoon)
- Horn 1 and 2
- Trumpet 1
- Trumpet 2
- Trumpet 3
- Trombone 1
- Trombone 2
- Keyboard
- Guitar (classical, electric)
- Drums
- 2 percussion players (castanets, chimes, claves, conga, finger cymbals, glockenspiel, gourd, guiro, maracas, police whistle, ratchet, slide whistle, small maracas, snare drum, tam-tam, tambourines, temple blocks, timbales, triangle, vibraphone, woodblock, xylophone, 2 suspended cymbals, 3 bongos, 3 cowbells, 4 pitched drums)
- Violin 1 and 2
- Violin 3 and 4
- Violin 5 and 6
- Violin 7
- Cello 1 and 2
- Cello 3 and 4
- Double bass

Musical numbers and analysis

Act One

- 'Prologue' (instrumental)

There is no **overture** written for the original 1957 production, although one was later added and included in the 1961 film. The action begins immediately with a carefully choreographed prologue which establishes the rivalry between the two gangs. The music begins with 8 **syncopated** chords which feature the major and minor third together and are unresolved harmonically, followed by three finger snaps and a solo saxophone playing a five note phrase which finishes with the **tritone** interval. Four pitched drums signify the entrance of the leader of the Sharks. The music also contains a **walking bass** and a huge contrast in **textures** and **dynamics** before returning to its opening 12 bars after a police whistle is sounded.

■ Jet Song' (Riff and the Jets)

The 'Jet Song' begins with material from the prologue and then develops the earlier chords into a syncopated accompaniment in $\frac{6}{8}$ while Riff's vocal **melody** is clearly in $\frac{3}{4}$ time. The main part of the song actually uses a slight variation on a 32 bar song format. In the B section the saxophone melody including the **tritone** is used.

■ 'Something's Coming' (Tony)

Tony's solo song immediately shows the unrest in his character with the two bar **ostinato** accompaniment and the vocal **syncopation**. The main opening of the song also uses the **augmented** 4th/diminished 5th (tritone interval).

■ 'The Dance at the Gym' (Instrumental)

'The Dance at the Gym' begins with the 'who knows' tritone theme played by the orchestra, as well as an inversion of the same interval, which is later heard in the song 'Maria' as a **leitmotif** for her character. This implies that Tony's premonitions were correct, in that Maria's music is already present in the music he sings even before they meet. The orchestra then play a blues, promenade, mambo, cha cha and a jump. During the cha cha, Tony and Maria meet and dance together, and when they speak to each other the underscoring is provided by solo violin and celesta using the tritone once again. The range of musical styles in this whole section is very impressive from the Latin American **rhythms** in the mambo to the bebop style of the jump.

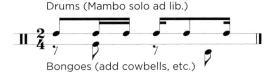

■ 'Maria' (Tony)

In this, one of the most famous songs from the show, and a fantastic show piece for the tenor voice, the singer has to sing the name Maria some 29 times. The song starts softly and is centred around one note, D♯, this then is enharmonically changed to E♭ and this becomes the key of the piece (E♭ major). The main theme again uses the tritone interval, and again it's actually the 'who knows' phrase from 'Something's Coming', but inverted.

■ 'Balcony Scene' (Maria and Tony)

The balcony scene for Maria and Tony contains the love duet 'Tonight', it is a masterful display of underscoring dialogue and accompanying singing, with the soloists taking it in turn to sing and then singing in unison. Under this beautiful melody Bernstein uses an accompaniment of rhythmic urgency, conveying the excitement and danger for the couple.

Also, before the last section of dialogue in the scene, Tony sings alone for 8 bars, and underneath the cello plays the music for the lyric 'There's a place for us' from the song 'Somewhere', a precursor of what's to come.

■ **'America' (Anita, Rosalia and girls)**

An energetic ensemble number based on Latin American **rhythms**, starting with claves and guiro creating a cross rhythm using **syncopation** and triplets respectively. The main **melody** is instantly recognisable and one of the great 'take home tunes' from the show. Based on chords with the notes of each **triad** and in alternating bars of $\frac{6}{8}$ and $\frac{3}{4}$ time, creating a rhythmic **hemiola**.

I like to be in A - me - ri - ca

■ **'Cool' (Riff and the Jets)**

There is a lot of use of the **tritone** again in this song, Bernstein also incorporates a **fugue** which is almost twelve-tone in the dance **break**. Use of the tritone and syncopation are the main features of the melody.

■ **'One Hand, One Heart' (Maria and Tony)**

A slow duet in triple time, again the tritone appears in the accompaniment to this song, most notably in the closing bars, echoing the previous meeting scene from the dance at the gym. Maria and Tony also sing in **harmony** for the last 16 bars.

■ **'Tonight' (Maria, Tony, Anita, Bernardo and Riff and chorus of Jets and Sharks)**

A fast and rhythmic ensemble piece which is also known as the 'Tonight quintet' as it has five parts and is based upon Tony & Maria's balcony scene duet.

■ **'The Rumble' (Instrumental)**

Like the prologue which begins the show, Bernstein writes an instrumental piece to close the Act. Syncopated chords, heard earlier in the prologue, pitched drums and the use of the tritone are used in a carefully choreographed piece of music which portrays a knife fight and leaves two of the main characters dead on the stage as the curtain falls.

Act Two

■ **'I Feel Pretty' (Maria and the girls)**

After the shock of the ending to Act One, Act Two begins with a bright and cheerful song, in $\frac{3}{4}$ time and in a major key.

■ **'Ballet Sequence' (Instrumental, Tony, Maria and company)**

Bernstein uses a number of different techniques in the ballet. The piece starts with a repeated timpani note, with other instruments joining on a simple two note semitone motif in $\frac{3}{2}$ time. Bernstein then uses a range of different time signatures during the following **scherzo**. This then makes way for another very well known song from the show, 'Somewhere'. 'Somewhere' begins with a minor 7th interval and also uses triad figures, step-wise melody and triplets in the melody. The dream soon becomes a nightmare, as music from the rumble is reprised.

There's   a   place   for   us

- **'Gee, Officer Krupke' (Jets)**

After all the tragic events that have happened in the show so far, the writers decided it would be good to insert a light hearted song for the audience. This song is written in a vaudeville style, with the Jets imitating different characters. There is also use of falsetto in the song. A music hall style **vamp** is used in the song, while the Jets perform spoken skits, but even this includes the **tritone** interval motif.

- **'A Boy Like That/I Have a Love' (Maria and Anita)**

Two duets for Anita and Maria. 'A Boy Like That' has a very low register for Anita and a chromatic and syncopated vocal line, this contrasts with the more lyrical 'I Have a Love' which as well as step-wise **melody** also contains minor 7th intervals heard earlier in 'Somewhere'. The tritone makes an appearance in the accompaniment when Maria sings the lyric 'right or wrong', an E♭ major chord sounds with an A♮ in the bass of the chord as she sings the word 'wrong'.

- **'Finale' (Maria and Tony)**

The show finishes with a 6 bar **a capella** reprise of 'Somewhere', a further 7 bars of instrumental, then a pause for Maria's speech, after which the orchestra play 14 bars first heard in the ballet incorporating 'There's a place for us'. The last three bars contain a C major chord and the tritone note of F♯ sounds in the bass.

DEVELOPMENT AND HISTORY OF MUSICAL THEATRE

The film adaptation of *West Side Story* (1961) won 10 Academy Awards including best picture, the most any film musical has ever had. The songs 'Cool' and 'Gee Officer Krupke' were swapped around in the order of songs for the film adaptation.

TEST YOURSELF: LEONARD BERNSTEIN

Listen to 'Some Other Time' from the musical *On The Town* and answer the following questions. You should listen to the extract a maximum of three times.

(1)   State two features heard in this extract that demonstrate a jazz influence.   [2]

(2)   State the interval between the two notes heard on the lyrics 'oh well' choosing from the list below.   [1]

      Perfect 5th   Octave   Perfect fourth   Tritone

Stephen Sondheim (born 1930)

Sondheim was a pupil of Oscar Hammerstein II (the lyricist from the Rodgers and Hammerstein partnership) and he wrote lyrics for the musicals *West Side Story* (1957) and *Gypsy* (1959).

He has also composed and written the lyrics for many of his own musicals.

Sondheim's musicals:

- *A Funny Thing Happened on the Way to the Forum* (1962)
- *Anyone Can Whistle* (1964)
- *Company* (1970)
- *Follies* (1971)
- *A Little Night Music* (1973)
- *Pacific Overtures* (1976)
- *Sweeney Todd* (1979)
- *Merrily We Roll Along* (1981)
- *Sunday in the Park with George* (1984)
- *Into the Woods* (1987)
- *Assassins* (1990)
- *Passion* (1994)
- *Bounce* (2003) rewritten as *Road Show* (2008)

Sondheim in around 1970

Musical features and style

Sondheim's ability to write both lyrics and music for his songs allows a complete unity in style for each character and scene. His musical settings very often follow the inflection of speech patterns, both in tempo and in **pitch**. This could be deemed to be a typical feature of Sondheim's style.

In each of his musicals, Sondheim also manages to **pastiche** different musical styles to suit the period and style of drama. *Sweeney Todd* has an operatic quality, consider the aria 'Greenfinch and Linnet Bird'; *A Little Night Music* feels like an operetta and is largely in waltz time. *Follies* draws upon 1930s show tunes in the style of Gershwin and also earlier operetta styles to invoke a sense of a theatrical reunion. *Company* has a largely 1970s feel to it, largely due to the opening number and **orchestration**. In *Assassins*, Sondheim ingeniously assigned various American music styles (folk song, spiritual, Western movie theme, Sousa march, Carpenters-style pop) to each of his characters, who in real life tried to kill a US president.

EXAMPLE WORK:

Assassins (1990)

Assassins is a musical revue in one act with music and lyrics by Stephen Sondheim, set in a fairground or carnival setting where people are invited to take part in a game: 'come here and shoot a president'. The people who take part in the carnival activity are all real life people who have attempted to assassinate American presidents, both successfully and unsuccessfully, throughout history – ranging from the assassination of Abraham Lincoln through to the attempted assassination of Ronald Reagan. The music varies to reflect the different eras portrayed.

Orchestration

- Reed 1 (soprano sax, clarinet, flute, piccolo)
- Reed 2 (flute, clarinet, bass clarinet, E♭ clarinet)
- Reed 3 (soprano sax, tenor sax, bassoon, flute)
- 2 trumpets
- Horn
- Trombone
- Guitar
- 2 keyboards
- 2 percussion
- String quintet

Musical numbers and analysis

- **Opening: 'Everybody's Got the Right' (Proprietor, Assassins)**

The music begins with 'Hail to the Chief' played in the style of a carnival waltz in $\frac{3}{4}$ time instead of the usual martial style associated with this **melody**. The music then moves to a bluesy, darker sound with some **chromaticism** and the triplet phrase 'Come here and shoot a President' before giving way to the deliberately melodic and catchy melody 'Everybody's Got the Right' with its **pentatonic** melody to start.

- **'The Ballad of Booth' (Balladeer, Booth)**

The balladeer appears with his guitar or banjo, like a Woody Guthrie style singer and performs, after some short statements, a bluegrass tune featuring the banjo.

This ballad begins with a **pentatonic melody** and simple folk harmonies (emphasising **tonic**, **subdominant** and **dominant triads**).

■ **'How I Saved Roosevelt' (Ensemble, Zangara)**

This song is in an American marching band style, including quotes from American composer John Philip Sousa, especially 'The Washington Post' which forms the main melody of the song:

■ **'Gun Song' (Czolgosz, Booth, Guiteau, Moore)**

There is a mixture of styles in this quartet, from dark and brooding to a fast waltz finishing with an unaccompanied barber shop style quartet.

■ **'The Ballad of Czolgosz' (Balladeer)**

A cowboy song style, with a melody influenced by a pentatonic scale. This later develops into a hoedown style.

■ **'Unworthy of Your Love' (Hinckley, Fromme)**

A folk-rock style song resembling The Carpenters, this is sung as a love song to the two characters' respective idols (Jodie Foster and Charles Manson).

■ **'The Ballad of Guiteau' (Guiteau, Balladeer)**

Written in a **cakewalk** style, using **ragtime rhythms** and **syncopation**.

■ **'Another National Anthem' (Balladeer, Assassins)**

A march sung by the assassins as they turn on the balladeer, a catchy tune with dotted rhythms.

■ **'Something Just Broke' (Ensemble)**

Using harmonic blurring with understated vocals, this song portrays the shock of recalling the aftermath of John F Kennedy's assassination.

■ Finale: 'Everybody's Got the Right'

A reprise of the opening, emphatically sung by all of the assassins, this is in $\frac{4}{4}$ and a major key. Notice the **diatonic** harmonies and use of added 2nd chords.

A little more Sondheim

Listen to the opening 'Ballad of Sweeney Todd' from the 1979 musical *Sweeney Todd.*

If you try speaking the lyrics of this 20-bar theme (from 'Attend the tale of Sweeney Todd' to 'The Demon Barber of Fleet Street'), you will notice that it is a perfect word-setting in tempo and inflection, with the right number of pauses, falling between each line. Each phrase begins with an **anacrusis**, notice the syllabic and largely stepwise movement of the **melody**, how the melodic intervals are the same for his name, 'Sweeney Todd', and how the **pitch** deliberately descends on the last phrase.

The next part of the ballad, on the words 'Swing your razor wide, Sweeney' uses a quotation from the **plainchant** 'Dies irae' (Day of wrath).

DEVELOPMENT AND HISTORY OF MUSICAL THEATRE

Sondheim also used rap in his musicals, long before *Hamilton* the musical. The 'Witches' Rap' is a great moment in the openings of Acts One and Two in *Into the woods*. This was also pre-dated by the opening song from *Sunday in the Park With George*, and also the chorus number 'It's Hot Up Here!' from the start of Act Two of the same show.

TEST YOURSELF: STEPHEN SONDHEIM

Listen to 'Pretty Lady' from the musical *Pacific Overtures* and answer the following questions. You should listen to the extract a maximum of three times.

(1) Comment on the composer's use of texture in his writing for voices. [2]

(2) Comment on the vocal writing of the first four lines of the song. [3]

Pretty lady in the pretty garden can't 'cher stay?

Pretty lady we got leave, and we got paid today

Pretty lady with the flower

Give a lonely sailor 'alf an hour

Andrew Lloyd Webber (born 1948)

Andrew Lloyd Webber is an award winning British composer most noted for his contribution to musical theatre.

He has worked with a number of different lyricists over his career and his work has been performed all over the world, with his musicals running for decades. His show *The Phantom of the Opera* has been running since 1988 on Broadway and is the longest running show in Broadway history. Songs from Lloyd Webber's musicals have been recorded many times, and many have become well known hit songs in their own right.

Notable songs:

'Memory', 'Don't Cry for me Argentina', 'Music of the Night', 'I Don't Know How to Love Him', 'Any Dream Will Do', 'The Perfect Year', 'You Must Love Me', 'With One Look'.

Main stage musicals:

- *Joseph and the Amazing Technicolor Dreamcoat* (1968)
- *Jesus Christ Superstar* (1970)
- *Evita* (1976)
- *Tell me on a Sunday* (1979)
- *Cats* (1981)
- *Starlight Express* (1984)
- *The Phantom of the Opera* (1986)
- *Aspects of Love* (1989)

Andrew Lloyd Webber in 2008

- *Sunset Boulevard* (1993)
- *Whistle Down the Wind* (1996)
- *The Beautiful Game* (2000)
- *The Woman in White* (2004)
- *Love Never Dies* (2010)
- *Stephen Ward the Musical* (2013)

EXAMPLE WORK:

Jesus Christ Superstar (1970)

Jesus Christ Superstar is a through-sung musical with a rock style score, known sometimes as a 'rock opera'. The story is based loosely on the Gospels, describing the last few weeks of the life of Jesus, with original lyrics by Tim Rice. The musical began life as a 'concept album' released in 1970, and was then staged on Broadway a year later and in the West End in 1972. A film adaptation was made in 1973.

Orchestration

The original orchestration is based on a 35 piece orchestra, however the number of strings can also be increased.

- Woodwind: flute I, flute II (flute, piccolo), flute III (flute, piccolo), oboe I, oboe II, clarinet I (B♭ clarinet, E♭ clarinet), clarinet II (B♭ clarinet, tenor sax), bassoon I, bassoon II
- Brass: horn I, horn II, horn III, horn IV, trumpet I, trumpet II, trumpet III, trombone I, trombone II, trombone III, tuba
- Percussion: four players including drum kit
- Keyboards: three players (piano, organ, Moog synthesiser)
- Guitar I, guitar II (electric and acoustic), bass guitar
- Strings: violin I, violin II, viola, cello, double bass

Theatres now tend to use a smaller orchestra, due to budget and orchestra pit size. The following 11 piece and rock combo is most common now for performances:

11 piece	Rock combo
<ul><li>Woodwind I (B♭ Clarinet, Flute, Tenor Sax)</li><li>Horn</li><li>Trumpet</li><li>Keyboard I</li><li>Keyboard II</li><li>Keyboard III</li><li>Percussion</li><li>Guitar I</li><li>Guitar II</li><li>Bass Guitar</li><li>Drums</li></ul>	<ul><li>Keyboard I</li><li>Keyboard II</li><li>Guitar</li><li>Bass</li><li>Drums</li></ul>

Selected musical numbers and analysis

■ **'Heaven on Their Minds'**

Judas starts the show with this rock style song based in D minor. It uses an **ostinato** pattern throughout the verse which is later repeated in the show when Jesus receives his 39 lashes.

■ **'What's the Buzz'**

A chorus piece featuring Jesus which has a funky soul feel mostly based around two chords, A7 and D7.

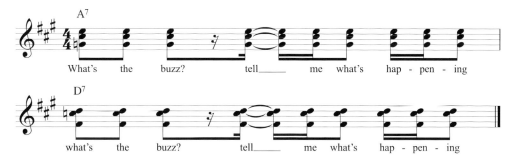

■ **'Pilate's Dream'**

This is in a minor key, starting with acoustic guitar, and vocals are of a limited range. The song is in a more reflective mood than most of the others in the show.

■ **'Everything's alright'**

This song has a $\frac{5}{4}$ time signature and alternates between major and minor **tonality** throughout.

■ **'Gethsemane'**

Jesus's solo begins in the same key as 'Pilate's Dream' and builds into a great show piece song for a rock tenor voice, containing an ad lib section for the singer. Notice the arch shape of each phrase of the **melody**, the use of sequences and stepwise movement. The bass line as indicated in the chords also moves down by step.

■ **'King Herod's Song'**

A complete contrast of style, this solo for King Herod is written in a **ragtime** style in a major key, complete with honky-tonk style piano solos.

■ 'Jesus Christ Superstar'

The title song of the show is an up-tempo funk/soul style piece sung by Judas and backing singers. It has an instantly catchy **melody** thanks to its main chorus which is based on **triadic** movement and then rising to a **blue note** (flattened 7th).

■ 'John 19:41'

This is an instrumental piece which is based upon the music of 'Gethsemane'. After the crucifixion scene it provides a slow and reflective response and is a hugely different ending to a show, with no up-tempo song which many shows rely upon.

DEVELOPMENT AND HISTORY OF MUSICAL THEATRE

The original production on Broadway caused much controversy. Many religious groups considered the show to be blasphemous and thought the story was over sympathetic towards Judas' character.

TEST YOURSELF: ANDREW LLOYD WEBBER

Listen to 'And the Money Kept Rolling in' from the musical *Evita* and answer the following questions. You should listen to the extract a maximum of three times.

(1)   Identify the time signature used in this song.   [1]

(2)   Place a tick in the box which best describes the **tonality** heard in
      this extract.   [1]

Tonality	Tick
Moves between a minor key and the relative major	
Moves between a minor key and the tonic major	
Moves between a minor key and the dominant major	
Moves between a minor key and the sub-dominant major	

Claude-Michel Schönberg (born 1944)

Claude-Michel Schönberg is a French composer who is best known for his theatre collaborations with lyricist Alain Boublil.

Main stage musicals:

- *La Révolution Française* (1973)
- *Les Misérables* (1980)
- *Miss Saigon* (1989)
- *Martin Guerre* (1996)
- *The Pirate Queen* (2006)
- *Margueritte* (2008)

EXAMPLE WORK:

Les Misérables (1980)

Les Misérables was originally written by Schönberg and Boublil in France in 1980. It was later discovered by theatre impresario Cameron Mackintosh and it opened in London in 1985, becoming the longest running musical in West End history. The musical's success has been worldwide, performed in 42 different cities and translated into 21 different languages. *Les Misérables* is through-sung, and is based on the novel by Victor Hugo telling the story of Jean Valjean in 19th Century France.

Les Miserables has enjoyed extremely long-running success in the West End of London

Orchestration

- Reed 1 (alto flute, alto recorder, flute, piccolo)
- Reed 2 (cor anglais, oboe)
- Reed 3 (B♭ clarinet, bass clarinet, E♭ clarinet, tenor recorder)
- Trumpet/flugel horn
- Trombone
- Horn 1 and 2
- Keyboard 1 and 2
- Percussion
- Violin
- Viola
- Cello
- Bass

Musical features of the score

Les Misérables is known for its popular and catchy melodies with many 'take home' tunes. Part of its success is Schönberg's gift for writing these memorable tunes, and it is interesting to see that some common features prevail in much of the score.

A number of the popular songs in the show contain:

- Step-wise melodies
- Intervals of 4ths and 5ths
- Traditional harmonic progressions (I-IV-V)

Selected musical numbers and analysis

- **'Look Down'**

Notice the **cadence**-like intervals of a 4th with harmonies over a **tonic** pedal and step-wise **melody** of the opening convict song.

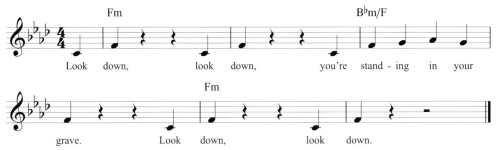

- **'At the End of the Day'**

This song features harmonies over a tonic pedal again, and step-wise melody for the beggars' chorus. It moves from minor to tonic major.

■ **'I Dreamed a Dream'**

In this song, note the descending bass line under the harmonies, with a rising step-wise **melody**.

■ **'Castle on a Cloud'**

Young Cosette's song has a childlike nature with a step-wise melody in a minor key, using standard chord progressions.

■ **'Do You Hear the People Sing'**

The student marching song, which is also the closing song of the show, is **rhythmically** interesting with its dotted rhythms and triplets. The melody moves by step, and the song also modulates to the minor and then to the **dominant** keys. In the finale of Act Two, the song is heard a capella from the chorus who sing in the remote key of A♭ major after the previous scene finishes in C major.

■ **'Empty Chairs at Empty Tables'**

Marius' song in Act Two, which is the same music sung by the Bishop in the prologue, is based on a step-wise melody in the key of A minor, before modulating to C♯ minor.

■ **'On My Own'**

Eponine's song in Act Two, which is also sung by Fantine and Valjean in the finale of Act Two, is based upon intervals of a fourth and step-wise movement. Again the bass line stays rooted to the **tonic** note when the **harmony** changes at the start of the song.

■ 'Master of the House'

The most contrasting character in the musical is Thenardier, who is a portrayed as a comic character despite his villainous activities. His main song, 'Master of the House' is an energetic number. The verse is in a minor key making good use of **syncopation** and **chromaticism** to show the character's unpredictability, the chorus then moves to the **tonic** major, relying very much on tonic and **dominant** harmonies and repeated notes in the **melody**.

DEVELOPMENT AND HISTORY OF MUSICAL THEATRE

Les Miserables has been running continuously in the West End since 1985, making it the second longest running musical in the world after *The Fantasticks*.

TEST YOURSELF: CLAUDE-MICHEL SCHÖNBERG

Listen to 'I'd give my life for you' from the musical *Miss Saigon* and answer the following questions. You should listen to the extract a maximum of three times.

(1) Describe the instrumental introduction before the singing starts.   [2]

(2) Comment on the vocal writing up until the lyric 'I know I'd give my life for you.'   [2]

A LEVEL EXTENSION
Stephen Schwartz (born 1948)

For your A Level you must also study Stephen Schwartz. Schwartz is best known for writing music and lyrics for the musicals *Godspell* and *Wicked* along with lyrics for a number of Disney films including *Pocahontas*, *The Hunchback of Notre Dame* and *The Prince of Egypt*.

Main stage musicals:

- *Godspell* (1971)
- *Pippin* (1972)
- *The Magic Show* (1974)
- *The Baker's Wife* (1976)
- *Working* (1978)
- *Children of Eden* (1993)
- *Wicked* (2003)

Style and musical features

Like Sondheim, Schwartz's ability to write both lyrics and music for his songs allows a complete unity in style for each character and scene.

Schwartz is quoted as describing his style as 'a mishmash'. This is due to the varying styles and popular genres that he uses throughout his musicals. Schwartz's musicals are very melodic and in all of them there are 'take home tunes'. His style is eclectic, encompassing a range to suit characters and plot. He doesn't always stick to one style throughout a show, especially in *Godspell* and *Children of Eden*.

FURTHER LISTENING

- **Patter songs**   'War is a Science' from *Pippin*
    'Two's Company' from *The Magic Show*
- **Music hall**   'All for the Best' from *Godspell*
- **Vaudeville**   'Wonderful' from *Wicked*
- **World music**   'Generations' from *Children of Eden*
- **Gospel**   'Children of Eden' from *Children of Eden*
    'You are the Light of the World' from *Godspell*
- **Jazz**   'Turn back o' Man' from *Godspell*
- **Jazz/rock**   'Simple Joys' from *Pippin*
- **Modern**   'Alas for You', 'Tower of Babble' from *Godspell*
- **Folk**   'Chanson' from *The Baker's wife*
    'On the Willows' from Godspell
- **Pop**   'Day by Day' from *Godspell*
    'The Wizard and I', 'Defying Gravity',
    'As Long as You're Mine' from *Wicked*

EXAMPLE WORK:

Children of Eden (1991)

Children of Eden is based upon the book of Genesis, with Act One dealing with stories of Adam and Eve and Cain and Abel, and Act Two with Noah and the flood. The musical first opened on the West End in January 1991 and closed some three months later. The show has been rewritten and was produced on Broadway. It is now a popular choice of production for amateur dramatic societies and schools.

Orchestration

- Reed 1 (alto saxophone, clarinet, flute, piccolo)
- Reed 2 (bass clarinet, clarinet, tenor saxophone)
- Reed 3 (clarinet, cor anglais, oboe, tenor saxophone)
- French horn
- Keyboard (3 players)
- Guitar (2 players: acoustic, electric and mandolin)
- Percussion (the list of percussion instruments required is large, and in the original London production a digeridoo was also included)
- Drums
- Cello
- Bass

Selected musical numbers and analysis

- 'The Wasteland'

This song starts with a bass **ostinato** pattern that is similar to the bass pattern from 'Dancing Through Life' in *Wicked*. The **melody** is written in a pop style, with **syncopation** and a limited vocal range which doesn't move too far away from the **tonic** note F.

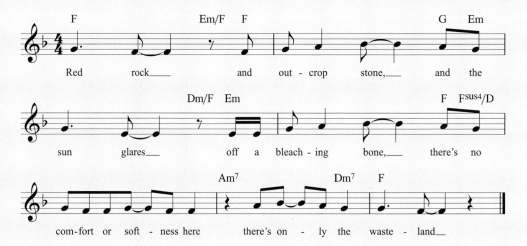

■ **'Stranger to the Rain'**

Notice that this song, in a pop style, changes time signature every bar to create the **rhythmic** effect that Schwartz wants to capture specifically.

Some notable features of style included here are:

■ the limited vocal range

■ the use of the **syncopation**

■ use of **anacrusis** in bars 2, 4 and 6

■ the use of repeated notes in the **melody**

■ the slight change in bars 5-8 to make it not an exact repeat with the downward scale in bar 5

■ the mainly syllabic writing

■ the use of **melisma** on the words 'me' and 'speed', which give it a 'pop' feel

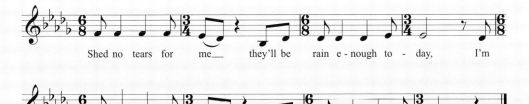

■ **'The Spark of Creation'**

This song centres around the **tonic** note, using a repeated note as a feature to create the excitement and energy, much in the same way 'The Wizard and I' does in *Wicked*.

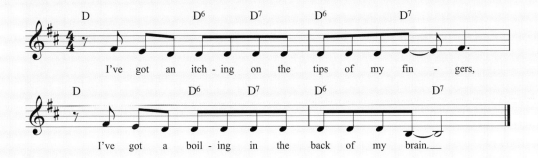

DEVELOPMENT AND HISTORY OF MUSICAL THEATRE

Schwartz wrote lyrics for Leonard Bernstein's *Mass* and it is interesting to make the comparison between the changing time signature of 'Stranger to the Rain' with 'America' from *West Side Story* which also has the same changes each bar. Also Bernstein's use of leitmotif in the same show was clearly an influence on Schwartz's use of leitmotif in *Wicked*.

Furthermore, as the characters and story of *Wicked* are based on *The Wizard of Oz*, Schwartz used the first seven notes of 'Somewhere Over the Rainbow' from *The Wizard of Oz* to create a leitmotif for Elphaba in *Wicked*. Listen to the phrase with the lyrics 'Unlimited, my future is...' from the song 'Defying Gravity' and you will hear the notes of the opening phrase: 'Somewhere over the rainbow...'

Stephen Schwartz has his own website where you will find many interesting articles about his work: www.stephenschwartz.com

Wicked has had long-running success both in London and on Broadway

TEST YOURSELF: STEPHEN SCHWARTZ

Listen to 'Love song' from the musical *Pippin* and answer the following questions. You should listen to the extract a maximum of three times.

(1) Comment on the composer's use of time signatures from the start of the solo singing up until both voices sing together in harmony.   [2]

(2) State the interval between the two voices when they sing together in harmony, choosing from the list below: [1]

   3rd/6th   Octave   4th/5th

AS Level Component 3 Practice Paper

Area of Study C: Musical Theatre

In the exam, you will be given **three** questions for this part of the paper. The first two will be divided into between 5 and 7 parts (a-e or perhaps a-g), and each worth **15 marks**. Both of these will require you to listen to extracts of unprepared works and answer multiple choice or 'describe' questions about them. The third question is an essay question, beginning with the word 'Explain'. This question will be worth **10 marks** and will require you to use your more general knowledge about the genre. Here we have given you examples of questions 1 and 2. Sample assessment papers are also available to download from the Eduqas website, and you should practise answering these as much as possible, particularly the third question, which is not included here.

**Listen to 'I'm Martin Guerre' from *Martin Guerre*
by Claude Michel Schönberg and Alain Boublil.**

The original London cast recording with Matt Rawle as the lead vocal is available at www.youtube.com/watch?v=8tApgUz0xGo – play until 1 min 37 seconds

1. You will hear an extract from a musical theatre song, the lyrics of which are written below.

   In the exam, The extract will be played **3 times** with a **45 second** pause between each playing and a **2 minute** silence after the final playing for you to complete your answer.

   You now have 30 seconds to read the questions.   [15]

   1.   All the insults, and the names, the kicks, the tricks, the vicious games to make a young man reach his prime.

   2.   They say he's weak, they say he's snapped, a man who's scared, a man who's trapped when all a young man needs is time,

   3.   Let them try, with the thrill of the pack,

   4.   Hold your breath, till the day he comes back.

   5.   Enough, no more, I don't give a damn. Why stay, what for? I know who I am,

   6.   A man above the lie that they live, A man who'll love when he's ready to give

   7.   But I'll come back one day, after ten years away

   8.   And they'll stop and they'll say, Look! Look!

   9.   Look it's Martin Guerre,

   10. We need him here, no need to fear, never despair,

   11. Yes! It's Martin Guerre,

   12. Back home at last, those from the past better beware.

   13. Strides through the town,

   14. Laughs, waves them away.

   15. They all think he must be the same

   16. But by heaven they're sure to see there's more to Martin Guerre,

   17. Than a name.

(a)   Underline the **type of voice** heard in the extract.   [1]

Bass   Baritone   Tenor

(b)   Identify the **time signature** at [i] the start of the extract and [ii] from
line 5 onwards.   [2]

(i) ....

(ii) ....

(c)   Tick **one** box which most accurately describes the bass line in the opening
two lines of this extract.   [1]

The bass line is chromatic	
The bass line moves by step	
The bass line uses a tonic pedal	
The bass line has triadic movement	

(d)   Comment on the **vocal writing** in the first two lines of the extract.   [3]

....

....

....

(e)   Describe the use of **tonality** in this extract. Refer to line numbers in your answer.   [3]

....

....

....

(f)   Describe how the writing for the **accompanying instruments** heard in the
extract help to add to the dramatic content of the song. Refer to line numbers.   [4]

....

....

....

....

(g)   Suggest a **composer** of this extract from the list below.   [1]

Andrew Lloyd Webber   Claude Michel Schönberg   Stephen Schwartz

Listen to 'Wishing you Were Somehow Here Again'
from *Phantom of the Opera* by Andrew Lloyd Webber.

It can be found at https://youtu.be/7Z8bBQmbXRk?t=1m21s and for this extract you should play it
from 1 minute 21 seconds in until the end)

2. You will hear an extract from a musical theatre song, the lyrics of which are written below.

In the exam, The extract will be played **3 times** with a **45 second** pause between each
playing and a **2 minute** silence after the final playing for you to complete your answer.

You now have 30 seconds to read the questions.   **[15]**

1.   Passing bells and sculpted angels, cold and monumental

2.   Seem for you the wrong companions, you were warm and gentle.

       (Four bar musical interlude)

3.   Too many years fighting back tears,

4.   Why can't the past just die?

5.   Wishing you were somehow here again,

6.   Knowing we must say goodbye.

7.   Try to forgive, teach me to live,

8.   Give me the strength to try.

9.   No more memories, no more silent tears,

10.   No more gazing across the wasted years,

11.   Help me say goodbye.

(a)   Underline the **type of voice** heard in the extract.   **[1]**

      Contralto   **Mezzo-Soprano**   **Soprano**

(b)   Identify the **time signature** of the extract.   **[1]**

      ....

(c)   Tick **one** box which most accurately describes the cadence at the start of
      line 9 of the extract.   **[1]**

Perfect cadence in a minor key	
Plagal cadence in a minor key	
Perfect cadence in a major key	
Plagal cadence in a minor key	

d)   Comment on the **vocal writing** in the extract, refer to line numbers in your answer.   [3]

....

....

....

(e)   Describe the use of **tonality** in this extract. Refer to line numbers and/or sections in your answer.   [3]

....

....

....

(f)   Describe how the writing for the **accompanying instruments** heard in the extract help to add to the dramatic content of the song. Refer to line numbers in your answer.   [4]

....

....

....

....

(g)   Underline the **composer** of this extract from the list below and suggest a suitable **date** of composition.   [2]

(i)   **Andrew Lloyd Webber**   **Stephen Schwartz**   **Richard Rodgers**

(ii)   Date of composition: ....

A Level Component 3 Practice Paper

Area of Study C: Musical Theatre

In the exam, you will be given **two** questions for this part of the paper. The first will be divided into several parts (perhaps a-d or a-e), and worth a total of **10 marks**. You will listen to an extract of an unprepared work and answer 'identify' or 'describe'-type questions about it. For the second question you will listen to **two** unprepared extracts, answering a number of 'identify' or 'describe' short-answer questions about the first, after which you will write a **10 mark** comparison essay about the two pieces. In total, question 2 will be worth **20 marks** so that in total this section is worth **30**. Here we have given you one example paper. Sample assessment papers are also available to download from the Eduqas website, and you should practise answering these as much as possible.

Listen to 'Weekend in the Country' from the musical
A Little Night Music by Stephen Sondheim

You can find it here: https://youtu.be/dW53pwS1P6o?t=5m and should play from 5 minutes to the end.

1. You will hear an extract from a musical theatre song, the lyrics of which are written below.

In the exam, The extract will be played **3 times** with a **45 second** pause between each playing and a **5 minute** silence after the final playing for you to complete your answer.

You now have 30 seconds to read the questions. [10]

1.   A weekend in the country, the bees in their hives,
2.   The shallow worldly figures, the frivolous lives:
3.   The devil's companions know not whom they serve.
4.   It might be instructive to observe
5.   We're off we are? We'll take the car, We'll bring champagne and caviar

      (Charlotte, I'm thinking it out, Charlotte, there's no need to shout)

6.   We're off and away, what a beautiful day, surveying each other while playing croquet,
7.   Controlling our feelings while strolling the lawns and confiding our motives while hiding our yawns.
8.   With riotous laughter we quietly suffer the season in town which is reason enough for
9.   A weekend in the country, how amusing, how delightfully droll!
10.   A weekend in the country, while we're losing our control
11.   A weekend in the country, how enchanting on the manicured lawns
12.   A weekend in the country with the panting and the yawns
13.   With the crickets and the pheasants and the orchards and the hay
14.   With the servants and the peasants we'll be laying our plans while we're playing croquet for
15.   A weekend in the country so inactive that one has to lie down
16.   A weekend in the country where
17.   We're twice as upset as in (a weekend, are you sure you want to go and leave)
18.   Town!

(a)   State the **two** different **time signatures** in the following sections of the extract: [2]

(i)   Lines 1-4: ....

(ii)   Line 9 to the end of the extract: ....

(b)   Name the **solo instrument** that plays an ascending counter melody in line 15 and also a descending motif in line 18.   [1]

....

(c)   Tick **two** of these statements which are correct.   [2]

At line 17 there is a tonic pedal for 12 bars	
At line 17 there is a dominant pedal for 12 bars	
At line 17 there is a sub-dominant pedal for 12 bars	
There is a perfect cadence between lines 8 and 9	
There is a plagal cadence between lines 8 and 9	
There is an imperfect cadence between lines 8 and 9	

(d)   Comment on the use of **tonality** in this extract (refer to line numbers in your answer).   [3]

....

....

....

(e)   Describe the composer's writing for **voices** in this extract (refer to line numbers in your answer).   [2]

....

....

Listen to 'Oh Happy We' from *Candide*

You can find it here: https://youtu.be/-oN3lQOUHwY?t=7s – Start at 7 seconds and end at 1 minute
47 seconds; then listen to 'One hand, One Heart' from West Side Story, which you will find here:
https://youtu.be/RWnsm5HVdXU?t=4m8s – Start at 4 minutes 8 seconds and end at 5 minutes 41 seconds)

2. You will hear **two** extracts of music, both love duets written by the same composer.
   You may wish to place a **tick** in the box each time you hear the extract. 5 mins

Answer questions (a-e) in relation to **extract 1 only**. Question (f) is a comparison
of extract 1 with extract 2.

Each extract will be played **3 times** with a **30 second pause** between each playing,
a **5 minute pause** after the second playing of extract 2 and a **7 minute silence** after
the last playing for you to complete your answer.

You now have 30 seconds to read the questions. [10]

First, you will hear an extract taken from the end of the song '*Oh Happy We'*,
from the musical '*Candide'* by Leonard Bernstein.

The lyrics are printed below.

1. Soon, when we feel we can afford it, we'll build a modest little farm.

2. We'll buy a yacht and live aboard it, rolling in luxury and stylish charm.

3. Cows and chickens. Social whirls.

4. Peas and cabbage. Ropes of pearls.

5. Soon there'll be little ones beside us; We'll have a sweet Westphalian home.

6. Somehow we'll grow as rich as Midas; We'll live in Paris when we're not in Rome.

7. Smiling babies. Marble halls.

8. Sunday picnics. Costume balls.

9. Oh, won't my robes of silk and satin be chic! I'll have all that I desire

10. Pangloss will tutor us in Latin and Greek, while we sit before the fire.

11. Glowing rubies. Glowing logs.

12. Faithful servants. Faithful dogs.

13. We'll round the world enjoying high life; All will be pink champagne and gold.

14. We'll lead a rustic and a shy life, feeding the pigs and sweetly growing old.

15. Breast of peacock. Apple pie.

16. I love marriage. So do I.

17. Oh, happy pair! Oh happy we! It's very rare how we agree

18. Oh happy pair! Oh happy we! It's very rare how we agree

19. Oh happy pair! Oh happy we! It's very rare how we agree.

(a)   State the **two** different **time signatures** heard in the following lines of the extract: [2]

(i)   Lines 1-2, 5-6, 9-10, 13-14: ....

(ii)   Line 17 to the end of the extract: ....

(b)   Underline the pair of solo voices heard in the extract.   [1]

Soprano and Tenor   **Soprano and Bass**   **Alto and Tenor**   **Alto and Bass**

(c)   Tick **two devices** heard in the vocal writing.   [2]

Augmentation	
Ostinato	
Riff	
Sequence	
Stretto imitation	

(d)   Comment on the use of **harmony** from line 17 to the end of the extract (refer to line numbers/lyrics in your answer).   [2]

....

....

(e)   Describe the **structure** of the song and comment on the **tonality** in each section. (refer to line numbers in your answer).   [3]

....

....

....

(f)   Next, you will hear an extract from the ending of the song 'One Hand, One Heart' from the musical *West Side Story* by Leonard Bernstein. Compare and contrast the stylistic features of this song with those of extract 1. You may wish to mention details of **structure**, **harmony**, **tonality**, the use of **voices** and **instruments**, and any other points of interest relating to the musical style.   [10]

The lyrics for extract two are printed below.

1.   Make of our lives one life

2.   Day after day, one life

3.   Now it begins, now we start

4.   One hand, one heart

5.   Even death wont part us now. (Death won't part us now.)

Jazz

FROM 1920 ONWARDS

Jazz is one of the optional Areas of Study (AoS). The AoS covers the development and stylistic features of jazz music between 1920 and 1950 for AS level, and between 1920 and 1960 for A level.

If you ask a group of people 'What is jazz?', each one of them will probably have a different answer, a different concept of what it is, a different sound in their head. This is because jazz has come to mean so many things.

In fact you could say it is an 'umbrella' term that embraces many diverse genres and sub-genres. Perhaps it has always been so as it was born out of a fusion (or amalgam) of different pre-existing kinds of music, brought together due to particular circumstances. Whether your idea of jazz is Louis Armstrong, Charlie Parker, Weather Report or Snarky Puppy, it is vital to understand the roots and early developments of the music.

What do I have to study at AS level?

For AS level, you will study the period from 1920–1950, with particular reference to:

- Ragtime
- Dixieland
- Early Jazz
- Big Band (including swing)
- Bebop

What do I have to study at A level?

At A level, the time-span is slightly extended to cover music of the 1950s:
up to 1960, and you will study an extra genre in addition to those listed above:

- 'Cool' jazz.

Throughout both AS and A Level, you will focus on a range of topics including:

- Form/structure
- **Harmony**
- **Rhythmic** elements
- Melodic devices
- Instrumental techniques and roles
- **Sonority/texture**
- Approaches to **improvisation**
- Performance environments

Jazz is surrounded by many mythologies and misconceptions, so this chapter will try to clarify as much as possible. One example would be, 'Oh you play jazz, that's when you play anything you like isn't it?'

Well, not quite! A musician might get to a stage where they can play with absolute freedom, but that is usually a very well-informed freedom, a freedom which comes from hours of listening and practice.

Background and Context

Jazz emerged in the early years of the 20th Century. Despite claims by individuals to have 'invented' the music (namely Jelly Roll Morton), it is more the case that a set of circumstances bringing communities of musicians with a variety of cultural and musical traditions together allowed this unique fusion of sounds to generate a new musical language.

There are three particularly important historical and sociological facts that can help us understand the circumstances which made jazz emerge in the way that it did.

1. The abolition of slavery. This took place over a number of years and succeeded in different parts of The United States at different times. It became the major goal of The American Civil War. The Emancipation Proclamation was delivered by Abraham Lincoln in 1865.

2. The end of The American Civil War. The official proclamation of this was in 1866, and its relevance to the history of jazz is that many abandoned brass instruments were taken up by players who made a new sound with them, using blues inflections and giving the impression of 'making the instrument sing'. They played with a different timbre and, more particularly, a different approach to vibrato.

3. In 1880 the State of Louisiana passed a bill that classified all people with any 'coloured blood' in the same way as those of direct African descent. This changed the lives of the Creole population who had previously lived elegantly, learning the musical culture of their French or Spanish ancestors in the European manner.

New Orleans

It is commonly accepted that New Orleans was the birthplace of jazz. It was probably one of the most cosmopolitan cities in the world at the turn of the century.

As a major port it had a population derived from all corners of the world. There were African-Americans, Creoles (people from mixed European and African descent), and

An artist's impression of Congo Square

Western Europeans (namely French and Spanish). In earlier days, before the abolition of slavery, slaves were only permitted to gather in one place on one day of the week. This was called Place Congo, now known as Congo Square. On a Sunday the slaves would gather and share their music; it was the only day drumming was permitted. A constant $\frac{12}{8}$ or triplet crotchet/quaver pattern, often played on a gourd, underpinned the performance of Praise Songs and other musical heritage from West Africa.

Musical precursors

Here is a list of musical forms which pre-dated jazz and undoubtedly influenced it. Some forms are related to each other. Significant forms such as blues and ragtime will be studied in more depth later in this chapter.

- Blues

- Ragtime

- Vaudeville and minstrel shows – rather like a variety show, these performances would include various musical acts such as virtuoso ragtime on banjo (Fred Van Eps: *Ragtime Oriel*) and novelty brass band (Sodero's Military Band: *Slidus Trombonus*)

- Work Song – these were typically sung by slaves when they were having to carry out repetitive and strenuous tasks. Work songs are usually rhythmic and have call and response phrases

- Spirituals – like the work song, the spiritual provided solace to the slave population. Some spirituals have been found to have elements of French, Spanish and even Scottish folk melodies. The Fisk Jubilee Singers were a highly respected university choir, specialising in singing spirituals. They visited Swansea, South Wales in 1874, raising money for their university, The Fisk University of Nashville, which was set up following the emancipation to offer an education to the freed slaves. They returned to Swansea several times, proving so popular that they undertook a tour of South Wales in 1907. You can hear the original choir singing *Swing Low, Sweet Chariot* on YouTube. There are also examples of a contemporary Fisk Jubilee Choir available

- Music of the Baptist church – the intoning of the preacher followed by improvised responses of the congregation suggest two important elements in jazz: the call and response, and collective or simultaneous improvisation. Listen to Rev. J.M. Gates: *I'm Going to Heaven if it Takes My Life*

- West African drumming – before the Emancipation Proclamation, African slaves were mostly isolated within their own community. This meant they were able to maintain their musical heritage and cultural identity. As well as drums and percussion, slaves were known to play flutes, fiddles and banjos

- Rhythmic chanting of Southern street vendors – using a simple phrase to describe and 'advertise' their goods, the vendors would intone and inflect the words with references to the blues. An example of this can be heard on 'Riverside – History of Classic Jazz', Disc 1, Track 2.

LISTEN

With the exception of the Fisk Jubilee Singers, all the tracks named above are available on one 3 CD collection:

- 'Riverside – History of Classic Jazz'

Stylistic Studies

The Blues

Although the blues is inextricably linked with jazz, it is also its own category, having many different sub-genres. It started as an oral tradition, and could be thought of as a folk music. Subjects sung about would focus on hardship, love and relationships. We will look at three types of blues:

- **Country Blues** – this was usually sung by a soloist who would accompany themselves on a guitar, banjo or fiddle. These blues would be led by the vocal line. Usually each verse would have three phrases of four bars. There was a basic harmonic blueprint which was:

Chord 1 (tonic) for 4 bars

Chord 4 (subdominant) for two bars, chord I for 2 bars

Chord 5 (dominant) for two bars, chord I for 2 bars

However, this structure was not rigid and the forms may be stretched or pushed, depending on the lyric and melodic line. Blind Lemon Jefferson can be heard singing *Shuckin' Sugar* on a recording made in 1926, (although it would have been performed many years earlier than this), and you can hear how he takes liberties with the final phrases. Sometimes you may hear eleven and a half bars, others closer to thirteen! Another of his recordings, *Black Snake*, doesn't even make the harmonic change to the subdominant (or chord IV) in bar five, something which would seem to epitomise the blues.

- **Classic Blues** – this was usually performed by a female vocalist and accompanied by jazz band or piano. This form of the blues was more commonly performed in theatres, as it developed in minstrel shows which toured to a number of venues. One of the first great singers of the classic blues was Gertrude 'Ma' Rainey. She recorded between 1923 and 1929 and you can hear several titles on YouTube. When you listen, try to check the form of the songs – they are the blues, but not all blues are twelve bars long.

W.C. Handy was a cornet player, composer and band-leader. He called himself the 'Father of the Blues'. We could think of him as a musicologist as well. He collected traditional African American themes and often incorporated them into his own compositions. One of his most famous songs was *St. Louis Blues*. This was performed by Bessie Smith, 'Empress of the Blues' in 1929, alongside Louis Armstrong on trumpet. You can hear this extraordinary recording on YouTube. Listen to how Armstrong matches the vocal inflections of Smith in his trumpet 'responses' to the vocal phrases. Much of the song has two bar vocal phrases followed by two bars of (improvised) trumpet commentary. Once again the structure of this blues is altered from the standard twelve bars. Although the song has a twelve bar form (which is repeated), it also has an eight bar 'bridge', (more on this on song structures to follow).

- **Instrumental Blues** – this is a rather generic term that expresses how jazz players and composers adopted the blues for instrumental performance. We will look at how the standard twelve bar form was developed (particularly harmonically), through the decades.

The music theory of the blues

The underlying harmonic principles of the blues appear to be contradictory: we may call a blues 'Blues in F' but it is not as we know it in conventional theory. The blues has '**blue notes**', notes that lie outside the major scale and create melodic tension. The significant blue notes are the minor third, the flattened fifth and the flattened seventh.

It is the flattened seventh note that creates the biggest seemingly contradictory statement, as it is present in all of the chords used in the blues. This means that the 'tonic' chord is actually a dominant 7th, the chord that we expect to lead to the tonic.

So a basic twelve bar blues will look like this:

F7 | F7 | F7 | F7 | B♭7 | B♭7 | F7 | F7 | C7 | C7 | F7 | F7

Now it becomes clear that Blues in F is not in F at all, as there is an E♭ in the tonic chord!

The blues also has its own scale(s – there are variations). Let's have a look at a basic blues scale that is derived from the minor **pentatonic** scale:

Place this over a dominant 7th chord and we can see that there are two thirds – a minor and a major, (A♭ in the scale and A♮ in the chord), causing the greatest discrepancy of **tonality** you can imagine. It is this very **dissonance** that is at the heart of the blues. Sometimes the **blue notes** are used as chromatic passing notes, often sliding (using **glissando**, **portamento**), to a resolution note, or falling off a resolved note. Sometimes they are resolutely held in dissonance creating a crying, mournful sound which is very difficult to describe in words. These are the tonal inflections of the blues.

Largely, it is perhaps not such a good idea to try to theorise too much, but just to enjoy the very human expression of the blues.

Ragtime

Ragtime was also known as 'ragged' music, due its **rhythmic** qualities. It is not jazz but certainly contributed enormously to what was to come, overlapping with the emergence of jazz and jazz players. It was popular from 1890-1917.

One of the reasons it is not considered jazz is because it was composed, very meticulously. Ragtime compositions were made available as sheet music before the end of the nineteenth century. They were widely performed by their composers and travelling minstrel musicians. The usual vehicle was the solo piano but other examples can be found, such as banjo solo and arrangement for small ensemble (cornet, clarinet, trombone and so on). Ragtime became extremely popular worldwide, with prominent composers including Charles Ives and Claude Debussy adding to the catalogue of compositions in the style.

The most famous of the classic ragtime composers was Scott Joplin (1868-1917). His greatest hit was *Maple Leaf Rag*, published in 1899. It sold hundreds of thousands of copies, which enabled Joplin to retire from his job as honkey-tonk pianist. Another extremely popular piece is *The Entertainer*, which was used as the soundtrack for the film 'The Sting'. On several of the covers of Joplin's publications you can see the name of the piece followed by 'a two-step' or 'march two-step', confirming that this music was designed for dancing. One of the most popular dances was the **Cakewalk**. Becoming the new popular dance music of its day added to the huge success of **ragtime**.

Joplin was an extremely talented piano player and a very thorough composer. He was particularly consumed with structure and form. He researched the form of the march and adhered strictly to this throughout his writings.

The music theory of ragtime

■ **Rhythm**

a) The Entertainer

b) Maple Leaf Rag

N.B. Pitches as guide only

Rags are generally written in $\frac{2}{4}$. Right hand melodies consist of semiquaver groupings while the left hand is mostly playing quavers. You can see from the examples above that the rhythm of the right hand is very syncopated, with tied notes over the main pulse beats and/or bar lines. Another rhythmic element to listen out for is a 'pick-up', otherwise known as an **anacrusis** or sometimes simply an upbeat, where the beginning of each section starts before beat 1.

We will look at jazz notation more specifically later on in this chapter, but take a look at the above rhythms expressed in $\frac{4}{4}$: it starts to look a lot more like jazz.

a) The Entertainer

b) Maple Leaf Rag

■ **Form**

Joplin was particularly precise with the structure of his rags, seeking to find a good balance and flow. Each section would be 16 bars of $\frac{2}{4}$. The material would essentially be organised like this: AA BB CC DD, i.e. in four different sections.

Sometimes there would be an additional A section before the first C section: AA BB A CC DD. Other features could include an introduction (I): I AA BB A CC DD. Try listening to as many rags as you can, identifying the structure and gaining confidence in recognising different material.

■ **Tonality and Harmony**

There is usually a pattern to the general tonality, which is linked to the structure. Sections A and B are in the **tonic** and Section C in the **subdominant**. Section D can be either.

Within each section, much of the harmonic movement is quite straightforward tonic and **dominant** relationships. Joplin has a trick of including a suggestion of the tonic minor on occasions, even when the general tonality is major. Quite often the left hand will mark out the harmonic movement with **roots** and fifths, connecting root movement with chromatic steps or leading notes.

A LEVEL EXTENSION

Also listen out for:

- Tonic, dominant, secondary dominant and diminished chord qualities
- Chromatic harmonic movement
- In *Maple Leaf Rag* (tonic A♭), bar 5 has an F♭ arpeggio falling to an E♭ root-only chord in octaves. How else could this be expressed, and why is it not?

■ Melody

Listen out for:

- Arpeggiated material
- Scalic runs
- Chromatic runs
- Question and answer phrases
- Repetition of musical 'cells' (little groups of notes that form a musical idea)
- Range and contrasts, for example very low to very high.

■ Texture

There can be a variety of textures within each rag. Some things to consider are:

- Octaves, or tenths (an octave plus a third), between the hands
- Left hand accompaniment, eg. <u>oom</u> pah, oom pah or <u>oom</u> cha cha a <u>oom</u> cha cha (beats 1 are underlined). In these examples 'pah' and 'cha' represent chords and 'oom' and 'a' roots and fifths or connecting root movement on beats 2 and 4
- **Counterpoint** (especially question and answer phrases between the hands)
- **Homophonic** texture.

■ **Performance Technique**

There is little or no pedal used.

Joplin had two disciples, James Scott and Joseph Lamb. You can hear examples of their contributions to **ragtime** thanks to the fact that their performances have been preserved as piano rolls. You can also hear Joplin playing *The Entertainer* in this way. Have a careful listen – can you hear a slight lilt, a tiny hint of swing towards the end?

The 1920s

In the 1920s, the Jazz Age had arrived. It was a decade of huge consolidation and development in jazz and popular music. Despite prohibition still being in place following the end of the First World War, jazz was flourishing and being widely performed, (albeit often in illegal clubs and bars known as 'speakeasies' or for 'private parties').

The jazz age is also associated with a particular style of clothing

Some of the greatest names in jazz became household names at this time, including Louis Armstrong, Bix Beiderbecke, Sidney Bechet, Jelly Roll Morton and Duke Ellington. In popular music, composers and songwriters, notably Gershwin and Cole Porter, were penning the songs that became the staple (or 'standard') repertoire of future jazz musicians – ' The American Songbook'. The blues and **ragtime** were still prevalent but approaches to performance were changing. The arrival of sound recording and the phonograph was instrumental to the rise in the popularity of jazz, suddenly making the music available to a much wider audience.

IMPORTANT THINGS TO CONSIDER WHEN LISTENING TO EARLY RECORDINGS

Musicians had to play into a single, large cone for their performances to be captured – this was 'live' recording.

The sound quality can appear faint, muffled or have a layer of 'dust' over it. To our contemporary ears this can make the sound old-fashioned and we have to work quite hard to imagine the fullness of sound that the original performance would have made. This old-fashioned sound can fool us into thinking that the musicians were old as well, but the opposite was often the case, with many young players turning 'professional' during their teens. The music was vibrant, youthful and fun!

Early Jazz

There isn't a single form that encapsulates early jazz, but there were two vital features that united the various styles:

- Rhythm
- Improvisation

We will look at these musical elements through the study of some of the great exponents:

- Jelly Roll Morton (1890–1941)
- James P. Johnson (1894–1955)
- Louis Armstrong (1900–1971)
- Bix Beiderbecke (1903–1931)

Our study will be split into two main categories:

1. Piano Styles
2. Dixieland

Note that every track listed in this chapter is available on YouTube, and many supporting materials such as lead sheets are also available as images online.

Piano Styles

We will study the progression from ragtime to early jazz piano, stride and boogie woogie.

Jelly Roll Morton

Jelly Roll Morton was a member of the Creole population of New Orleans, the 'melting pot' that gave birth to jazz. In fact Morton claimed to have invented jazz. This was obviously an overstatement (he was not the most modest of characters), but he could lay claim to being the first jazz composer. He was a piano player coming out of the ragtime tradition, a composer, and band-leader.

Listen to Jelly Roll Morton playing Joplin's *Maple Leaf Rag*. A good version can be found on YouTube labelled 'Jelly Roll Morton plays *Maple Leaf Rag* (The Complete Library of Congress Recordings by Alan Lomax)'. You will hear two versions of the rag and a short interview. Although this recording is later than the 1920s it clearly reflects the nature of the playing of the time.

What makes version 2 a 'jazz performance'?

1. Rhythm

This version is employing 'swing' quavers. Does this mean Morton is playing in triplets rather than the original semiquavers? Well…

Jelly Roll Morton aged about 17, in around 1906

Swing is a highly complex beast: it is a combination of several **rhythmic** attributes coming together. Textbooks tell us that swing quavers are triplets:

But try beating out the above rhythm. Does it sound like 'swing', or does it sound like *Humpty Dumpty*, or any other nursery rhyme in compound time?

So, we can assume that other elements are needed to create 'swing'. Important factors are **syncopation**, (as in **ragtime**) and **articulation** (which of a pair of swing quavers is long/short, **accented**/slurred, and so on?)

The degree to which a pair of quavers are 'tripletised' very much depends on the tempo; the faster the tempo the straighter the quavers. So the triplets are not precise. Swing is more of a 'feel' and trying to notate this 'feel' proves limiting. That is why it has become more common to notate 'swing' as quavers.

One more thing – try tapping your foot, or clicking your fingers on firstly beats 1 and 3, and then beats 2 and 4. Which feels better? The answer to this will tell you that there is a rhythmic stress on the off-beats of the bar.

The left hand gives a firm suggestion of $\frac{4}{4}$ swing: Some bars have a strong oom cha oom cha feel, where the 'cha' is slightly stressed. In other passages Morton suggests a **walking bass** line in which four single note crotchets join the **root** notes in a smooth ascending or descending fashion, using scalar runs and chromatic passing notes.

2. Improvisation

Morton is not playing exactly what Joplin wrote.

This tells us that there must be an element of interpretation or **improvisation** in his performance.

We can recognise that the piece is *Maple Leaf Rag* but there are some additions and subtractions to the score:

- The **melody** is frequently embellished with ornaments and fast runs
- The phrasing is stretched or compressed
- Arpeggiated passages are elaborated with rhythmic variations
- Some melodic phrases (especially single notes) are harmonised, so although the original harmonic framework is preserved, Morton provides more complex harmonic movement and colour by creating inner voices.

James P. Johnson

One of Johnson's legacies that we may be most familiar with is the *Charleston*, of 1923. This popular song (and dance) is synonymous with 'The Roaring Twenties'. The piece is still frequently performed, and the dance is even featured on the BBC's 'Strictly Come Dancing!'

One of the most important features of the *Charleston* is the **rhythmic** figure of the opening bars of the theme:

Charle - ston,   Charle - ston!

This rhythm is derived from the Spanish or Latin American rhythms, the 'Habanera' and the 'Clave':

Habanera rhythm   The 3 2 Clave

The *Charleston* rhythmic cell is still used as a '**comping**' figure in contemporary jazz.

James P. Johnson was the first great player of the **stride piano**. Stride is characteristically when the left hand plays a single bass note or intervals of an octave, seventh or tenth on beats one and three (the 'on-beats') and strides up to a chord on beats two and four (the 'off-beats'). It is said to be a direct descendant of **ragtime** and the blues.

Listen to *Carolina Shout*, recorded by Johnson in Harlem, New York, in 1921, (this was not the first recording: he had previously recorded the piece on piano rolls in 1918 and earlier in 1921.)

Things to listen out for:

- 4 bar introduction
- Melodic phrases in groups of 4 bars
- Major **tonality**
- Descending melodic 'question' phrases with a variety of 'answers'
- Imperfect **cadence** at the end of the first 8 bars
- Rolling quavers (swing quavers) and triplets in the right hand
- The repeat of section A (16 bars) has different melodic material (variation, embellishment and **improvisation**) but the harmonic movement is the same
- Variations of feel in the left hand
- The left hand defines the **harmony**
- The third 'strain' (section) about 1 minute 5 seconds in, has **dissonance** in the right hand 'shout' (this is a blues technique where the major and minor 3rds are struck together)
- Call and response between right and left hands
- Driving rhythm
- About 2 minutes in, the left hand starts to anticipate the bar line (on beat 4-and) and, therefore, the harmonic change (rhythmic and harmonic anticipation)
- The coda uses the 'habanera' rhythm.

In summary, although this piece draws heavily on ragtime, particularly in its structure, there are some marked differences that give it a sense of freedom and drive. Johnson was known as the first master of stride but in this piece he uses a variety of left hand techniques and the stride is not obviously consistent.

You can see a version of *Carolina Shout and Harlem Strut* (also 1921) on YouTube, labelled: 'stride piano:james p. johnson/willie the lion smith', where the piano rolls are played on a digital keyboard. Watching the keys move literally shows you the stride action of the left hand.

James P. Johnson was also renowned for being the teacher of Fats Waller, who will be featured in the 1930s.

Dixieland

The term Dixieland describes a form a jazz that is ensemble based, and definitely had its roots in the 1920s. However, at the time of creating and performing the Dixieland sound, musicians were more likely to label their music either 'jazz' (there were multiple spellings such as jas, jass and jaz) or 'hot jazz'.

Remember at this time there hadn't yet been the creation of sub-genres such as 'swing' or 'bebop' – it was all just called 'jazz'. Several bands had 'hot' in their names, such Jelly Roll Morton's 'Red Hot Peppers' and Louis Armstrong's 'Hot Five' and 'Hot Seven'.

There were bands that had Dixieland in their names and, in fact, the first recording that had 'jazz' in its description was made in 1917 by a band called 'The Original Dixieland Band'. This was a quintet of white musicians led by cornet player, Nick La Rocca.

So, it was at the time of a revival of this music (a backlash against the later forms of 'swing' and 'bebop') in the 1940s that the term became widely adopted. In the UK the term traditional or 'trad' jazz is also widely used.

We will now study some of the sounds of this music from the 1920s by listening to three of its greats.

Jelly Roll Morton as Composer and Band-leader

First on the listening list is *Black Bottom Stomp* (Jelly Roll Morton) Victor BVE-36239 which was recorded in 1926 and performed by his band, 'The Red Hot Peppers'.

This has to be one of the most superlative pieces of composition and performance of its day. In many ways it was looking forward to what would become standard practice in the coming years, but in others it drew on what had come before, especially some of the melodic and harmonic concepts of **ragtime**.

Let's look at compositional devices to start with:

- The piece is formed of different sections (repeated)
- The sections are different lengths
- Some sections are used as a vehicle for **improvisation**
- There is a linking section that leads the **modulation** into the third idea. This is a reflection of the introduction used as a '**vamp**' before the C sections in ragtime
- The third idea is in the **subdominant** (as in ragtime)
- There are **rhythmic**, melodic fragments of ensemble work (the 'stomp')
- There are 'stops' (played by the whole ensemble)
- There are '**breaks**', where a soloist improvises in the space provided by the 'stops'.

So what is particularly forward-looking about this performance? One of the key things is the nature of the improvisation. It was typical of the time that improvisation was collective, i.e. all of the frontline players would be **improvising** simultaneously. Each would use their instrument to its strengths to create a **polyphonic texture**. You would hear call and response, countermelodies, harmonic 'weaving' and **rhythmic** punctuations. All of this came from a real sense of collaboration and interaction. In *Black Bottom Stomp* there are individual solos (improvisations), as well as collective improvisation. Each musician is featured apart from the double bass.

1. Rhythm

This performance has a keen sense of swing. This is probably due to each and every musician's feel, but one of the other groundbreaking things about this recording is that the double bass is played **pizzicato**. This provides a strong rhythmic and harmonic foundation to the music. Although the piece begins with a cut time feel, ie. ¢ with the bass playing two in a bar (on beats 1 and 3), as it progresses you can hear the bass clearly moving to four in a bar. This is an extremely early example of the **walking bass**. There is a more percussive sound to the bass then brass bass or arco string bass and it gives a greater propulsion or drive to the music.

A rolling quaver feel is present throughout. Listen to the banjo accompaniment.

There is emphasis on beats 2 and 4. Initially this is more obvious in the piano **comping** in the left hand (as described in *Maple Leaf Rag*), but listen to the bass drum towards the end of the track; there is no way of missing the strong 2 and 4 then!

Performance techniques and musical elements to listen out for:

- Contrary motion chromatic backings
- **Glissandi** – especially on trombone, but listen also to the clarinet bending its way up to a note
- Ornaments – triplet decorations (rather like mordents) in piano and clarinet lines
- Arpeggios
- Repeated patterns (often three notes) which provide **syncopation**

- Pizzicato bass
- Continuous light but driving banjo accompaniment
- Variety of percussion sounds (including triangle)
- Repeated ensemble rhythms
- Instrumental drop-outs – for example listen to who accompanies the banjo and piano solos.

A LEVEL EXTENSION

At A Level it is recommended that you do further study of harmonic trends in popular and jazz music of the 1920s. Look at the use of the mediant major, such as the **tonic** chord C followed by E7, and how secondary **dominants** are used. A good starting point would be *The Charleston* by James P. Johnson (1923).

Louis Armstrong

Louis Armstrong, nicknamed 'Satchmo', was one of the leading and most enduring of the New Orleans jazz musicians. His career spanned from the beginning of the 1920s right through to the 1960s. It was his extraordinary cornet and trumpet playing that first earned him recognition, but he was also a great entertainer, film star and singer. He had huge recording success and topped the charts in 1968, with *What a Wonderful World*.

Armstrong had a hard childhood and was ordered into care at a very young age, after being arrested for firing a gun on the street (it was New Year's Eve and nobody was injured). However, there was a positive outcome to this situation because, while he was in The New Orleans Home for Waifs, he was

Louis Armstrong in 1953

introduced to music; firstly he excelled at choral singing, then percussion, a range of horns and bugles and, finally, the cornet. He left the home and started working as a musician straight away as a teenager, while delivering coal during the day. He soon grabbed the attention of the king of cornet players in New Orleans, Joe 'King' Oliver. Oliver mentored Armstrong and gave the young player his first big break. Oliver, like many New Orleans musicians, moved to Chicago in search of work. Once there he established his band, 'King Oliver's Creole Jazz Band' and soon sent for Armstrong to join them.

Here is an example one of their recordings:

King Oliver's Creole Jazz Band: *Dippermouth Blues*, 1923, Chicago

Listening notes:

- 4 bar arpeggiated introduction, and note the diminished chord
- The form is a 12 bar blues, note the developed chord sequence
- The 'head' (the theme or **melody**) is played within collective (or simultaneous) **improvisation**, which creates **polyphony**
- Stops on choruses three and four
- The trombone plays glissandi
- The percussionist is playing one instrument (woodblock)
- The cornet has distinctive **vibrato**
- The cornet solo has blues inflections
- The final two bars are repeated as a 'tag' or coda.

SOME KEY VOCABULARY

Head:	theme or melody
Chorus:	the form of the melody or harmonic sequence used for improvisation
Stops:	the whole band plays chords together (in this case on beats 1, 2, 3 as accompaniment to the solo clarinet)
Glissandi:	Slides – literally sliding from one note to another
Vibrato:	Playing (or singing) a little above and below the note, producing a 'wobble'

The next piece to listen to is Louis Armstrong & His Hot Five: *The Heebie Jeebies* 1926

This recording is a little clearer and it is easier to hear the warm sound that Armstrong makes on the cornet. Many of the musical elements studied are present in this performance but, more importantly, there is a new technique to look at: **scat**.

There are two myths associated with scat and this recording:

1. Armstrong invented scat on this performance. This is false, it was a known technique.

2. He started to scat because his lyrics fell off the music stand… well, have a listen yourself and see what you think. One thing for certain is that he was very convincing.

What is scat?

Put simply, it is when a singer improvises in the same way as an instrumentalist, often imitating the sounds of a particular **instrument**. There are the same demands put on scatting as creating any improvisation, i.e. you have to create melodic contours which reflect the **harmony** with convincing **rhythmic** flow and feel. You could think of this as the **melody** generating the harmony – J.S. Bach was the master of this, especially in his suites for solo instrument.

There are usually no words when you are scatting, although some singers have used nonsense words. It is better to think of the sounds that are made as copying the sounds of an instrument, eg. bwe, bwe, bway (once you've got over the giggles of trying to say it) can sound like a trumpet cry – try saying it on beats 1, 2, 3 where beat 3 has a little more weight and is longer. Other consonant sounds can be more percussive, such as sk, b, g, and are useful for making strongly articulated, **accented** rhythms. Remember, it won't sound very convincing if you try to make a swinging scat using 'la, la, la, la, la'!

So, despite the comic associations with scat, in the right hands (or voice) it can be one of the most expressive forms of improvisation.

FURTHER LISTENING

If you want to hear more of Armstrong's fabulous sound take a listen to Louis Armstrong & His Hot Five: *West End Blues*, 1928, which includes the legendary opening cadenza, clearly demonstrating his outstanding technique and huge range.

Bix Beiderbecke

Beiderbecke was born in Iowa, into a family of German descent. As a cornet player he was renowned for his tone and impeccable **intonation**; something that he owed to his European musical heritage perhaps. Despite starting piano lessons at the age of seven, Beiderbecke never got to grips with reading music (this was something that continued to frustrate his ideas of becoming a composer in later years). However, he took up the cornet at fourteen and, self-taught, continued the aural tradition for learning jazz. He had early gramophone records, including the one mentioned earlier by 'The Original Dixieland Band' and taught himself the sound. So, though not a sightreader, Beiderbecke created 'elegant' melodic improvisations that not only captured the right notes but did so with flair and musicality.

Bix Beiderbecke is in the centre of this photo with his trumpet, as part of the Wolverine Orchestra, in 1924

FURTHER LISTENING

Frank Trumbauer & His Orchestra (featuring Bix Beiderbecke):
Singin' The Blues 1927, Chicago

Listening notes:

- Despite the word 'blues' in the title, this is a 32 bar song form: ABAC
- The 4 bar introduction is constructed of block chords, and is therefore **homophonic**
- The first solo is on C melody saxophone and starts with a 'scoop' or **portamento** up to the first note
- The guitar accompaniment is sometimes chordal and sometimes provides single note countermelodies
- There is piano accompaniment but this is quite quiet and only obvious when the guitar drops down to single note lines
- At bar 15 of the sax solo there is a '**break**' (the rest of the band stops and the sax leads into the second half of the solo)
- The second solo is Beiderbecke on cornet
- The cornet solo uses a great variety of note values including crotchets, lilting 'swing' quavers, triplets and even semiquavers
- The cornet solo uses all melodic devices: arpeggios, scalar passages, chromatic runs, interval leaps and **blue notes**
- The third 'chorus' is the only time the actual melody of the piece is stated
- The melody is embellished with collective **improvisation**
- The melody is split by a clarinet solo
- The guitar has a one bar break and plays a fast diminished arpeggio pattern.

Note that this recording has elements of more modern approaches. There are solo improvisations as well as collective improvisation.

General notes on 1920s jazz

Orchestration

In this period a typical jazz ensemble, band, or orchestra was made up of six or seven players.

These could be split into two units:

1. The **rhythm** section – drums/percussion, bass, '**comping**' instrument(s)
2. The frontline – cornet/trumpet, 1 or 2 reeds, trombone

More detail on instrumentation:

- The drums were not yet the modern drum-kit as we know it. Often there would be a bass drum (sometimes like a concert bass drum), splash cymbals, trap drum and woodblocks (or skulls). Other instruments used by the percussionist were the washboard and bock a da bock

- The bass was often a brass bass instrument such as tuba or sousaphone (these were obviously used in the marching bands of New Orleans). The double bass or string bass was not particularly common at this time, and certainly not the 'norm'. In many instances the bass instrument was omitted altogether

- A 'comping' instrument is one that provides a chordal 'accompaniment', such as piano, banjo and guitar

- Reeds refer to clarinet and saxophone. The alto sax was the most prevalent but tenor, soprano (especially in the hands of Sidney Bechet) and C melody were also seen

- Frontline could include (but more rarely) violin and, of course, voice.

Key points

If you can hear:

- Collective **improvisation** (**polyphony**, countermelodies)
- A strong 2 in the bar feel
- The instrumentation detailed above
- Trombone glissandi, big brass **vibrato**

You are probably listening to Dixieland, hot jazz, classic jazz, or trad jazz, as it is variously named.

The 1930s

In 1929 the American stock market crashed to an all time low. The ten years of economic hardship that followed was called The Great Depression.

This had a huge impact on the lives of all Americans (particularly on the working lives of musicians) and changed the nature of the development of jazz. There was no longer such an appetite for the hot jazz gigs; popular music and jazz was becoming more reflective and sentimental, with songs such as *Wrap Your Troubles in Dreams*, *How Deep is the Ocean* and *I've Got The World on a String*. However, audiences still wanted to hear music and go dancing, spurred on by the music they were hearing on more widely available radio broadcasts.

The need to deliver a big sound to large numbers of dancers in big venues started the movement towards the 'Big Band' and 'Swing Era'. To achieve this bigger sound the frontline instrumentation had to be expanded. As more instruments were added so there was a need for greater organisation between the players and this led towards big band style arrangement and **orchestration**. Jazz became the music of the composer and arranger, whereas previously it was the music of the player.

In 1930 George Gershwin composed *I Got Rhythm* which, second only to the blues format, became the most re-worked jazz form.

In 1936 Walt Disney brought out the first animated film, 'Snow White'. Why is this important in jazz history? Well, one of the songs in the film has become an iconic part of the jazz repertoire: *One Day My Prince Will Come*. Not only is it a beautiful **melody** and **harmony** but it has the time signature of $\frac{3}{4}$, something we have not come across yet in our studies.

This guide will focus on three key personalities of this music and this era:

- Duke Ellington (1899-1974)
- Benny Goodman (1909-1986)
- Glenn Miller (1904-1944* missing in action)

Duke Ellington

The title of Ellington's biography is *Beyond Category*, which sums up his musical life perfectly. It was actually Ellington himself who coined this phrase to describe his musical influences. He was hugely interested in the work of the **Impressionists**, particularly Debussy. So, although Ellington is known as a jazz composer really he should be thought of as simply a composer. His work stretches from blues to jazz standards, and ballads to symphonic work.

Duke Ellington in 1943

Ellington was a great collaborator. He wrote with others (Billy Strayhorn became a long lasting collaborator) and he wrote specifically for particular musicians. His writing therefore, made the most of his musicians' strengths and specialisms.

The Cotton Club days

Ellington started as a pianist and arranger before becoming a bandleader. Shortly after taking on this role, his band got a very important gig at The Cotton Club, New York (1927–1931). You can see an archive film of Ellington with The Cotton Club Orchestra playing *Old Man Blues* in 1930. Note that this is part of a film called 'Check and Double Check' and the piece begins at 1 minute and 5 seconds in.

Note the following:

- Two bar introduction on rhythm section (piano, banjo, bass and drums) plus two trombones

- Extended introduction over a pedal point
- Introduction first theme on reeds
- Introduction second theme on trumpets
- Form after introduction AABA
- Trombone solo on the bridge of the head with reeds backing
- Derby mutes on stands
- Double bass moves from two in a bar feel to $\frac{4}{4}$ **walking bass**
- Solos from baritone sax, soprano sax and trumpet
- Trombone 'backings' behind the baritone solo at bridge with harmon mutes
- Extended quaver passages in the baritone sax solo
- Derby mutes used for signature railroad sound on trumpets.

You can hear, even from this very early ensemble, that the material is very well-organised with instruments working in their families (in units such as reeds, trombones and trumpets). The melodic material of the head is divided between the families. There are backings which provide **texture** and **harmony** behind **improvised** solos. There is timbral variety added by the use of different mutes in the brass section.

A LITTLE NOTE ON MUTES

The Derby was actually a type of hat. When it is hand-held it can make a '**wah wah**' effect. Other times it is kept on a stand and players would play into it for a quieter effect. The Harmon mute creates more of a sizzling, thin sound, which can be adjusted by a tube that goes through its centre.

The **rhythmic** feel clearly moves to a four in the bar: Drums, banjo and piano **accent** the second and fourth beats, while the double bass plays a driving **pizzicato** four in the bar.

FURTHER LISTENING

Notable Compositions of the '30s by Duke Ellington:

- *Mood Indigo* (1930)
- *It Don't Mean A Thing If It Ain't Got That Swing* (1932)
- *In A Sentimental Mood* (1935)
- *Caravan* (1936)

Following the Cotton Club years, Ellington and His Orchestra toured extensively in Europe. He had an enduring career that lasted far beyond the 1930s but even from this short snapshot of some of his compositions from this period we can see how broad his compositional style was. He also kept on re-inventing his work, re-arranging, and re-recording.

Listen to *In A Sentimental Mood* played by Duke Ellington and His Orchestra (1935) and then by Duke Ellington and John Coltrane (1962) as an example of this constant development. Note how one of the key ingredients of the original composition, the chromatic descending line, is omitted from the later recording.

A LEVEL EXTENSION
Duke Ellington's *Caravan*

For A Level further study, examine Ellington's Caravan. Take a look at the opening few bars of the melody:

Work out the mode of this melody. Can you see an association with the given chord? Think about the differences between the A and B sections. What is the relationship of the two key centres?

In one early arrangement (which has been transcribed for the Jazz at the Lincoln Center Library) Ellington starts each frontline instrument on a different degree of the opening chord. The two trombones start on C and D♭, just a semitone apart! Every part follows the melody precisely, i.e. the melodic movement is perfectly parallel. The result is an astounding feat of 'linear' writing; every instrument's path makes sense and so, even though you may think that it shouldn't work, it does; a great wall of **homophonic** sound.

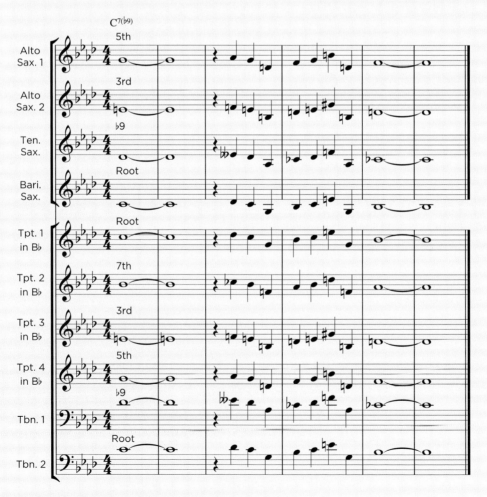

Fats Waller (1904-1943)

It is important to remember that as new styles were emerging, earlier forms were still being played (and developed). Fats Waller took the art of **stride piano** to new heights. Listen to *Alligator Crawl* (1935). You can clearly hear that 'oom pah' of the left hand, as well as short passages of boogie-woogie left hand riffs. The right hand is clear and precise with detailed ornamentations, flowing quavers and triplet quavers. The melodies are played chordally in some passages (the **melody** is harmonised).

Fats Waller was an all-round musician and entertainer. Some of his best-known compositions became part of the Jazz Standard repertoire: *Honeysuckle Rose* and *Ain't Misbehavin'*, both written in 1929.

The Swing Era

Although swing music started to emerge in the late 1920s and early 1930s, the swing era became defined as 1935-1945. It is from within this decade that the next two of our studies come.

Fats Waller in 1938

Benny Goodman

Benny Goodman was a clarinettist who became known as The King of Swing. He is said to have popularised the big band and turned it into the most exciting form of dance music known. He was also an incredibly fluent player who created extremely polished **improvisations**. Much of the Goodman Orchestra repertoire demonstrates the changing approach to the various roles within a jazz ensemble. We are going to focus on one particular piece that has a particularly unusual dimension: the piece is built around a series of drum kit features (Goodman's drummer was Gene Krupa). The piece is *Sing, Sing, Sing*. There are many versions available to watch or listen to online, so try to find *Sing, Sing, Sing (with a swing)* from 1935. There is some great dancing to boot, just to prove how popular this music was at the time.

Listening notes:

- Time signature $\frac{4}{4}$
- Starts with drum solo on floor tom-tom
- Unison riff from bass instruments

Benny Goodman in 1971

- Trumpet section joins with melodic feature using 'growls'
- Main theme enters on reeds
- The form of the theme is AABA
- Brass take the role of commentators with punctuations and counter melodies before taking the main thematic material
- **Antiphony**, or call and response: question and answer between the instrumental families
- Solo clarinet (Goodman) includes new phrasing; rolling quavers (swing) and often eight to a bar, **accented** on beats 1 and 3. This is a particularly significant **rhythmic** development of swing
- **Blue notes** and scoops or swoops used in the clarinet solo
- The piece is delineated by drum features
- There are riffs which build up **polyphonic textures** family by family of instruments
- The **tonality** is minor with most of the melodic fragments (riffs) based on the blues scale.

This tune was ground breaking in many ways, not least due to the featured drum **breaks** throughout and the riff based composition of many of the sections.

LISTEN

For more typical swing from Benny Goodman and His Orchestra listen to:

- *Stompin' at The Savoy* (1936)
- *One O'Clock Jump Live at Carnegie Hall* (1938)

IMPORTANT CHANGES IN THE ROLES OF THE RHYTHM SECTION IN THE SWING BAND

- The modern drum kit has evolved. The addition of foot pedals allows the drummer to play the time with both feet: the bass drum on beats 1, 2, 3 and 4 and the hi-hat cymbals on beats 2 and 4. This leaves the hands free to add punctuations, comping patterns or, in the case of *Sing, Sing, Sing*, to play solos!

- The double bass plays four in the bar, providing pulse and outlining harmony

- The guitar plays four even chords in the bar, reinforcing the pulse

- The piano player is now freed up from keeping time in the left hand and can offer more responsive comping (sometimes in the left hand) and single line fills.

Glenn Miller

In 1939, the Second World War broke out. American swing during the years of the war was, for many, the Glenn Miller sound. He created, with careful **orchestration**, a hugely recognisable sound. This was extremely popular in America for the years preceding the US joining the fight, through extensive recording and radio broadcast. So, when the American troops went to fight in Europe, Miller and his band were sent to entertain them. It was in December 1944, when crossing the English Channel, that Miller's plane was lost and he was deemed 'missing in action'.

The Miller sound was particularly created by very closely orchestrated reeds. The section consisted of clarinet, two alto saxophones and two tenor saxophones. The clarinet **melody** was doubled by the second tenor sax part then the other three reeds harmonised as closely as possible between the octave produced. This close **harmony** is often referred to as 4-way close. The harmonies usually contained a 'colour' tone (a consonant note that is not in the **triad** or the seventh – usually a sixth or ninth). These additional notes do not change the function of a chord but they add a richness to the sound.

Note that the lowest voice doubles the top voice in octaves

It is worth noting that part of Miller's success was a result of crafting his arrangements to be a perfect length for 'air' time. Radio broadcast did not usually allow for extended solos or **improvisations**.

Listen to *Moonlight Serenade* by Glenn Miller and His Orchestra. Listen for the following:

- The reeds have a slow moving **legato** melody played tutti
- Muted brass play repeated accompaniment figures which develop into counter melody
- Swing ballad tempo
- Matched **vibrato** and **articulation**
- Guitar plays four in a bar
- Piano plays single note fills
- **Dynamic** builds and brass becomes unmuted
- Clarinet takes improvised, embellished phrases leading into the melodic lines
- Subtle dramatic surprises in the **texture**, creating a stop
- Tutti coda with **double time** feel.

Glenn Miller was a Major in the US Army Air Corps

This is one of Miller's greatest danceable ballads. Be sure to listen to some of his up-tempo pieces such as *In The Mood*, *Little Brown Jug* and *String of Pearls*.

Strange Fruit

In 1939 Billie Holiday (known as Lady Day) released *Strange Fruit*. It was written as a poem by school teacher Abel Meeropol under his pseudonym Lewis Allan. The poem is a protest against lynchings – public hangings of African American people, usually inflicted by community members taking the law into their own hands with dubious justification. This was one of the most violent aspects of American life living in a state of racial segregation, and we should reflect on the fact that life was extremely difficult for the black musicians we have been studying. They were forced to travel in separate railway carriages, for example, and even to enter venues by the back door. Listen to the song, which says everything.

The 1940s

We have already started to look at the 1940s with the 'Swing Era' lasting well into the decade but there were other major developments in jazz and the music of the 1940s was extremely diverse.

Alongside the popular swing band or big band, another form of jazz was being developed; this was called bebop, and as a rejection of the organised sound of the swing bands and the 'chaos' of this new music, bebop, there was a major revival of hot jazz, now known as Dixieland.

Bebop

Bebop was developed by jazz musicians who aspired to elevate the status of the music and its players. It was a deliberate move toward creating an art form rather than popular music. It was also a move towards seeing the jazz musician as an artist.

The bebop sound is highly complex in its harmonic content. For years musicians had practised their instruments hard in order to participate in jam sessions and get work. Now highly complicated chord sequences were deliberately played to challenge those who couldn't cut it.

The name bebop came from the **scat** vocabulary. As this music is very highly syncopated many phrases ended on two swing quavers – producing the sound 'bebop'.

Key musical features of bebop include:

- Fast moving harmonic changes (two chords per bar)
- Complex **syncopation**
- Very fast tempos
- **Dissonance**.

We will study some of the music by two of bebop's leading figures.

- Charlie Parker (1920-1955)
- Dizzy Gillespie (1917-1993)

Before we look at details in the music of Parker and Gillespie it is probably worth a short focus on **harmony**, in order to understand quite how far they developed it.

Harmony

Jazz **improvisation** requires the player to 'make the changes' (play the correct harmony) but this does not just mean playing chord tones and **diatonic** scale notes; there can be more choices if you understand the functionality of the harmony and that, essentially, every chord and/or every note will have the 'function' of either the **tonic** or the **dominant**. You could think of this as *home* and *away* or *tension* and *release* or *suspension* and *resolution*.

During the early part of the twentieth century, popular music and therefore jazz that 'covered' or imitated these songs had two traits:

1. The home key (tonic) often had an added sixth, eg. C6 = C, E, G, A
2. Chord progressions and **cadences** were frequently composed of strings of dominant 7th chords, such as C7 F7 B♭7 E♭6.

The 2-5-1

Jazz musicians most frequently used this pattern of chords to make a **cadence**. It is written here as 2-5-1 simply to stand for chord 2 (supertonic), chord 5 (**dominant**) and chord 1 (**tonic**). You might have seen this expressed as ii V I – this symbolises the qualities of the chord (ie. major/minor) as well as the number/degree of the chord. In most jazz **improvisation** the qualities of the chords in a major '2-5-1' are different to those in a minor '2-5-1'

MAJOR 2 5 1

Major 2 5 1: Dm7 G7 C6 (or CΔ – which means Cmaj7)

Δ is a commonly used symbol for a major 7 chord   CΔ = C, E, G, B

7 is used as the symbol for a dominant 7 chord   C7 = C, E, G, B♭

m7 is the symbol for a minor seventh chord   Cm7 = C, E♭, G, B♭

Minor 2-5-1: Dm7(♭5) G7(♭9♭13) CmΔ

m7(♭5) ∅

Cm7(♭5) = C, E♭, G♭, B♭

7(♭9♭13)

C7(♭9♭13) = C,E, G, B♭, D♭, A♭

Note: alternative, earlier minor 2-5-1s could be Dm7 G7(♭13) Cm6

A LEVEL EXTENSION

In a 2-5-1 cadence it became popular to substitute the dominant 7th for a chord a **tritone** away (this is also called the flat five substitution).

Dm7 | G7 | CΔ

becomes:

Dm7 | D♭7 | CΔ

The Turnaround

In jazz performances the form of a song or piece (chorus) may be repeated many times, to allow for extended improvisations. To allow for a smooth transition back to the beginning of a chorus, players insert a 'turnaround'. This would often replace a perfect cadence, which would effectively produce a musical 'full stop'. Let's look at an example:

Dm7 G7 | CΔ | CΔ ||

becomes

Dm7 G7 | Em7 A7 | Dm7 G7 ||

which would lead you back to a C major **tonality**.

This principal of creating a sequence of V-I movement can also be used to lead to a **modulation** (for example into the bridge). An example of this can be heard in Duke

Ellington's *Take The A Train*. The form is AABA. The tonal centre of the A section is C major and the tonal centre of the B section (bridge) is F major. So the first time ending of A is:

Dm7 | **G7** | **C6** | **Dm7 G7** ‖

which leads back to C major. The second time ending is:

Dm7 | **G7** | **C6** | **(Gm7) C7** ‖

which leads to F major.

Circle of fifths

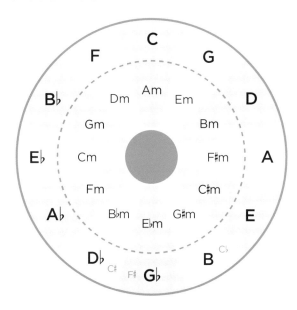

Charlie Parker and Dizzy Gillespie

Charlie Parker and Dizzy Gillespie didn't invent bebop, (certainly not on their own), but their names are synonymous with the music. It is said that Parker used to practise up to fourteen hours a day in order to be able to play this music that he and his colleagues were working on tirelessly. This music was not designed to be easy dancing or easy listening. It demanded a tremendous amount of technical skill on the instrument and preparation. There is a good film called *Bird* (that was Parker's nickname) that illuminates the story behind bebop. It was directed by Clint Eastwood in 1988.

Have a listen to a tune written by Parker and Gillespie. It is called *Anthropology* and is based on the 1930 composition by George Gershwin, *I Got Rhythm*.

Anthropology (1945)

- Tempo is over 300bpm!
- 4 bars drum
- The form is AABA
- A frontline of alto sax and trumpet play the head in unison
- Piano and drums **comping** follow the **accents** of the **melody**
- The saxophone plays two choruses of solo
- There are extended lines of quavers which accent **syncopations**
- Triplet semiquavers embellish the quaver lines

- A trumpet plays two choruses of solo including very high passages in the second chorus
- Piano plays two choruses of solo
- Drums 'trade fours'.

Notes about the rhythm section roles:

- The drums no longer play bass drum on all four beats and the pulse is maintained on the ride cymbal in a 10 to 2 pattern. You can see this pattern in the following musical example:

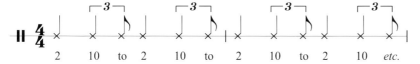

- While **comping** the soloists, the drummer plays a lot of **accents** which a) comment on the phrasing of the solo or head (punctuation), b) complement the soloist's lines (interaction), and c) delineate the form (especially marking out the transitions into the **middle 8** and back to the top of the chorus). These accents are called 'dropping bombs' and are usually played on the snare and/or bass drums
- 'Trading' fours is when the band plays four bars and then the drummer solos for four bars, unaccompanied. The form of the piece is maintained throughout
- The double bass plays a **walking bass** line. Here are two examples of how you can construct walking lines through this chord sequence:

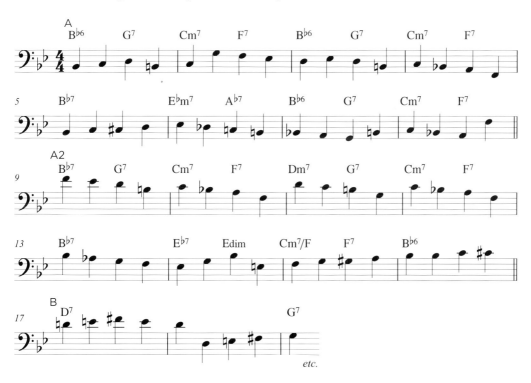

Look at how the line is constructed from chord tones, **diatonic** passing notes and chromatic passing/leading notes:

- The piano plays chords between both hands, clearly outlining the fast moving **harmony** while comping the solos and the head
- A note about the swing: notice how little of a triplet you can hear in the quaver lines at this tempo!

A LEVEL EXTENSION

Many bebop compositions were composed using existing harmonic forms. The new melodies were highly complex and feel like **improvised** lines in many respects. Have a look at some of the detail in the writing of the **melody**:

Note ( ) show ghost notes

- In bar 1, note that the **rhythmic** phrase ends on the last two quavers ('bebop'!)
- The pick up note (**anacrusis**) provides a strong V-I melody stating the **harmony**
- In bar 1, the first four notes are simply **diatonic**
- In bar 1, the second four notes have a classic bebop 'enclosure', i.e. a chord tone (D) is preceded by a semitone above and below. You could think of the D as being a target note. This device produces the heightened sense of tension and release that is heard in bebop
- Bar 4 has the bebop phrase ending on beat 2
- Bars 5 and 6 are anticipated and are very syncopated throughout
- Much of the melody is diatonic until another enclosure at the end of bar 7.

Listen to *A Night in Tunisia* by Dizzy Gillespie (1945). This piece is quite different to many of the $\frac{4}{4}$ swing pieces in the bebop catalogue. It starts with a straight 8s (quavers) rhythmic feel. Notice that the bass plays a two bar riff alternating in semitones:

E♭7 | Dm6 |

- The structure is (Intro) AABAC
- A is 6 bars straight 8s, 2 bars swing
- B is swing
- C is 12 bars swing with a 4 bar **break**.

This changing time feel is something to listen out for in other tunes such as *Love For Sale*. Musicians often heightened the impact of the swing by preceding it with a straight 8s (often inadequately described as 'Latin').

Ella Fitzgerald (1917-1996)

It would be possible to study Ella in the 1930s or the 1940s (or the 1950s and 1960s for that matter) as the breadth of her singing styles encompassed the music of all of these decades. She was certainly swing and she could comfortably perform the complex material of bebop. In her interpretations of The American Songbook she transformed many songs. Ira Gershwin (brother and writing partner of George) is said to have commented, 'I never knew how good our songs were until I heard Ella Fitzgerald sing them.'

Listen to Ella singing *How High the Moon* written by Morgan Lewis and Nancy Hamilton in 1940. There are many versions of Ella singing this as it became one of her signature tunes. In several live versions she quotes the 'contrafact' (this is a form of composition that was frequently used by bebop (and later) musicians. They would write a new **melody** over the harmonic (chord) sequence of an existing piece. This new melody was usually more complex than the original one and had an **improvisatory** feel to it) bebop version of the song by Charlie Parker: *Ornithology*.

A great version which is more contemporary but fully reflects Ella's vocal style in the period you are studying is the recording of *How High the Moon* with The Paul Smith Quartet, live in Berlin 1960 from the Album 'The Complete Ella in Berlin'.

Ella Fitzgerald in 1968

Listening notes:

- The opening phrase of the song would look like this:

- Ella starts with an improvisational interpretation of the song, embellishing the melody in a swing feel
- A drum **break** after the first verse leads into **double time**
- The tempo is now over 300bpm
- The second verse is sung in this double time with further extemporisation of the melody
- The third chorus is **scat** improvisation demonstrating Ella's skill as a musician, perhaps imitating a saxophone
- Her lines have motifs, sequencing and development
- The next chorus is Parker's reworking of the song, *Ornithology*
- Following this is another chorus of scat, this time perhaps imitating a trumpet with two sequenced arpeggios demonstrating her high range
- Ella starts to use some of the lyric in her improvisation
- She introduces quotes from other popular songs
- There are seven minutes of vocal gymnastics!
- The band drops down to drums only and Ella imitates an arco double bass by producing overtones
- The performance ends with virtuosity and humour as she references the physical energy involved in this astonishing vocal feat.

A LEVEL EXTENSION
The 1950s

The 1950s heralded even greater diversity in jazz. New genres and sub-genres emerged but let's remember that each individual musician's interpretation of an existing style will inject some new element, some personal way of playing, a new approach to sound and, therefore, a new direction.

We will look at the music of the 1950s by studying some of the music of:

- Stan Getz (1927-1991)
- Miles Davis (1926-1991)
- Dave Brubeck (1920-2012)

Cool Jazz

There are said to be three strands to cool jazz but one element that unites them: sound. Cool jazz is softer, with instrumental sounds unfettered (less vibrato, less use of overtones) and the music is generally more reflective in its nature, allowing for a purity of melodic improvisation.

Simply, you could describe it as less showy. The sheer attack and heavy accents of bebop are left behind and the big, bold and brassy sounds of the big band swing era are replaced by orchestrations using more traditionally classical instruments. Even Charlie Parker made an album with a string section: 'Charlie Parker with Strings', released in 1950.

Stan Getz is one of the leading 'cool' saxophonists. Although he was active as a bebopper, listen to his recordings of the early 1950s, *Stella By Starlight* (Victor Young) and *Autumn Leaves* (Joseph Kosma).

Two things strike you immediately:

- Relaxed tempo – *Stella* is just under 160bpm and *Autumn Leaves* c.70bpm
- Airy sound (you can hear the breath escaping from the mouthpiece at the ends of phrases).

Then there is evidence of a refinement of melodic invention. There are still elements of bebop phraseology heard, such as triplet ornamentation of quaver lines but the overall effect is smoother, less accented. The melodies often extend beyond the confines of the harmonic structures, particularly spilling over into the beginning of a new chorus giving a sense of flow and true 'in the moment' invention.

Getz went on to make a further revolution to the development of jazz, making the bossa-nova compositions of Brazilian composer Antonio Carlos Jobim famous worldwide in the early 1960s.

LISTEN
Desafinado and *Girl From Ipanema* by Antonio Carlos Jobim.

'Birth of The Cool'

This seminal album was finally released in 1957 although it had been recorded in a series of sessions right at the beginning of the 1950s. It is in Miles Davis' name but is actually the result of collaboration between Davis, Gil Evans (arranger) and Gerry Mulligan (baritone saxophone). The aim was to create a new sound in contemporary music using harmonies inspired by the Impressionists, new tonal colours and melodic (linear) invention.

Listen to *Moon Dreams* by Gil Evans and listen for:

- Chamber instrumentation: this is a nine piece ensemble which comprises a rhythm section of piano, double bass and drums with frontline of trumpet, alto sax, baritone sax, French horn, trombone and tuba
- Relaxed tempo of about 74bpm
- Passages of parallel orchestration (homophony)
- Sections of counterpoint (listen particularly to the bass instruments)
- Passages with fugal entries in the different voices
- Short solo features with backings (notice that the orchestration is very different to that of the big band because there are not enough of each family (e.g. reeds) to produce an entire harmonic backing)
- The variety of note values in the melodic material
- Shortly after 2 minutes the orchestration and harmony sounds more like atonal polyphony
- This sense of a new sound in jazz is added to by entries (first on French horn) of a rhythmic cell which cuts against the underlying swing feel
- The overall structure differs from the pattern of playing head, solos and head out. It is through-composed.

Listen to *Boplicity* by Davis and Evans, and compare notes from your previous listening exercise. As the name suggests it owes much to the 'bebop' style. In what ways does it contrast strongly with bebop?

1959

The 1950s was a rich decade for jazz. Recording quality was much improved. Jazz was featured on radio, television and became film-score. Many American musicians continued to tour in Europe.

In London Ronnie Scott's Jazz Club opened its doors for the first time and in America two of the most popular jazz albums of all time were released:

- 'Time Out' by The Dave Brubeck Quartet, and
- 'Kind of Blue' by Miles Davis

Both of these albums offered another new approach to jazz composition and performance. 'Time Out' was all about rhythmic elements. Many of the tunes have irregular time signatures (apparently inspired by Turkish street music heard by Brubeck when he was on a tour of Eurasia). As you might imagine, this created quite a division between musicians, many complaining that you can't swing in $\frac{7}{4}$ or $\frac{9}{8}$! Audiences, however, totally embraced this new rhythmic feel and one of the best known tracks, *Take Five*, even entered the top 40 chart.

Let's listen to *Blue Rondo à la Turk* from 'Time Out':

- The time-signature is $\frac{9}{8}$ but not in the compound triple arrangement: quavers are grouped as 2+2+2+3 (with the fourth bar of each 4 being 3+3+3)

- Repetition of ideas (the composition is motivic, or riff based)
- Instrumentation is standard **rhythm** section plus alto saxophone
- The alto sax (Paul Desmond) has the 'cool' sound
- The left hand of the piano descends then ascends chromatically
- The material is organised in blocks which alternate between two tonalities (8 bars each)
- The piano part contains **counterpoint** in the interlude before the solo section
- The solos are blues form (the first chorus has two bars of $\frac{4}{4}$ swing then reverts to the $\frac{9}{8}$ for two bars)
- The remainder of the solos are straightforward blues form until the final chorus reverts to trading 2 bars of $\frac{4}{4}$, 2 bars of $\frac{9}{8}$ in order to lead more fluently back into the final head.

In sharp contrast to 'Time Out', 'Kind of Blue' by Miles Davis is all about **melody** and **harmony**, or rather lack of harmony! Despite there being two blues compositions on the album, the main aim of the writing was to create a **modal** approach, i.e. the pieces are based on **modes** (scales) rather than chord sequences. This is an entirely different approach to the music that had preceded this album. You could think of this new concept as being 'linear' (horizontal or melodic) as opposed to the vertical (harmonic) approach of bebop.

Let's have a listen to arguably one of the most iconic jazz compositions of all time: *So What*:

- There is (a reputedly **improvised**) introduction on double bass and piano
- The theme (riff-based) is played on the bass (the call)
- There is a chordal response using a charleston rhythm (dotted crotchet – quaver) in quartal harmony (building the notes of the chord in intervals of a fourth rather than thirds)
- The mode employed is a dorian mode (this is a minor mode which has a flattened 7th note but the 6th degree is major)
- The structure is AABA (each 8 bars)
- The B section is one semitone higher than the A section (so A = D dorian and B = E♭ dorian)
- The first solo is two choruses long, using simple melodic ideas, lots of space and natural development
- The second solo is tenor sax (John Coltrane) and clearly demonstrates the challenge of playing in this new way. The phrases almost sound as if they are searching for new notes in the mode. The time values are varied and non-metronomic, creating a very human effect, perhaps reminiscent of the 'imperfect' nature of the blues. (Please note that this word is not designed to be a criticism.)
- The third solo is alto saxophone (Cannonball Adderley) and has some evidence of bebop language within it. Beautiful motivic work and sequencing (using ideas through **transpositions**) creates the effect of harmonic movement despite it being absent from the composition
- The final, brief solo is piano (Bill Evans) which has an even greater sense of exploration. He plays with more and more **dissonance** as the solo progresses (as this is modal music you should be able to use any notes from the mode together and it should still work).

Miles Davis is known to have insisted on the 'first take' being the one to use on a recording. This may result in some imperfections but it also results in a very fresh and creative sound.

Revision

Jazz education is still a relatively new phenomenon. In its early days jazz was an oral and aural tradition, like a lot of folk music.

So, your revision should be based on further listening; remember that all the developments that have taken place in the decades we have studied are due to individuals listening and adding their own twist to the music around them.

If you are keen to be a jazz performer or composer, then you should be transcribing work. You can transcribe and notate work, or you can transcribe through performance; this is how the greats did it. Also remember that practising, often extended practising, is vital. Aspiring swing players were 'wood-shedding', (practising scales and arpeggios in their room) and beboppers like Charlie Parker practised 11 to 14 hours a day (depending on which book you read). Remember that no-one was born playing this music; it takes time and application!

The other revision you should do is to study the **harmony** exercises. Try playing simple parts of the harmony, eg. What does the **root** movement of a 2-5-1 sound like? Try playing a **tritone** substitution in a II-V-I **cadence**; what do you identify in the root movement? Listen to the change between a C6 chord and a C7: this will help you to identify **modulations**.

A LEVEL EXTENSION

HARMONIC STUDIES, THE DEVELOPMENT OF THE BLUES

Here is a commonly heard variation of the twelve bar blues, sometimes called a 'jazz blues':

| F7 | B♭7 | F7 | F7 |

| B♭7 | Bdim | F7 | D7(♭9) |

| Gm7 | C7 | Am7 D7 | Gm7 C7 ‖

Note the use of an extended **dominant** in bar 8 and the turnaround in bars 11 and 12.

Here is a Parker Blues (sometimes called 'round the clock' changes as it employs the **cycle of fifths** to create forward motion). There are strings of 2 Vs (sometimes creating a 'tritone' relationship: bars 6-9).

| FΔ | Em7(♭5) A7 | Dm7 G7 | Cm7 F7 |

| B♭7 | Bbm7 E♭7 | Am7 D7 | A♭7 D♭7 |

| Gm7 | C7 | F7 D7 | Gm7 C7 ‖

Note that the rate of harmonic movement is mostly every two beats. Investigate further blues repertoire such as *Billie's Bounce*, *Blues For Alice* (Charlie Parker), *Blue Monk*, *Misterioso* (Thelonius Monk), *Freddie Freeloader*, *All Blues* (Miles Davis) specifically looking at how the harmonic sequences have been developed.

When you are doing your listening, here are some ideas of what to listen out for:

- Overall form (can you hear a 12 bar blues or AABA form, and so on?)
- Instrumentation (this will often give you a big clue to the period of the music, even if it is a modern replication)
- Time feel (swing, straight quavers etc.)
- Time signatures
- Harmonic movement (how frequently is there a chord change?)
- Sound (recording techniques can give the game away but, again, don't be fooled by contemporary versions)
- **Improvisation** – is there collective improvisation? Is there very little improvisation? Are there extended improvisations?
- Phraseology – are the swing quavers grouped in fours (swing), syncopated with **accents** (bebop) or syncopated without accents (cool)?
- **Texture** (unison, **homophonic**, **polyphonic**, solo).

And here are some ideas of whom to listen to:

- Early jazz: Sidney Bechet, Django Reinhardt
- Swing: Charlie Christian, Lester Young
- Big Band: Count Basie, later Duke Ellington
- Bebop: Tadd Dameron, Coleman Hawkins
- The 50s: Horace Silver, Art Blakey, Wes Montgomery

AS Level Component 3 Practice Questions

Area of Study D: Jazz

In the exam, you will be given **three** questions for this part of the paper. The first two will be divided into between 5 and 7 parts (a-e or perhaps a-g), and each worth **15 marks**. Both of these will require you to listen to extracts of unprepared works and answer multiple choice or 'describe' questions about them. The third question is an essay question, beginning with the word 'Explain'. This question will be worth **10 marks** and will require you to use your more general knowledge about the genre.

Here, instead of a sample paper, we have given you individual questions designed to expand your listening – each one is therefore about a different unheard piece of music. Sample assessment papers are available to download from the Eduqas website, however, and you should also practise answering these as much as possible.

1. Listen to *Cakewalking Babies From Home* by Red Onion Jazz Babies

(a)   Which term most accurately describes this genre of jazz?   [1]

Bebop   **Swing**   **Dixieland**   **Classic Blues**

(b)   Give three reasons for your choice (you may refer to sound, instrumentation, time feel, performance technique and improvisation):   [3]

1. ....

2. ....

3. ....

2. Listen to *In The Mood* by Glenn Miller and his Orchestra

(a)   This music was first played in the early years of which decade?   [1]

1920s   **1930s**   **1940s**

(b)   Make three observations about the introduction (focus on orchestration and key musical elements):   [3]

1. ....

2. ....

3. ....

(c)   What is the form of the A section?   [1]

....

(d)   What is the nature of the material for: [3]

i. Reeds ....

ii. Brass ....

iii. Rhythm section ....

3. Listen to *Moose The Mooche* by Charlie Parker

(a)   Which genre best describes this piece?   [1]

Swing   **Bebop**   **Dixieland**   **Early Jazz**

(b)   Give three reasons you have made this choice: [3]

1. ....

2. ....

3. ....

(c)   Which popular song of 1930 is this piece built upon?   [1]

....

A Level Component 3 Practice Questions

Area of Study D: Jazz

Here, instead of a sample paper, we have given you individual questions designed to expand your listening – each one is therefore about a different unheard piece of music. Sample assessment papers are available to download from the Eduqas website, however, and you should also practise answering these as much as possible.

1. Listen to *One O'Clock Jump* by Count Basie (1943)

(a)   Draw a comparison of this with Miller's *In The Mood* noting five points of similarity or difference.   [5]

....

....

....

....

....

2. Listen to *Milestones* by Miles Davis (1958)

(a)   What style best describes this piece?   [1]

Bebop   Modal   Swing   Cool

(b)   Identify two musical elements that are in the playing of: [3]

(i)   The double bass   ....

....

(ii)   The drum kit   ....

....

(c)   What is the form of this piece? (Include how many bars are in each section).   [2]

....

....

(d)   Write a description of the compositional elements in this piece.   [4]

....

....

....

....

3. Listen to *Flamenco Sketches* by Miles Davis (1959)

(a)   This piece is based on a series of modes (scales) and does not have a 'head'. Each soloist may determine the length of improvisation on each mode. Identify how many modes (tonal centres) are contained in each solo.   [1]

....

(b)   Identify the order of instrumental solos that follow the rhythm section introduction.   [5]

....

....

....

....

....

(c)   Comment on five points of comparison between *Milestones* and *Flamenco Sketches*.   [5]

....

....

....

....

....

4. Listen to Lee Konitz and Gerry Mulligan playing *All The Things You Are* (1953)

(a)   What is this an example of?   [1]

Bebop   Modal   Swing   Cool

(b)   Give two reasons why you have chosen the above: [2]

1. ....

2. ....

5. Listen to *Blues For Alice* by Charlie Parker, *Billie's Bounce* by Charlie Parker, *St. Louis Blues* by Bessie Smith and *Oh, Black Betty* by Lead Belly (1939).

(a)   Which of these tracks is: [4]

(i)   Classic blues ....

(ii)   Parker blues ....

(iii)   Jazz blues ....

(iv)   Country blues ....

Into the Twentieth Century

A LEVEL ONLY

This is an A Level-only module, and you will study either this area of study OR Area of Study F: Into the Twenty-first Century. Whichever you take accounts for **30%** of the Component 3 exam.

You will study how composers at the turn of the 20th Century (1895-1935) reshaped musical language for new circumstances and audiences. You will focus on three specific **styles** of music and two **set works** as outlined here:

Styles

Eduqas has specified three early 20th Century styles for study but it is up to your teacher to decide exactly which pieces (alongside the set works) will be used to illustrate the various features of each style. Eight composers are specifically mentioned by the exam board:

- **Impressionism** (page 211): Claude Debussy; Maurice Ravel

- **Expressionism** and **Serialism** (pages 217 and 222): Arnold Schoenberg, Alban Berg, Anton Webern

- **Neo-classicism** (page 227): Sergei Prokofiev, Igor Stravinsky, Francis Poulenc

Set works

You will also study two set works in detail. In the exam you will be asked to answer detailed questions about technical features of **ONE** of these works, with reference to a score.

- Debussy – Three Nocturnes, No. 1: *Nuages* (1899 – Impressionist) (page 233)
- Poulenc – Trio for Oboe, Bassoon and Piano: Movement II (1926 – Neo-classical) (page 237)

Your exam will be structured in the following way:

Musical extract	Question types	Marks (30)
Extract from EITHER set work (with blank score)	■ Short questions on musical elements and devices, including comparisons of passages ■ Longer question discussing one aspect of the piece (e.g. form, tonality and so on).	10 5
Unseen extract	■ Short questions on musical elements and devices, including comparisons of passages. These might also ask about composer and style ■ Asked to discuss one musical element in the context of other pieces studied in wider listening.	10 5

Music and change

'[The music] introduced new rules, new modes, and new turns of phrase, these were harsh and little pleasing to the ear, nor could they be otherwise; for so long as they violate the good rules... [they are] far removed from the object of music'
Giovanni Artusi writing about the music of Monteverdi in 1600

'Almost incessantly the odd and dazzling effects strike the ear... it seems to us that Wagner has reached the point beyond which he cannot possibly go'
Eduard Hanslick writing about the music of Wagner in 1869

'Schoenberg is one of the extremists; here cacophony is elevated to a law'
Music critic for Signale writing about Schoenberg in 1907

Listeners in the 20th Century were not the first to complain that new music was giving them earache. While more experimental composers were accused of wrecking music with their innovations, many of their contemporaries continued to compose as before or incorporate their ideas into more traditional styles.

We will tend to focus on the more experimental composers, but we could tell a different story by choosing composers who developed their styles more gradually. Listen to works by the following composers to get a taste of this alternative narrative: Edward Elgar, Richard Strauss, Carl Nielsen, Jean Sibelius, Sergei Rachmaninov, Samuel Barber and Ralph Vaughan-Williams.

The early 20th Century was a time of extraordinary change. On the one hand there were advances in science and technology but, on the other, there was massive upheaval, not least that caused by the First World War. When Claude Debussy wrote that 'the century of airplanes has a right to its own music' he spoke for many composers who tried to forge new styles for a new era.

SOME KEY EVENTS IN THE EARLY TWENTIETH CENTURY

- 1903 – Wright brothers make first powered flight
- 1905 – Einstein publishes paper on special relativity
- 1908 – Model T Ford first produced
- 1914 – Beginning of First World War
- 1917 – Czar deposed in Russian Revolution
- 1928 – Alexander Fleming discovers penicillin
- 1929 – Wall Street crash causes Great Depression

A Model T Ford from the turn of the century

Modernism

Debussy's search for new forms of expression to suit a new era is a typically modernist attitude.

Modernism is defined not only by new techniques but by a radical rejection of the past in favour of a new, better and more exciting future. Modernists had to have great confidence in their vision of how music should be, as their bold rejection of musical conventions presented a serious challenge to listeners.

Despite the complaints of critics, the conventions of musical language had been relatively stable for at least two-hundred years. While **harmony** and **tonality** had continually evolved, the fundamental building blocks of **triads**, **cadences** and keys had remained more or less the same. Starting in the last decades of the nineteenth century, some composers started to stretch traditional harmony and tonality so much that it reached breaking point. The collapse of these conventions had a dramatic and fundamental effect both on how music worked and sounded.

As we shall see later in this chapter, modernists often have a complex attitude towards the music of the past, and are not always as willing or able to reject it as fully as they might pretend. Most of the pieces that we will look at (with the exception of some **Expressionist** and **Impressionist** ones) look back to the music of the past in one way or another.

Maximalism

One of the most important trends in Modernism is the expansion and intensification of musical resources.

Composers tried to heighten the power and expressiveness of their music by, for example, adding more instruments, making their works longer; or by increasing the levels of **chromaticism** and **dissonance**. Richard Taruskin has called this tendency **Maximalism** and suggests that it continues a process started by the **Romantic** composers of the previous century.

The following table shows the expansion from the **Classical** orchestra of Mozart through the **Romantic** ones of Beethoven and Wagner to that of Mahler's Eighth Symphony, which was known as the 'symphony of a thousand' due to the vast forces it required.

Mozart Symphony No.38 (1787)	Strings, 2 flutes, 2 oboes, 2 bassoons, 2 horns, 2 trumpets, timpani.
Beethoven Symphony No.9 (1824)	Strings, 2 flutes, 2 oboes, 2 clarinets, 2 bassoons (plus contra bassoon), 4 horns, 2 trumpets, 2 trombones, timpani, percussion, choir, vocal soloists.
Wagner *Parsifal* (1882)	Strings, 3 flutes, 3 oboes (plus cor anglais), 3 clarinets (plus bass clarinet), 3 bassoons (plus contra bassoon), 4 horns, 3 trumpets, 3 trombones, tuba, two harps, timpani, percussion, chorus, vocal soloists.
Mahler Symphony No.8 (1906)	Strings, 4 flutes (plus 2 piccolos), 4 oboes (plus cor anglais), 3 clarinets (plus 2 E♭ clarinets and bass clarinet), 4 bassoons (plus contra bassoon), 8 horns, 7 trumpets, 7 trombones, tuba, 4 harps, organ, harmonium, piano, mandolin, celesta, two choirs, children's choir, vocal soloists.

You can trace a similar tendency in Romantic music towards increasing length, particularly in the symphony. As you can see below, in the space of a hundred years the overall duration is more than tripled from a Mozart symphony to Bruckner's first.

Mozart Symphony No.38 (1787)	about 22 minutes (last movement – 5 minutes)
Beethoven Symphony No.3 (1805)	about 50 minutes (last movement – 12 minutes)
Bruckner Symphony No.1 (1887)	about 1 hour and 15 minutes (last movement – 25 minutes)

Mahler's Symphony No.3, completed in 1896, is close to an hour and a half, but like many maximalist trends, this type of expansion begs the question of how much further it is possible to go.

EXAMPLE WORK:

The Rite of Spring, by Igor Stravinsky

One of the most extreme examples of **Maximalism** is Igor Stravinsky's ballet *The Rite of Spring*. The brutal intensity of this piece has made it one of the most famous and influential early 20th Century works. The orchestra is a similar size to Mahler's Eighth Symphony (without the choirs and soloists), but it is the violence with which Stravinsky deploys these forces that really makes it stand out.

Igor Stravinsky (1882-1971): *The Rite of Spring* (1913)

Stravinsky pitched this ballet to Sergei Diaghilev, who had become famous for his lavish and exotic *Ballets Russes* productions in Paris. The scenario on which *The Rite* is based is a series of rituals performed to usher in the spring. The ballet ends with a young girl dancing herself to death. The brutality of the music, together with the deliberately ugly choreography by Vaslav Nijinsky, caused a near-riot at the premiere. This scandal provided just the sort of publicity upon which Diaghilev (and indeed Stravinsky) thrived.

Dancers in the original production of *The Rite of Spring*

It is worth looking briefly at one of the most famous passages from *The Rite of Spring* in order to see how Stravinsky creates maximum **dissonance**, **rhythmic** unpredictability and fragmentation. As with all musical examples, you should obviously listen to this extract in order to hear the effect.

- The chord played by the strings is highly dissonant, consisting of an F♭ major (or E major!) chord against an E♭ **dominant 7th**. Not only is this a very harsh dissonance but Stravinsky seems to have no interest in resolving it

- The rhythm is very simple, but savage and irregular **accents** destroy any sense of metre

- After eight bars, Stravinsky suddenly breaks off and begins a new dissonant idea, adding C major and E minor arpeggios into the mix. In more traditional music, ideas are developed and linked with transitions, but here Stravinsky just repeats and juxtaposes (incidentally, C major and E♭ dominant 7th, a minor third apart, can both be derived from an **octatonic scale**, which we will encounter again later in the Debussy and the Poulenc set works).

EXAMPLE 1:

Stravinsky, *The Rite of Spring*, Part I: 'The Augurs of Spring'

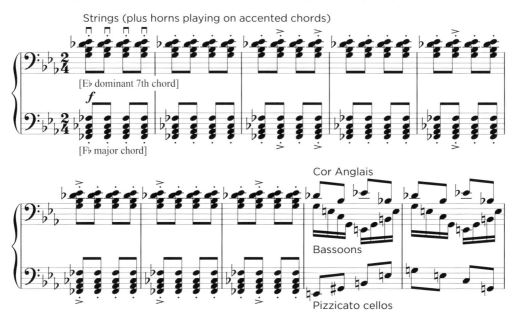

While this section of *The Rite of Spring* ends with maximum brutality on a $\boldsymbol{fff}$ tutti that cuts the frenetic **rhythms** suddenly short, our last example of Maximalist writing (for now) does nearly the opposite. The end of Arnold Schoenberg's *Erwartung* has a similar level of rhythmic activity but ends $\boldsymbol{ppp}$ in a mist of chromatic oblivion. It is from his Expressionist period, a style of music (to which we will return shortly) in which composers express heightened emotion with extreme **dissonances** and other distortions of traditional musical language.

EXAMPLE WORK:

Arnold Schoenberg (1874-1951): *Erwartung* (1909)

Schoenberg's *Erwartung* is one of the most famous pieces of musical **Expressionism** and was written in a white heat of creativity in just under three weeks (not including the **orchestration** which took another three). The work lasts around half an hour and features a single female singer (with orchestra) who becomes increasingly crazed as she searches for her lover in a forest. The increasing hysteria of the solo singer is matched by anguished dissonance and dense **textures** in the orchestra.

We will return to *Erwartung* later in this chapter but the extraordinary final page, of which example 2 is a much simplified reduction, is worthy of a chapter in itself. This is **chromaticism** taken to its absolute limit, as multiple chromatic lines ascend and descend at different rates. The individual chords are all based on the whole tone scale, which means that the only possible type of **triad** is that which is most uncommon in tonal music, the unstable and ambiguous **augmented** triad (a clear example in **root** position is the C, E, G♯ in the second chord of the violas and cellos). The incredibly high level of chromaticism along with these augmented chords makes any sense of tonal centre absolutely impossible.

EXAMPLE 2:

Schoenberg, *Erwartung*, last half-bar (reduced and simplified)

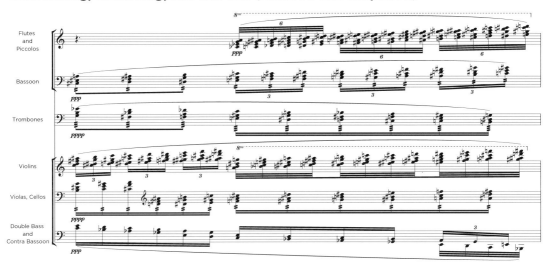

These maximalist scores are used by Stravinsky and Schoenberg to portray emotional and physical violence, but both of these composers and many of their contemporaries struggled to use this expressively distorted musical language to write music for less extreme circumstances. The **serial technique** later employed by Schoenberg and the **Neo-classical** style adopted by Stravinsky are two responses to this problem which we will study later in this chapter.

We will now begin to look at the styles that Eduqas have prescribed for this area of study. The focus is on a series of representative works to which you can refer when you are asked to describe a feature of an unprepared work in relation to your wider listening. In order to do this properly **it is important that you listen to the extracts and works discussed**.

Impressionism

Impressionism is a term borrowed from art history. French painters at the end of the nineteenth century aimed not at exact representation but in capturing an *impression* of a scene.

The most famous artist associated with **Impressionism** is Claude Monet (1840-1926), who was interested in how the same view could be shown in different lights. In such paintings, the colour of morning or evening light, for example, is more important than the details of the scene itself, which are often blurred and vague. Another relevant movement from the late nineteenth century is that of the Symbolist poets, who aimed not to describe precisely but to evoke and suggest meanings.

The term 'Impressionist' was first used in music to describe the work of Claude Debussy. Like many names for musical styles it was meant as a criticism. Debussy had sent a piece to the *Prix de Rome* committee in 1887 and they described it as showing a 'vague impressionism', probably referring to the **tonality** and structure.

The other composer associated with this style is Maurice Ravel, and both certainly show an intense interest in colourful orchestral and harmonic effects. To look in a bit more detail at what is different about this music, let's compare it to a passage by Richard Wagner (1813-1883), who was one of the most influential musical figures of late **Romanticism**.

EXAMPLE 3:

Wagner, *Tristan and Isolde*, Prelude, opening

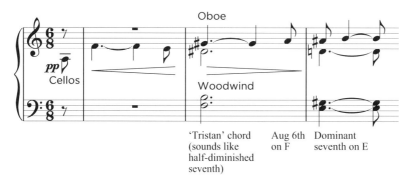

Wagner's famous opera *Tristan and Isolde* tells the tale of lovers whose circumstances mean that they can never be together, other than in death. The **harmony** communicates this sense of striving for something impossible.

Listen to the opening of the opera and note the following features:

- The first chord of the Prelude (the 'Tristan chord') is one of the most famous in music history, creating both ambiguity and an unresolved harmonic tension

- The third full bar ends on a **dominant 7th**, which is also left unresolved (as it is the next two times)

- The semitone is important in tonal music because it is the interval of the leading note to the **tonic** as well as the resolution of chromatic chords. Here the semitones seem to seek resolution without ever achieving it.

The **chromaticism** and **dissonance** found in Wagner made a big impact on composers at the end of the nineteenth century, as did his colourful use of the orchestra. However, Debussy and other French composers were not so keen on the use to which these musical resources were put. They thought Wagner's huge quasi-religious operas (and the hero-worship of the composer himself) pretentious, and resented the influence of this on French music.

The lovers Tristan and Isolde

Claude Debussy (1862-1918)

Debussy, influenced by older composers such as Emmanuel Chabrier (1841-94), began to develop similar harmonic resources but to very different effect. Rather than creating a sense of yearning through a constant need for resolution, Debussy used dissonance and chromaticism in a much more colourful (and indeed impressionistic) way.

> **Claude Debussy (1862-1918): *Pour le piano*, 'Sarabande' (1894), *Preludes* (Book 1) 'Voiles' (1909)**

Claude Debussy had a huge influence both in his native France and on European composers more generally. Debussy's anti-establishment attitude can be seen in a conversation that he was reported as having with a professor from the conservatory: 'There is no theory. You have only to listen. Pleasure is the law'. This attitude was one he apparently followed in his personal life too, with a series of affairs and short-lived engagements that scandalised both the public and friends of the composer.

We can see a relatively early instance of this in example 4, in which you should listen for the following:

Claude Debussy

- As in the Wagner there are unresolved seventh chords but at the beginning of the Debussy they no longer sound like chords that need resolving and become instead colourful rather than functional

- The first chord is a half **diminished seventh** which, organised differently, would be the same as a Tristan chord. Here it is not anguished but, is just part of a string of colourful chords

- The sense of key (a sort of **modal** C♯ minor) is only very weakly established.

EXAMPLE 4:

Debussy, *Pour le piano*, 'Sarabande', opening

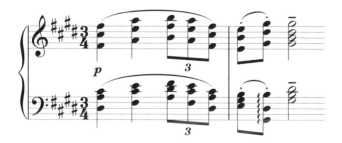

'Voiles' (meaning sails or veils), shown in example 5 was written fifteen years later and is much more radical in the way that it avoids harmonic resolution:

■ The whole extract (and most of the piece) is based on a **whole-tone scale**. The striving chromatic lines with their semitone resolutions seen in the Wagner are avoided by a complete lack of semitones!

■ Notice how Debussy asks for the sustaining pedal on the piano to be depressed for the last two bars, creating a haze of **harmony** rather than clear harmonies. The emphasis is on colour rather than function.

■ The **rhythm** is quite free and based on flourishes and pauses.

EXAMPLE 5:

Debussy, *Preludes* (Book 1), 'Voiles', ending

Claude Debussy (1862-1918): *Prélude à l'après midi d'un faune* (1894)

The *Prelude* is based on a poem by the symbolist poet Stephane Mallarmé. In the poem a faun plays his panpipes in the heat of the afternoon, while gazing at nearby nymphs. Debussy wrote that 'The music of this prelude is a very free illustration of Mallarmé's beautiful poem... there is a succession of scenes through which pass the desires and dreams of the faun in the heat of the afternoon.'

The last example from Debussy is from one of his most well-known orchestral works. The brief extract (which begins at bar 3) shows some details of the harmony but it is very important that you listen to the rest of this work, paying attention to the lush and colourful **orchestration**, which together with the harmonies perfectly capture the sensual pleasures of the faun. Note how the first chord (an A♯ half-diminished seventh) is basically the same as the 'Tristan' chord from earlier (B♭, E, G♯, C♯). Rather than being an anguished chord in need of resolution, however, it just moves in a non-functional way to a B♭ **dominant 7th** chord, with which it shares the B♭/A♯.

EXAMPLE 6:

Debussy, *Prélude à l'après midi d'un faune*, bars 3-5

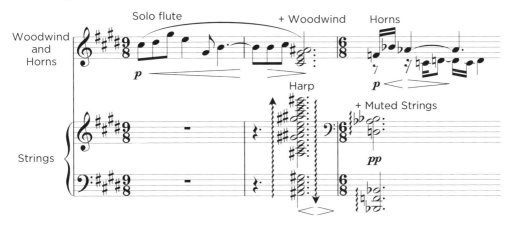

Maurice Ravel (1875-1937)

Although he was a composition student of the much more conservative Gabriel Fauré, Maurice Ravel was heavily influenced by Debussy.

The two composers were often bracketed together, but Ravel himself was clear that he did not consider himself to be cast in the same Impressionist/Symbolist mould: he said, 'For Debussy, the musician and the man, I have had profound admiration, but by nature I am different'. Nevertheless, there are strong similarities in their emphasis on orchestral colour and harmonic innovation in particular. Ravel's famous *Bolero* showcases both, in the context of a piece of music that is otherwise highly repetitive.

Maurice Ravel

Maurice Ravel (1875-1937): *Rapsodie Espagnole* (1908)

In writing music inspired by Spain, Ravel was following in the footsteps of many French composers, including Debussy, Chabrier and Saint-Saens. More than any of these, however, Ravel had strong connections with Spain through the Basque origins of his mother, who spoke Spanish and had lived in Madrid.

Example 7 shows a particularly pungent harmonic idea in 'Prélude à la Nuit' from *Rapsodie Espagnole*, but it is important first to listen to the whole first movement, paying attention to the following:

- The movement is based on a four-note stepwise descending ostinato (later changed to three)
- Melodic material develops from and around this idea but the emphasis is on changing orchestral and harmonic colours shifting around the ostinato

■ Although in three time, the metre and pulse is quite flexible, not least because the **ostinato** idea is initially two beats and later one and a half beats long, and works against the basic triple time.

EXAMPLE 7:

Ravel, *Rapsodie Espagnole*, 'Prélude à la nuit', Figure 6

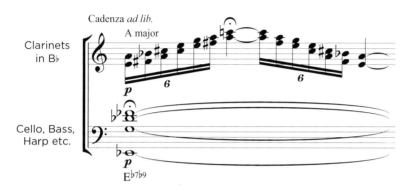

Example 7 shows the beginning of one of two cadenzas **that punctuate the first movement. The** harmony **is very exotic:**

■ The basic harmony combines E♭ major and A major **triads**, a polychord widely used by other composers, including Stravinsky, who made it famous in *Petrushka*. This **tritone** relation is associated with the **octatonic** scale (see the notes on Debussy's nocturne for an explanation)

■ The minor 9th (F♭) added to the E♭ major adds extra spice (and is also part of the same octatonic scale)

■ Similarly the C natural (again octatonic) at the top of the clarinet arpeggio (making it briefly A minor rather than major) adds further colour.

Maurice Ravel (1875-1937): String Quartet (1903)

Ravel's String Quartet is a student work written at the age of 27 and is dedicated to his teacher Fauré but, with the exception of some of the melodic writing, is much more influenced by Debussy.

Ravel's String Quartet is a very different work to *Rapsodie*, combining harmonic and textural novelty with **Classical** structures and forms. Listen to the first **movement**, which clearly follows a **sonata form** structure. You should be able to identify the traditional contrast between first and second subjects in relatively clear opposing keys.

Example 8, however, shows how Ravel is not using the traditional harmony and **tonality** of the Classical era. Rather than clear **dominant** to **tonic cadences**, the harmony drifts between extended chords a tone apart. Chord vii is often used in Classical harmony as a substitute for chord V, but here it is flattened so it loses any cadential meaning. Although it ends on a tonic chord, the harmony and the gestures show much more interest in 'impressionistic' colour. This idea of pouring new wine (in this case harmony) into old bottles (in this case sonata form) is something that we shall encounter again when we study the **Neo-classical** style in more detail.

EXAMPLE 8:

Ravel, String Quartet, first movement, ending

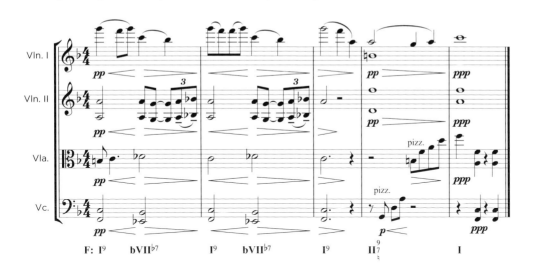

F: I^9 $bVII^{b7}$ I^9 $bVII^{b7}$ I^9 II^9_7 I

Expressionism

> **'One must express *oneself*! Express oneself *directly*! ... Not all those acquired characteristics, but that which is inborn, instinctive.'**
> Schoenberg in a letter to Kandinsky

Expressionism is a relatively brief phase in the history of music, concentrated in a period lasting just over a dozen years up to about 1921. As suggested in the quotation above, Schoenberg was trying to free himself from the conventions of musical language in order to express emotion more directly. The idea was that conventional form, **harmony** and phrase structure constrained a composer's ability to convey emotion and that these things needed therefore to be cast off.

As discussed in the introduction, the drive to express emotion through ever more extreme musical language continues a tendency found in late **Romanticism**. Schumann and Wagner, for example, both broke with convention in order to give their music more emotional impact; Expressionism can be understood as a maximalist extension of this idea.

Lovers – Self Portrait with Wally, an Expressionist painting by Egon Schiele

EXPRESSIONISM AND THE SECOND VIENNESE SCHOOL

The three composers most closely associated with Expressionism at the beginning of the twentieth century were Schoenberg and his two pupils Webern and Berg. After the First World War the younger two followed Schoenberg in his development of a new method of composition – the serialism that we will encounter in the next section. The close relationships between these composers (and some others in their circle) gave rise to the idea of a 'school' of composition based in Vienna. The title 'Second Viennese School' suggests an analogy with the way in which a 'First Viennese School' of Haydn, Mozart and Beethoven (also closely associated with Vienna) established the mature Classical style in the eighteenth century.

Schoenberg compared with Wagner

Even the subject matter of Schoenberg's *Erwartung*, which we discussed earlier, can be seen as a maximalist extension of the familiar Romantic idea of the mad woman.

Example 9a is sung by the Kundry, the central (and mad) female character in Wagner's *Parsifal* (1882), who is cursed to live forever because she mocked Christ at his crucifixion. It is interesting to compare her vocal line as she is awoken and those of the 'woman' in Schoenberg's *Erwartung*, shown in Example 9b. In both works we see a highly emotional state conveyed through chromaticism, large leaps and dissonant accompaniments.

EXAMPLES 9a AND 9b:

Wagner: *Parsifal*, Act II & Schoenberg, *Erwartung*, Figure 110

a) Kundry in Parsifal

b) Woman in Ewartung

Alban Berg (1885-1935)

On the face of it, Alban Berg's *Wozzeck* is a similar work. The anguish and alienation of the main character is reflected in fractured and dissonant music. There are, however, two important differences to *Erwartung*...

Alban Berg (1885-1935): *Wozzeck* (1922)

Berg's opera focuses on Wozzeck, a soldier, who is bullied by his Captain and his doctor (who has put him on an experimental diet of beans) and is furthermore being cheated on by his wife Marie. In the final act, he murders Marie and then drowns in a pond trying to hide the knife and wash blood off his clothing.

Although the opera caused something of a scandal at its premiere, the story seemed to strike a chord with post-war audiences and there were enough performances for Berg to make a decent income from the royalties until his premature death.

Alban Berg (left) with the conductor of *Wozzeck*, Corneille de Thoran

The first major difference to *Erwartung* is that although it uses a similarly heightened harmonic and melodic language, Berg contains the music of *Wozzeck* within familiar seventeenth and eighteenth century instrumental forms and structures. Although these are not always obvious to the listener, this clearly goes against the Expressionist idea that conventional forms and language get in the way of direct emotional writing.

TONALITY AND ATONALITY

The traditional tonality of the Western Classical Tradition establishes a hierarchy among the notes of the chromatic scale (i.e. some notes are emphasised as being more important):

More emphasised	Less emphasised
Diatonic notes of a minor or major scale	Surrounding chromatic notes
Tonic note/chord and dominant	Other notes/chords
Consonant notes that fit with triads	Dissonant notes that do not fit with triads (and therefore resolve to consonant ones)

Schoenberg and his pupils found the conventions of tonality too restrictive and tried to find new ways of writing that avoided emphasising a tonic or favouring consonances over dissonances. Many critics called such writing 'atonal', in other words 'without tonality', but Schoenberg did not like the negative implications of this term. He saw himself not as destroying tonality but expanding it, and preferred the term 'pantonality'.

The second major difference is that, at moments of extreme emotion, Berg occasionally retreats from atonality back into something much closer to tonality. In order to get a sense of what all this sounds like, you should listen to the last two scenes of the opera.

In between Act III scenes 4 and 5, at the climax of the drama when Wozzeck has just died, comes an instrumental interlude with some more tonal writing. It is almost as if, having pushed towards atonality to portray the extreme emotions of the characters, Berg now wants to make a plea for our sympathy with this more conventional writing.

Anton Webern (1883-1945)

If Berg's opera represents a bit of a softening of the ideals of Expressionism, his fellow pupil Webern was much more radical. This example from his *Six Bagatelles* is different from our previous examples in that it is not trying to tell a story but instead uses the distorted musical language of the Expressionists in the more abstract context of a string quartet.

Anton Webern

Anton Webern (1883-1945): *Six Bagatelles* (1913)

Anton Webern was Schoenberg's most uncompromising pupil, and his severe style and technique meant that his pieces were always very short. His Expressionist works take their inspiration not from Schoenberg's *Erwartung* but from the slightly earlier piano and orchestral pieces that are similarly brief and intense. Schoenberg wrote a preface to Webern's Bagatelles, praising the discipline needed 'to express oneself so briefly. Every glance can be expanded into a poem, every sigh into a novel'.

Webern's quartet **movements** have a similar intensity to the dramatic Expressionist works explored above. In the *Six Bagatelles*, however, everything is much more concentrated. None of the movements is longer than a page of score and No. 3 (excerpted below in Example 10) is only 9 bars in total. As well as listening to the beginning, you should listen to the rest of the movement (it will not take long!), which gets even more intense and anguished.

EXAMPLE 10:

Webern, *Six Bagatelles*, No. 3, opening

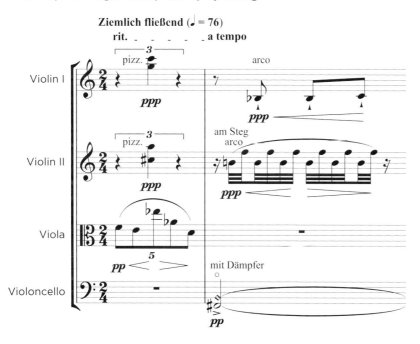

Look and listen out for the following:

- The anguished five-note viola idea
- The music is highly chromatic. All twelve notes of the chromatic scale are used in these first two bars
- There are lots of different instrumental colours including mute, **pizzicato**, playing on the bridge (*am Steg*) and false **harmonics** (in the cello).

Arnold Schoenberg (1874-1951)

The previous examples of Expressionism are complicated and sophisticated works, but it is at least clear what the composers are trying to achieve. Schoenberg's *Pierrot Lunaire*, however, is more ambiguous. It is easily the most popular and successful work from Schoenberg's Expressionist phase, but it is curious because it seems to be exploring not only the limits of the Expressionist style but also its limitations.

Arnold Schoenberg (1874-1951): *Pierrot Lunaire* (1912)

Pierrot Lunaire is a collection of twenty-one poems featuring Pierrot, a stock character from Commedia dell'Arte (Punch and Judy has the same origins). He is traditionally a sad clown-like figure, but in these poems he is on the edge of insanity. Schoenberg's settings were written for Albertine Zehme, a performer who was both an actor and singer. The score asks for a strange hybrid of song and speech called *Sprechstimme* in which the performer slides away from notes in the flexible manner of speech rather than sticking to a single pitch as in singing.

To get a proper sense of this bizarre work you need to listen to a few of its twenty-one movements. Two are suggested in the table below, along with some brief notes.

No. 5: **Valse de Chopin**	The poem for this movement begins with the line 'Like a pallid drop of blood / Colours a sick man's lips / So reposes in these tones' and later specifically mentions 'melancholic dusty waltzes'. Schoenberg's music is like a grotesque parody of a waltz, nearly submerged in the dissonant and complex texture.
No. 7: **Der kranke Monde**	'The Sick Moon' is about love, torment and death and the voice is pushed well below its normal range to E below middle C and asked to sing very quiet. If we suspect that Schoenberg may have an ironic awareness of the impossibility of these instructions, this is confirmed at the end where the singer is asked to sing grotesque and quavering mordents in a manner that is 'not yet tragic!!'.

In this piece Schoenberg draws attention to some of the potential absurdities of Expressionism in a humorous way. The popularity of this work with the general public irritated some of Schoenberg's followers, who felt that it was not representative. We will see in the following two sections of this chapter some of the directions which the Second Viennese School composers and others took in the 1920s, perhaps in response to the problems that Schoenberg alludes to in *Pierrot*.

Serialism

The suspicion with which some of Schoenberg's circle viewed the popularity of *Pierrot* is typical of some modernists and represents an exaggeration of yet another Romantic trait.

Beethoven was seen by the Romantics as a heroic figure, who overcame deafness and critical opinion to change the face of music. This idea of the composer as a struggling

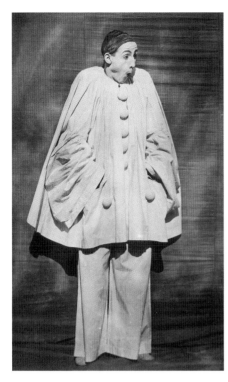

Pierrot

The original ensemble who played *Pierrot Lunaire*, pictured in 1912

hero was maximalised by composers and critics in Schoenberg's circle to the extent that success with the public was almost viewed as an artistic failure.

In his Expressionist music, Schoenberg uses **dissonance** to help convey extreme emotion, but his ambitions for dissonance were much grander than simply expressive effect. He would later write that his experiments in the first few decades of the twentieth century 'enabled me to establish the law of the emancipation of the dissonance... [in which] the comprehensibility of the dissonance is considered as important as the comprehensibility of the consonance.' Schoenberg's idea is that dissonances should be as free as consonances to make sense on their own.

EMANCIPATED DISSONANCE

In 1911 the Italian composer and writer Ferrucio Busoni wrote that when compared to the 'eternal **harmony**' the tonal system was 'a meagre pocket edition... artificial light instead of the sun... How strictly we divide 'consonances' from 'dissonances' – in a sphere where no dissonances can possibly exist.'

Schoenberg hoped to open up a totally new musical world, free from the old tonal hierarchies and controls on dissonance. Freeing (or emancipating) the dissonance from the traditional obligation to resolve would completely change how music worked.

Expressionism laid the foundations for a freely dissonant style in the first two decades of the century, but Schoenberg (and others) reached some sort of crisis point after the First World War, finding it difficult to continue writing in a very intense style in which there were no conventions or restrictions.

The answer for Schoenberg was in the end to develop a different method of composing, one which replaced the old conventions with some new ones. The method, known as **serialism**, involves the steps shown below.

SERIALISM METHOD

- An initial **tone row** is constructed, which is made up of all 12 notes of the chromatic scale put in a fixed order (with no repeated notes). This series of 12 notes is called the **prime**
- This 12-note row is then used to construct 47 new forms of the row that are all transformations of the original:
  - 12 transposed **primes** (moving the tone row so that you have a transposition starting on each note of the chromatic scale)
  - 12 **retrogrades** (the prime turned back to front – reading it from the end to the beginning)
  - 12 **inversions** (the prime turned upside-down – if the original goes up a major third, the inversion goes down a major third etc.)
  - 12 **retrograde inversions** (the 12 inversions turned back to front)
- The 48 forms of the tone row are then used to compose melodic lines and chords.
- Each form of the tone row is normally used in its entirety before moving on to the next.

In tonal music, composers had chosen their **pitches** from a menu of pre-existing scales, chords and chord progressions. In serial music, the composer choses their pitches from a menu of tone rows. The difference is that while the tonal menu was based on making certain notes and chords and intervals more important, the serial menu treats them all equally.

Arnold Schoenberg (1874-1951): Variations for Orchestra, Op. 31 (1928)

This set of **variations** was Schoenberg's first orchestral score that was fully serial. A set of variations is a good choice to showcase this new system, because, unlike in **sonata form**, the contrasts are created mainly through changes in **rhythm**, melodic decoration, **texture** and instrumentation (rather than through changes of key and **harmony**).

Example 11 shows the opening of the theme from Schoenberg's variations for orchestra. This is the moment in the piece when the prime form of the tone row is set out.

EXAMPLE 11:

Schoenberg, Variations for Orchestra, theme

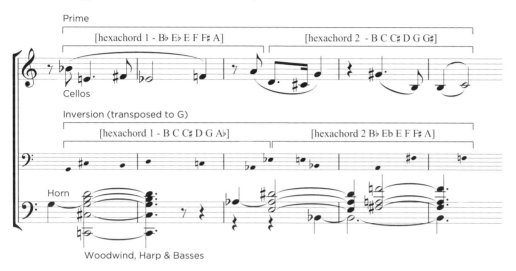

- The cellos play the theme, which is the **prime** version of the tone row. The **rhythm**, which octave the note appear in, and so on, are all down to the composer's choice – but the actual notes are used in strict order

- The small stave in the middle (not part of the music) shows an **inversion** of the prime, in this case **transposed** to start on G rather than B♭

- Schoenberg does not use this inversion as a **melody**, however, but uses the notes to build up accompanying chords

- There is an interesting relationship between the row and the inversion in this extract. It can be seen by comparing the notes in square brackets, which are presented in ascending alphabetical order from A. The first six notes (or hexachord) of the inversion has the same notes as the second hexachord of the original, which means it contains, by definition, none of the notes from the first hexachord. This makes the **chromaticism** in these bars more intense, as all 12 notes have already been used by the first beat of the third bar. The same thing is obviously true of the second half of the extract. This relationship is called *combinatorial*.

This short extract tells us quite a lot about Schoenberg's aims in using this system of composition. While on the one hand the intense chromaticism obliterates any sense of **tonality** and the **dissonant harmony** avoids **triads**, the form and the **texture** of this music is relatively traditional. In the music of his two pupils, who adopted the same basic method of composition, we shall see surprisingly different approaches.

Alban Berg (1885-1935): Violin Concerto (1935)

Alban Berg was commissioned to write his Violin Concerto for the American violinist Louis Krasner. Early in the composition process the death of Alma Mahler's daughter Manon at the age of only 18 led Berg to dedicate it to her memory.

Example 12 shows the row on which Alban Berg based his Violin Concerto, which was written at the very end of the period covered by this Area of Study.

EXAMPLE 12:

Berg, Violin concerto, row

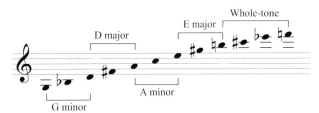

Note the following and listen for their consequences in the opening few minutes of the concerto

- The first part of the row contains four tonal **triads**. After an introduction (see next bullet point) Berg explicitly uses these triads as a chord progression that sounds plausibly tonal

- The **roots** of these triads are the open strings of the violin – G, D, A and E

- The last four notes of the triad are a whole tone scale. This seems much less tonal, but they turn out to the first four notes of a harmonised Bach chorale (or hymn tune) that Berg quotes in full later in the concerto.

Schoenberg's method is designed specifically to move away from the traditional tonal system so Berg's deliberate inclusion of triads within the tone row works strongly against the basic aims of **serialism**.

The instincts of Schoenberg's other pupil, Anton Webern, are in exactly the opposite direction. Rather than trying to soften the impact of serialism, Webern goes further than his teacher in avoiding not just traditional **tonality** but also conventional **melody**, **rhythm** and **texture**.

EXAMPLE 13:

Webern, Quartet Op. 22, first movement, development

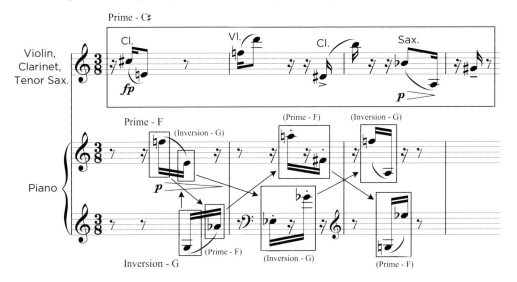

Anton Webern (1883-1945): Quartet Op. 22 (1930)

Webern wrote his quartet for violin, clarinet, tenor saxophone and piano for the 60th birthday of the architect Adam Loos. The music comes across as startlingly original, something that impressed both Schoenberg and Berg, but it was premiered in Vienna to the terrible reviews that usually accompanied Webern's works.

The apparently erratic and unpredictable nature of this kind of music has become almost a caricature of **Modernism** but Webern absolutely did not mean his music to come across as ugly or irrational. The composer is reported to have complained that an unmusical performance of one of his works came over as 'a high note, a low note, a note in the middle – like the music of a madman!'

The first **movement** of the quartet can be understood as a mini **sonata form** and this extract is the beginning of the **recapitulation**. Note the following features:

- The unusual choice of instruments for a chamber group
- The main '**melody**' can be seen in the violin, clarinet and saxophone parts. The way fragments of the melodic line pass between the instruments is called *Klangfarbenmelodie*
- The accompaniment on the piano is a **canon** between the two hands. The left hand plays an inversion against the prime starting one semiquaver later – this type of inverted imitation is called a mirror canon
- The overall **texture**, with its little bursts of two and three notes moving between different instruments is sometimes called pointillistic. This is an analogy with a style of painting in which the canvas is built up from little dots or points that together make up larger shapes
- The **rhythm** is made up of irregularly placed cells that frequently cut across the bar, so there is no real sense of metre.

To enjoy Webern's works you have to treat them like little jewels, which need to be contemplated in their miniature complexity and listened to carefully from all angles.

Neo-classicism

The term **Neo-classical** in music history has at least two overlapping meanings:

1. It can refer to a general musical trend that began in the 1920s to write music that is simpler, clearer and more economical than the maximalist music that preceded it. Calling a piece Neo-classical in this sense suggests an analogy with the **Classical** style of the eighteenth century which reacted to the complexity of **Baroque** music with greater simplicity.

2. It can also refer to pieces of music that take particular ideas from an older style, composer or piece of music and work them into a more contemporary context.

Of the pieces we have already encountered, Debussy's impressionistic Sarabande, Schoenberg's **theme and variations**, and Webern's sonata form movement all have elements of a broad Neo-classicism. In this section, however, we are going to concentrate on two composers who are more obviously Neo-classical, Sergei Prokofiev and Igor Stravinsky (in his middle period).

The idea of **pastiche** – writing something in the style of someone else – is not in itself a new one. Mozart wrote some pieces in the style of Bach, and Tchaikovsky in the style of Mozart to mention just two. Similarly, it is very common for composers to adopt techniques more often associated with an earlier period, for example Brahms basing the last **movement** of his fourth symphony on a **passacaglia** (ground bass). All these borrowings are potentially **Neo-classical** in the broadest sense, but the composers we are discussing use a borrowed style as a mask, one that becomes a prominent feature of the piece.

One of the earliest examples is Prokofiev's Classical Symphony, which was written in 1917. The Haydn-esque mask that the composer wears throughout the work makes a startling contrast from his brutal *Scythian Suite*, which he wrote just two years before under the influence of Stravinsky's *Rite of Spring*.

Sergei Prokofiev (1891-1953)

Sergei Prokofiev (1891-1953): *Classical Symphony* (1917)

Sergei Prokofiev is probably best known for his charming piece for children *Peter and the Wolf* (even though the apparently innocent tale could also be seen to be Soviet propaganda!) and his music for the ballet *Romeo and Juliet*. His music is very varied stylistically with these more accessible pieces at one end of the spectrum and some aggressively **modernist** early works at the other.

Prokofiev was trying to wean himself off composing at the piano when he started work on the symphony, and he wrote that 'it seemed it would be easier to dive into the deep waters of writing without the piano if I worked in a familiar setting' – i.e. in a **Classical** style and form.

The first movement of the Classical Symphony follows a clear **sonata form** pattern and the basic harmonic language is mostly that of Haydn and Mozart too, except that tonal shifts are sometimes more sudden and unexpected and Prokofiev adds in quite a few spicy **dissonant** notes that would be 'wrong' in the Classical style. The extract from the second subject in Example 14 gives a good idea of how the piece works.

Sergei Prokofiev

EXAMPLE 14:

Prokofiev, Classical Symphony, first movement, second subject

The main second subject idea at the start of the example is played quietly at the point of the bow in an exaggeration of a playful **Classical** theme. The change from A major to the flat **submediant** (F major) is not completely out of the question in the Classical style, but the sudden shift to this key and the equally quick return, all without any transition, certainly is. If you listen to the rest of the **movement** you will hear plenty of ironic touches, but this is not a work that comes across as a parody; it is rather trying to channel the wit and clarity of the Classical style while taking on board some twentieth century developments.

Sergei Prokofiev (1891-1953): Violin Concerto No. 2 (1935)

The second violin concerto represents part of Prokofiev's attempt to find a style that would be acceptable to the increasingly repressive regime in the Soviet Union to which he was about to return. A year before he finished, he wrote: 'The composer must bear in mind that in the Soviet Union music is addressed to millions of people who formerly had little or no contact with music... It should be primarily melodious, and the **melody** should be clear and simple without, however, becoming repetitive or trivial... It is not the old simplicity that is needed, but rather a new kind of simplicity'.

Prokofiev's second violin concerto has a much wider stylistic range than the *Classical Symphony*. It is still broadly tonal (in G minor) and follows the basic forms and structures of a Classical concerto, but right from the beginning the writing is more unstable and emotionally charged.

Listen to the first movement of the concerto, paying attention to the following moments:

- the first movement opens with an austere violin solo that is almost like (Russian) **plainchant** or folk song in its simplicity
- this gives way to a sugary-sweet second subject (a very obvious change of mask and one which he takes up again in the second movement)
- these two types of writing alternate and mingle along with others but the austere opening idea returns at the end
- this time, however, it suddenly takes a more sinister turn and the movement comes to a rather sombre close with tutti **pizzicato** chords.

In the *Classical Symphony* we heard Prokofiev putting on a Haydn-esque mask for a whole piece (a sort of experiment in **pastiche** writing), but the concerto is a more typical **Neo-classical** work. The composer is still constraining his musical expression within a broadly tonal **harmony** and the clarity of **Classical** form, but the mask he wears is more complex and indeed changes at various points in the piece. The resulting musical language is therefore more dramatic and personal; the composer behind the masks is much more apparent.

In both the playful second subject from the *Classical Symphony* and the sweetly lyrical one from the first movement of the concerto it is clear that Prokofiev the composer is putting on an act, or, as we have been describing it, wearing a mask. Writing in this way allows a composer to put a little emotional distance between them and their music – there is an element of irony. This ironic distance is a very typical feature of Neo-classical composers and we shall see it even more strongly in the Neo-classical work of Stravinsky, a style he adopted in the 1920s, perhaps reacting against the maximalist extremes of his earlier work.

Igor Stravinsky (1882-1971)

Stravinsky liked to talk about composing as an arranging of musical objects rather than creating emotional drama. His objective and rather severe approach to both composing and performing was very influential on other **modernists**. Stravinsky once famously wrote that 'music is, by its very nature, essentially powerless to express anything at all.' Stravinsky liked to exaggerate for dramatic effect, but even if this is more extreme than his actual views it still gives us an insight into what he was trying to achieve.

Igor Stravinsky (1882-1971): *Pulcinella Suite* (1920/1922)

Pulcinella marked the beginning of a different direction in Stravinsky's music. He re-worked a selection of music by Pergolesi to accompany a ballet. Diaghilev, who commissioned the work, expected Stravinsky simply to adapt and orchestrate the music, but the composer took a much more radical approach:

'I began by composing on the Pergolesi manuscripts themselves, as though I were correcting an old work of my own...I knew that I could not produce a 'forgery' of Pergolesi... at best, I could repeat him in my own accent.'

With his Classical Symphony, Prokofiev beat Stravinsky by three years to producing the 'first' example of **Neo-classicism** but Stravinsky's *Pulcinella* had a more immediate impact on its composer's style than the earlier work and is considered by many to be the first properly **Neo-classical** work. Given that most of the notes are taken directly from eighteenth century pieces, however, it is also a slightly dubious contender for that crown. What is indisputable, however, is that working on *Pulcinella* inspired Stravinsky to take his subsequent Neo-classical turn.

A brief listen to the 'Vivo' will give you the idea and, if possible, you should first listen to the Presto fourth **movement** of Pergolesi's *Sinfonia a tre for Violoncello and Basso Continuo* on which it is based. Note the deliberately clownish instrumentation (sliding trombone and high double bass writing) and the large number of **dissonances** added to the **texture**. If you listen really carefully you will notice that Stravinsky adds a written-in performance error in the middle. After the repeat of the first half the trombone tries to repeat again in the **tonic** only to be corrected by the double bass that scrambles up to the correct entry in the **dominant**. This sort of wry humour is very common in *Pulcinella*.

Igor Stravinsky

Igor Stravinsky (1882-1971): Concerto for Piano and Winds (1924)

Stravinsky wrote this concerto in order to have one of his own works that he could perform in concert. He had fled the Russian revolution and was living in Paris, but the chaos back home had led to earnings from his compositions with Russian publishers drying up.

The work is written without a string section (apart from double basses), which is a common feature of many Stravinsky works. He liked the clarity of wind instruments, with their purer tone and relative lack of **vibrato**, features that suit the severity and detachment of much of the writing.

The Concerto for Piano and Winds is a much more mature work from Stravinsky's Neo-classical period. There are echoes of various **Baroque** composers alongside some hints of jazz. The major difference, however, is that this music feels abstract and austere compared to the Prokofiev, which although clear and concise is much more of an emotional drama.

The opening (shown in Example 15) is like a Baroque **overture** with its dotted **rhythms** but at the same time it is unmistakably Stravinsky:

- Sparse **orchestration** (in this case just wind and brass, adding extra hardness to the sound compared to using strings as well)
- Lots of mixing major and minor: 1) C♮/C♯ hints at first A major then A minor (again, many of these are **octatonic** in origin) 2) G♮/G♯ are played at the same time at the end of the second bar – a harsh and very typical Stravinsky chord
- A lot of dissonances.

The dryness of this music seems to reinforce the quotation above about music's expressive power. The slow introduction soon gives way to a relentless **Allegro** and the second part of Example 15 shows a piano solo passage from near the beginning of this section.

Note the following features:

- Insistent busyness of the quaver and two semiquaver **rhythmic** motif (rather like much **Baroque** instrumental music)
- The sparse and **dissonant** harmonies (as with the slow introduction)
- Constantly shifting metre.

Somehow, by sheer force of musical personality (whatever else it sounds like it always is strongly Stravinsky), the composer makes the odd mixture of **textures** and ideas that make up this piece feel coherent.

EXAMPLE 15:

Stravinsky, Concerto for Piano and Winds, first movement

FURTHER READING

For more information about this period in music, see:

- Griffiths, Paul (1994) *Modern Music*, London: Thames and Hudson
- Ross, Alex (2009) *The Rest is Noise: Listening to the Twentieth Century*, New York: Harper
- Taruskin (2004) *Music in the Early Twentieth Century (Oxford History of Western Music)*, Oxford: Oxford University Press

Set work:
Debussy's 'Nuages'
from Three Nocturnes

We have already encountered Debussy in the Impressionists section above, and 'Nuages' (clouds) was completed in 1899 and therefore sits chronologically between the two Debussy pieces discussed. More than in *Prélude à l'après midi d'un faune* but perhaps slightly less than in 'Voiles', Debussy dissolves tonality in favour of colour and atmosphere.

The music drifts between different types of scales, chords and tonal centres without ever properly resolving a chord V onto a chord I. Although the centre of the piece is therefore clearly the opening and closing B, this is never established as a tonic in any conventional sense.

The notes below summarise some key points from the information provided in Eduqas's own extensive notes, which are available at:
http://resources.eduqas.co.uk/Pages/ResourceSingle.aspx?rlid=688
You will need to look at a score and the online analysis as well as the following.

Debussy's Musical Style

- **Dissonance**. Dissonances such as 7ths and 9ths are not used functionally (i.e. they do not resolve to consonances) but instead are used to create colourful sounds and sonorities. Dissonant chords are sometimes strung together in long chains that move in parallel motion (see the notes on Sarabande on page 213)

- **Modes**. Debussy does not only use traditional church modes (e.g. Aeolian, Dorian and so on) but also makes use of the **pentatonic** and **whole-tone scales**

- **Octatonic** scale. This is a special type of mode that is frequently found in early twentieth century music and is discussed below

- **Form**. Debussy avoided the formal **recapitulations** and developments of the Western Classical Tradition, preferring structures that loosely repeat and transform the material in a continuous way

- **Timbre**. Debussy explores new sounds in the orchestra to complement his colourful harmonies. The string section, for example, is often divided into more individual parts, wind instruments tend to be used in unusual registers and he makes extensive use of percussion and harp

- **Rhythm**. Rhythm, metre and tempo are usually very free and flexible.

Form in 'Nuages'

The very loose form of 'Nuages' can be understood in various ways, but in the Eduqas notes the main analysis presents it as a series of 'rotations' of two main melodic ideas, X and Y. Another more traditional way of analysing it is as ABA' (**ternary form**). The table below summarises the form in relation to both these analyses:

Bar 1	5	11	21	29	43	57	64	80	94	99
Rotation 1		Rotation 2		Rotation 3			Rotation 4		Rotation 5	
X	Y	X	Y	X	Y	X	(new material)	Y	X	Y
		A					B		A'	

Use of different modes and scales in 'Nuages'

The Eduqas notes refer to a number of scales and modes and it is worth explaining some of them briefly before moving on to the key points of the piece itself.

Whole-tone scale

The whole-tone scale is discussed in the notes on **Impressionism** in relation to 'Voiles' on page 214 of this book. The scale is only used a few times in 'Nuages' and its main properties are as follows: 1) because it has only one interval (the tone) there is no clear sense of **tonic** 2) the only possible **triad** is the tonally ambiguous and unusual-sounding **augmented** triad.

Whole tone

Pentatonic scale

The pentatonic scale is often associated with 'exotic' music – Debussy would have been familiar with it through his experience of Gamelan music in the Paris exhibition. The five notes in two groups of tones tend to create soft and gentle harmonies without any harsh (semitone) **dissonances**.

D♯ pentatonic minor

Octatonic scales

The octatonic (eight-note) scale alternates tones and semitones. It can also be understood as two overlapping diminished seventh chords. As shown in the example below, the notes of one of these diminished sevenths can be used as **roots** to construct a variety of familiar chords using only chords from the octatonic scale. In this example, there are **dominant 7ths** on each of the four notes of the C♯ diminished chord. These familiar chords organised in a symmetrical way create exotic combinations (e.g. a **tritone** apart) while completely avoiding chords that are fifth-related. There are three different octatonic scales starting with a tone on C, C♯ and D before you start repeating scales you have already encountered – the octatonic scale below, for example, has the same notes as the one starting on D.

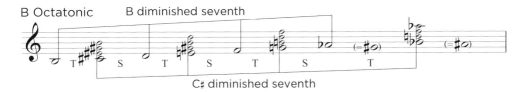

B Octatonic   B diminished seventh

C♯ diminished seventh

E octatonic

Acoustic Scale

The G acoustic scale is commonly found in folk music, and in 'Nuages' it seems to be used partly because it is a bit like a compromise between the **octatonic** and **whole-tone scales**. The distinctive features of this scale are the raised fourth and lowered seventh on what is basically a G major scale. It is called the acoustic scale because it is loosely based on some of the notes from the harmonic series.

G acoustic

KEY FEATURES OF EACH ROTATION

Rotation 1

■ X has a tonal centre of B but it uses two different scales – minor in the top part and octatonic in the lower part. As with many of the scales, Debussy is not too strict in the way he uses them, with extra notes sometimes added.

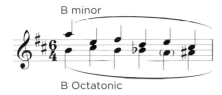

B minor

B Octatonic

■ The Y idea is based around a G **dominant 7th** but all the notes are also taken from the B octatonic scale.

■ While Debussy develops the X idea as the piece progresses, the Y **melody** is presented almost in the same form each time, with just the accompaniment around it slowly changing.

Rotation 2

- X is similar but then moves into a series of parallel ninth chords:

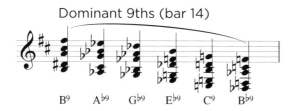

Dominant 9ths (bar 14)

B^9 A^{b9} G^{b9} E^{b9} C^9 B^{b9}

- The Y idea is given a more lush **dominant** ninth accompanying chord and the overall **harmony** is best understood as being based on the G **acoustic scale**, which combines some elements of the **octatonic** and whole tone scales.

Rotation 3

- After a brief nod towards the obligatory B minor as a tonal centre, the music suddenly shifts to a C major chord (perhaps related to the earlier G chords). After this the harmony becomes more exotic with whole tone and octatonic writing both evident

- After a similar start to the B section to before, the music shifts to end on a highly ambiguous and unexpected F major idea.

Rotation 4

- The central 'B' section shifts into D♯ minor. The few bars before come closest to a functional dominant as the last of the series of parallel **dominant 7th** chords in last inversion (bar 63) is a B♭, which enharmonically resolves to D♯ (i.e. E♭)

- The **pentatonic melody** and the use of flute and harp as well as some slightly more conventional harmony work together to make this sound like the moment at which the cloud comes closest to lifting

- When the Y section finally returns in bar 80, the harmony is a bit more mobile. Debussy, however, cycles between G, C♯ and E chords, which are all derived from the B octatonic scale.

Rotation 5

The final rotation is much shorter and only touches on fragments of the previous melodic material.

- The X material is more sharply **dissonant** as the B minor material is presented for the first time directly against the G material, creating a G/F♯ dissonance that we have not heard in this thematic idea before

- The Y material is only represented by a two note idea which comes from the accompaniment in previous rotations – the actual melody is not present

- There is also a hint of the earlier pentatonic melody in bar 98

- The harmony is similarly fading away, with a highly ambiguous G chord giving way to unison Bs at the end. B has remained a tonal centre throughout but has most certainly not been tonally established.

Set work:
Poulenc's Trio for Oboe, Bassoon and Piano, Movement 2

Poulenc

Unlike Debussy, we have not yet encountered Francis Poulenc (1899-1963) in our survey of the early twentieth century. The music he wrote from the early 1920s onwards (including this piece) is largely Neo-classical, although he also wrote some religious works later in life that do not so easily fit in this bracket.

Francis Poulenc

Poulenc was a key member of a group of young French composers known as *Les Six* (the others were Durey, Honegger, Milhaud, Auric and Tailleferre), whose music was promoted by the older maverick composer Erik Satie and also the novelist, playwright and filmmaker Cocteau. Their music was in part a reaction against the influence of what they saw as the excesses of German music represented by Wagner and the high seriousness of 1920s Modernism (such as the serial music that we looked at above). They aimed to write in a more straightforward and direct way than Debussy and other older French composers. The group did not last much past the mid-twenties but Poulenc and Auric continued to write at least some of their music in the light-hearted style with which *Les Six* are associated.

Poulenc's Musical Style

- **Form.** Form is often based on Classical models, but the relationship can be very loose, with various twists and modifications along the way. This Andante is less Classical in its form than is typical in Poulenc's works

- **Melody and motif.** Poulenc (in some respects like Stravinsky and Debussy) tends not to develop his melodies in the usual Classical way – often repeating them before moving on to a new idea without much attempt at transition. Although there are lots of motivic links between ideas, the ideas themselves are rarely subject to extensive development

- **Harmony and tonality.** Poulenc uses a harmonic language that incorporates some more recent innovations (e.g. plenty of 'wrong note' dissonances and some use of the octatonic scale) but is recognisably based on that of the Western Classical Tradition. There are plenty of surprising twists in terms of modulations, and the tonal structure is a long way from what you might expect in a 'real' Classical piece, particularly in this movement

- **Instrumentation.** Both the choices and uses of instruments in Poulenc are usually fairly traditional. In this piece, as in many of his chamber works, he includes the piano, on which he was very proficient, frequently performing his own music

- **Rhythm.** Poulenc's rhythmic writing is reasonably traditional, but he often throws the rhythm off balance with unexpected changes of metre.

Form in this movement

As discussed in the Eduqas notes, the division of the movement into **ternary form** is problematic, but it is a good way of getting to grips with the overall shape.

Bar 1	12	20	23	33	35	37	45	51	52
B♭	D♭	V of B (octatonic)	Bm	V of B (octatonic)	B(maj)	V of C (then chromatic)	C	ii-V in F	F maj/min
A	(A)		B1		(B2 – climax of movement)				A'

As is also shown in the online notes, another way of understanding the form is as a transition between the A major of the first movement and the D♭ major of the last. This is not without its problems either, in particular the way it minimises the role of F major at the end of the second movement.

Mov. I	Mov. II	Mov. III
A	[B♭ – B – C]	D♭

Key features

Section A (bars 1-22)

■ There is an unexpected shift from B♭ to D♭ major, after which the opening **tonality** never returns

■ The **harmony** is often basically 'correct' in that it follows normal progressions (in the example below, I6–V–I in F major), but the details seem to introduce notes that sound wrong or out of place. In the example, the B♭ passing notes clash with the arpeggiating semiquaver A naturals in the first half of the bar, then the same clash happens at the end of the bar, this time without even the justifying context of the B♭ being a passing note.

EXAMPLE 16:

Poulenc, Bars 3–4

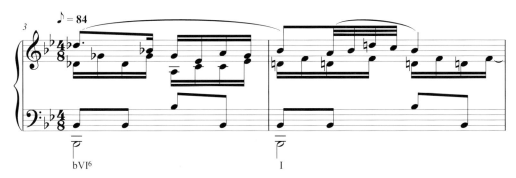

- The $\frac{3}{8}$ time signature in bar 8 at the end of the first phrase unbalances the metre
- The end of the A section is briefly **octatonic** as Poulenc combines two harmonies a **tritone** apart in bar 21: F♯ (the **dominant** of the following B minor) against C.

EXAMPLE 17:

Poulenc, bars 21-22

Section B1 (23-34)

- This is in B minor but it is not very strongly established with not a single **root** position **tonic** chord
- The thematic material is new but not very distinctive – this section seems to be part of a larger build up to the climax at the beginning of B2
- There are more **octatonic** harmonies in bar 29.

Section B2 (35-51)

- There is an *fff* climax in bar 35 on B major
- Poulenc hints at C major before a chromatic passage of ascending parallel first inversion chords
- After the approach to C major in bars 45-47 (a tonic followed by a cadential $\frac{6}{4}$), what should have been the dominant in bar 51 becomes G diminished instead and becomes chord **ii7** in F minor.

Section A' (53 to the end)

- This section is unexpectedly in F
- This is the most octatonic section of the piece (from bar 62)
- The final ambiguous chord – F minor with a major seventh – is part of the octatonic collection and helps to transition into the next movement, which is in D♭ major.

The notes above summarize some key points from the information provided in Eduqas's own extensive notes, which are available at:
http://resources.eduqas.co.uk/Pages/ResourceSingle.aspx?rlid=688
You will need to look at a score and the online analysis as well as the following.

Practice Paper

Area of Study E: Into the Twentieth Century

In the exam, you will be given **two** questions for this part of the paper, divided into between 5 and 7 parts (a-e or perhaps a-g), and each worth **15 marks**. The first question will be on one of your set works: the Poulenc or Debussy. The second question will be on an unprepared work. Here we have given you example questions for part 1, based on the set works. Sample assessment papers which cover unprepared works are also available to download from the Eduqas website, and you should practise answering these as much as possible.

Set work – Poulenc

1. You will hear an extract from the second movement of Poulenc's Trio for Oboe, Bassoon and Piano. Use an **unannotated copy of the score** for this question.

   The extract begins at bar 21 and ends at the end of bar 36. In an exam, the extract would be played **3 times** with a **1 minute pause** between each playing and a **7 minute silence** after the final playing for you to complete your answers. [15]

   You now have 30 seconds to read the questions below.

   (a)   State in full (e.g. G major) the key in bar 23. [1]

   ....

   (b)   Describe precisely the relationship between the oboe and bassoon parts in bar 26. [1]

   ....

   (c)   Describe the harmony in bars 21 and 22 in as much detail as possible. [4]

   ....

   ....

   ....

   ....

   (d)   State four **differences** between bar 23-4 and bar 35-6. [4]

   1. ....

   2. ....

   3. ....

   4. ....

(e) The extract starting from bar 23 could be described as the beginning of the B section of a ternary form structure. Discuss the extent to which you agree with this ternary form analysis of the movement, referring to specific musical features (using bar numbers) to support your argument. [5]

....

....

....

....

Set work – Debussy

2. You will hear an extract of 'Nuages' from Debussy's *Nocturnes*. Use an **unannotated copy of the score** for this question.

The extract begins at bar 94 and runs to the end of the movement. In an exam, the extract would be played **3 times** with a **1 minute pause** between each playing and a **7 minute silence** after the final playing for you to complete your answers. **[15]**

You now have 30 seconds to read the questions below.

(a) State in full (e.g. G major) the key implied by the bassoon parts in bar 94. [1]

....

(b) State precisely (e.g. F♯ dominant seventh) the chord on the first crotchet of bar 94. [1]

....

(c) What scale is most of the material in this extract drawn from? [1]

....

(d) Describe the string writing in this extract. [3]

....

....

....

(e) Identify a bar from 11-28 on which the following bars in this extract are based and describe how it differs in its later appearance. [4]

Bar number in extract	Bar number from 11-28	Difference
Bar 94		
Bar 99		

(f)   Discuss how Debussy uses different modes and scales in **the rest** of
this movement.   [5]

....

....

....

....

Unprepared work

3. Listen to Alban Berg, Four Songs, Op. 2, No. 3.

You will hear a song with piano accompaniment. The English translation of the title is
'Now I have overcome the strongest of the giants'. In an exam the extract would be
played **3 times** with a **45 second pause** between each playing and a **7 minute silence**
after the final playing for you to complete your answer.   [15]

You now have 30 seconds to read the questions.

(a)   Describe the texture at the very opening.   [1]

....

(b)   Describe the opening piano texture.   [1]

....

(c)   Comment on any repetitions or modified repetitions of the opening
melodic idea in the voice later in the song.   [2]

....

....

(d)   Comment on the harmony at the end of the song in comparison to the beginning.   [4]

....

....

....

(e)   Underline the style that best describes this music.   [1]

Impressionist   Serial   Expressionist   Neo-classical

(f)   Underline the composer that you consider to have written this music.   [1]

Ravel   Stravinsky   Prokofiev   Berg

(g)   Explain the composer's treatment of harmony and melody in one other
piece you have studied this year which is similar in style to this extract.   [5]

....

....

....

....

Unprepared work: you will have only one unprepared work to answer questions on in the exam, but here is a second practice question

4. Listen to Stravinsky, Appollon Musagete, Premiere tableau: Naissance.

Listen from the beginning until 2 mins 8 seconds. The recording used here is Decca, Stuttgart Chamber Orchestra with Dennis Russell Davies.

You will hear an extract from an orchestral piece taken from a ballet. In an exam the extract would be played **3 times** with a **45 second pause** between each playing and a **7 minute silence** after the final playing for you to complete your answer.   **[15]**

You now have 30 seconds to read the questions.

An outline of the structure is printed below:

Section A [about 1m15s]	Section B [about 25s]	Section A' [about 30s]
Opening idea includes a short transition into next section.	Contrasting material with distinctly different texture.	Shortened reprise of section A.

(a)   Describe the instrumentation.   [1]

....

(b)   Describe the first two textures heard at the beginning.   [2]

1. ....

2. ....

(c)   Describe the accompaniment in the B section.   [3]

....

....

(d)   Other than the length, give two differences between the first A section and the second.   [2]

1. ....

2. ....

(e)   Underline the composer that you consider to have written this music.   [1]

Ravel   Stravinsky   Prokofiev   Webern

(f)   Underline the style that best describes this piece.   [1]

Impressionist   Serial   Expressionist   Neo-classical

(g)   Explain the overall style and technique of one other piece you have studied this year which is similar to this extract.   [5]

....

....

....

....

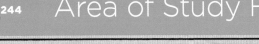

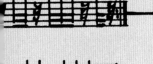

Into the Twenty-First Century

A LEVEL ONLY

This is an A Level-only module, and you will study either this area of study OR Area of Study E: Into the Twentieth Century. Whichever you take accounts for **30%** of the component 3 exam.

You will study how composers at the turn of the 21st Century (1980-the present) reshaped musical language for new circumstances and audiences.

Set works

There are **TWO** set works from this period to be studied in depth:

1. **Thomas Adès: *Asyla*, Movement 3, 'Ecstasio'.**
2. **Sally Beamish: String Quartet No. 2 (*Opus California*) Movements 1 ('Boardwalk')
   and 4 ('Natural Bridges').**

For the Adès, you can buy a full score from Faber Music (ISBN 10: 0-571-51863-X), or go to the Eduqas website to download movement 3 only. For the Beamish, again, you can buy a score from Norsk Musikforlag (ISMN: 979-0-065-12115-4), or find a link to Norsk Musikforlag on the Eduqas website. You will also find detailed background and analytical notes on these two works on the Eduqas website. Be sure to read these as well as the notes in this book.

Suggested composers

To provide a broader context of other developments in the period when these two works were composed, it is recommended that you explore other works by Adès and Beamish, and the following composers, including four current British composers, are also suggested by the exam board for study:

- Sofia Gubaidulina
- Hans Werner Henze
- Witold Lutosławski
- Kaija Saariaho
- Mark-Anthony Turnage
- Judith Weir

In this chapter, a well-known and characteristic work by each of these six composers has been chosen to help you focus on the main features of their styles. Note that many of the features identified are generally common to their music as a whole.

Your exam will be structured in the following way:

In Section 2 of the 'Appraising Music' paper (Component 3) **at A Level only**, there will be two questions on AOS F which account for 30 marks.

Musical extract	Question types	Marks (30)
Extract from EITHER set work (with blank score)	■ Short questions on musical elements and devices, including comparisons of passages	10
	■ Longer question discussing one aspect of the piece (e.g. form, **tonality** and so on)	5
Unseen extract	■ Short questions on musical elements and devices, including comparisons of passages. These might also ask about composer and style.	10
	■ Asked to discuss one musical element in the context of other pieces studied in wider listening.	5

Musical Language for this Area of Study

This AoS has some specialist vocabulary not found elsewhere, so here are some definitions of terms used in music written since 1980 that you might not encounter in your study of earlier music.

Additive rhythm: This is a repeated rhythm, 'displaced' either by adding notes to or subtracting notes from it – this is a well-known technique and can be found in Stravinsky.

Aleatoric: music in which some element is left to chance or to the performers to determine.

Cluster chords: chords containing three or more adjacent notes separated by a semitone. These are **dissonant** chords without resolutions and are not found in functional **harmony**.

Golden Section: A geometrical proportion that divides a line with a longer side and a shorter one. Many contemporary composers have used the proportion to mark climactic points or moments of significance in their music. It can be applied using Fibonacci numbers (where each number is the sum of the previous two: 1, 2, 3, 5, 8, 13, 21, 34, 55, and so on). So, in a piece 34 bars long, the Golden Section falls either at the end of bar 21 or bar 13.

Microtones: These are intervals smaller than a semitone, frequently used by contemporary composers. They are often divided into quarter tones (half of a semitone), but may also be divided in other ways.

Multiphonics: This is a technique on an instrument that can only play one note at a time (a **monophonic** instrument) in which several notes are produced simultaneously. They are usually found in music for woodwind using new fingerings or different embouchures. On brass instruments they usually consist of simultaneously playing the instrument and singing into it.

Pluralism: pluralism suggests a number of different approaches or styles, both in music generally and within a musical piece, rather than just one kind of style. It is a particular feature of the musical world since 1980.

Polyrhythm: A polyrhythm is where two different metres or musical pulses are played simultaneously. A very simple example would be two beats against three; or four against five.

Spectralism: See the section about Kaija Saariaho on page 259 for a detailed discussion of Spectralism.

Time-based notation: music in which normal **rhythmic** values are dispensed with and measured in seconds instead.

Who's who in music since 1980

Here are a few thumbnail sketches of some of the leading composers who have dominated music since 1980, and whose names you are likely to come across as part of your studies.

Pierre Boulez (1925-2016)

Dominated contemporary music as composer and conductor for seventy years, producing a stream of dazzling masterpieces developing the principles of 'total **serialism**' including *Le marteau sans maître* (1955), a work as influential as Stravinsky's *Rite of Spring* forty years earlier. He also instigated Paris's IRCAM, revolutionising the development of music technology.

Peter Maxwell Davies (1934-2016)

Along with Harrison Birtwistle, one of the leading British composers of his generation and a member of the Manchester School – a group of composers studying in Manchester in the 1950s, drawing on the most advanced techniques of the time. He later moved to the Orkney Islands in Scotland, and became Master of the Queen's Music in 2004.

Karlheinz Stockhausen (1928-2007)

The leading and most progressive German composer of his generation. He was a major force in the development of electronic music during the 1950s, and the development of serialism and **aleatoric forms**. Much of his time from the mid-1970s was devoted to an opera, *Licht* (Light) to be performed over seven nights.

Some other composers whose works and styles you could explore include György Ligeti, Krzysztof Penderecki and Luigi Nono.

Musical features of the period from 1980-the present day

If we were to try to sum up the main aspects of music written since 1980, these are some of the features linking many of the composers. You won't find all these in the work of each composer, but you will probably find several of them.

- **Style**: There is a wide variety of different musical styles of composition, with no one style predominating. This is usually called '**Pluralism**'.
- **Influences**: Many composers draw on other music as a basis for their own compositions (this a feature of the two set works). These might range from medieval to present day music and across popular, jazz and world music.
- **Tonality**: Composers use a wide variety of different tonal and harmonic styles, ranging from **serial** and **atonal** through to very simple **modal** idioms.
- **Harmony**: No two composers will have the same approach to **harmony**, which might range from **dissonant** twelve-note chords or **microtones** to simple **triadic** harmony.
- **Metre & rhythm**: Much music since 1980 explores changing time signatures, unusual metres, **polyrhythm**, **additive rhythm**, free and **aleatoric rhythm** and unconventionally notated rhythm.

- **Texture and sonority**: The use of texture and sonority is a very important element of music since 1980 and is sometimes more important to composers than even melody, harmony and rhythm.

- **Notation**: Although many composers continue to use conventional traditional notation, many have abandoned or modified this in favour of new ways of notating music. This might include graphic notation, aleatoric notation, time-based notation and other new systems.

- **Writing for instruments**: Many new scores feature new techniques of writing for instruments ranging through glissandi, multiphonics, microtones, key clicks, air tones and many other devices.

- **Forms**: Although traditional forms continue to be used, composers have invented many new types of form for their music such as chain form, moment form, narrative forms and so forth.

FIND OUT MORE

Online: You can find a series of easy-to-read blogs on The Guardian website called 'A Guide to Contemporary Classical Music by Tom Service', with profiles and listening links for 50 of the most important composers of recent times.
Go to www.theguardian.com/music/series/a-guide-to-contemporary-classical-music

In a book: Alex Ross's book *The Rest is Noise* (published by Fourth Estate) is a fascinating guide to music in the last century and contains a great resumé of the years leading up to 2008 when the book was written.

Case Studies:

Eight composers since 1980 and their music

Here are some notes on the eight composers recommended for study in order to gain a wider knowledge of music written since 1980.

A particular work by each of these (except for Thomas Adès and Sally Beamish) has been suggested as an example for further study, recordings of which are easily available online. These works are discussed below, but their main features also apply to other pieces by the same composers.

All the pieces of music discussed here can be found on Spotify, and (at the time of writing) on YouTube.

Sofia Gubaidulina (b.1931)

Sofia Gubaidulina and the Soviet Union

Sofia Gubaidulina (the composer herself told an American interviewer that her name was pronounced So-FEE-uh Goo-bye-DOO-lee-nuh) is one of the last surviving composers from the generation who grew up in the Soviet Union in the 1950s and 60s. Her own characteristic voice did not fully emerge until she was already in her fifties in the 1980s; it is noted for its deep spirituality combined with an openness to the latest developments in contemporary music. She has written:

'True art for me is always religious, it will always involve collaborating with God.'

Sofia Gubaidulina was born in poverty to a Slavic mother and Tatar father in Chistopol in 1931 and came to Moscow in 1954 for post-graduate studies. She met Shostakovich who encouraged her to continue down her 'incorrect path'.

Sofia Gubaildulina

In the 1960s and 70s she earned a living composing film music while her own more experimental concert works attracted Soviet disapproval.

In 1980 she composed her violin concerto *Offertorium* for Gidon Kremer which, by the end of the 1980s, brought her an international reputation.

She did not make her first visit to the west until 1985, and after the fall of the Soviet Union in 1991 moved to a small village outside Hamburg, Germany, saying:

'I need silence to write; here I have the woods around me where I can walk without interruption.'

Like Shostakovich and Prokofiev before her, Gubaidulina grew up and worked in the Soviet Union before its collapse in 1991. Although restrictions were not as severe after the mid-1950s, living under the communist regime was particularly hard for her because it discouraged religious observance. She came into conflict with the authorities early on when, in 1959, a symphony had to be withdrawn under Soviet pressure: 'Inner independence was unacceptable', she says, 'and wherever that was detected in music, it was objected to.'

Find out more about Gubaidulina at www.bruceduffie.com/gubaidulina.html

Gubaidulina often uses non-Western instruments in her music, such as the Koto

Main features of Gubaidulina's music

The most important aspect of Gubaidulina's music is her faith: 'I am a religious Orthodox person and I understand 'religion' in the literal meaning of the word, as 're-ligio', that is to say the restoration of connections, the restoration of the '**legato**' of life. There is no more serious task or music than this.' The music combines the ritual of the ancient Eastern Orthodox Church with many techniques of contemporary music.

Gubaidulina has been particularly drawn to concerto-type works, including several works for the Russian bayan, and non-western instruments and orchestra such as the koto and zheng. She has also composed much chamber and choral music.

Her music is intensely chromatic, based on motivic cells rather than long-breathed melodic lines. It is also driven by **rhythm** which she derives from the Fibonacci series (or **Golden Section**) where each successive number is the sum of the previous two numbers (1, 2, 3, 5, 8, 13, 21, 34 etc). Major climactic points or moments of significance in her music often coincide with the Golden Section. 'The Fibonacci series is always about approaching the divine,' she says.

Despite this rigorous approach Gubaidulina feels that intuition forms a very important part of composing; 'for me the most important thing is not to interfere with intuition, not to get in the way of intuition.'

EXAMPLE WORK:

Sofia Gubaidulina (b.1931): *Offertorium* (1980-86)

Offertorium is a violin concerto composed for Gidon Kremer, who premiered it in Vienna in May 1981 with Leif Segerstam conducting. It was extensively revised in 1982 and 1986. The piece lasts around 38 minutes and is published by Music Sales. It has been recorded by Gidon Kremer and the Boston Symphony Orchestra conducted by Charles Dutoit on Deutsch Grammophon 471 625.

The title *Offertorium* (Offering) indicates that the work is a sacred drama based on sacrifice and regeneration. It draws its material from Bach's *Musical Offering* of 1747 (hence the title) which is based on a **theme** given to Bach by Frederick the Great during a visit to Berlin:

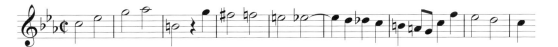

This theme dominates the whole work and is heard immediately at the beginning, in an arrangement made by the composer Anton Webern (1883-1945) in 1934-35, of the **Fugue** (Ricercare) from the *Musical Offering*. Webern fragmented the theme, distributing its notes around the different instruments of the orchestra to make its motivic construction clear. Gubaidulina starts with Webern to bring the theme's distant origin nearer to our own time.

Form:

- In the introduction, the theme is heard in a fragmented Webern-like form where it is passed around various instruments; it lacks only the last note (D) which is taken over by the entry of the violin
- When the soloist then enters, we hear a series of **variations**; each successive one removes one note from the beginning and end of the theme
- After the third variation, this process makes the original theme hard to recognise
- The second half now is dominated by the intervals that are left: a 2nd and 4th

- The final section is a slow string chorale underneath which the harps and piano play the theme in reverse (retrograde), leading to a complete statement from the solo violin, finally coming to rest on a high D – the note that remained unheard at the outset.

Melody:

- Gubaidulina's melodic lines tend to concentrate on outlining intervals, rather than long arching lines. Listen to the entry of the violin in *Offertorium* where the soloist moves obsessively between the same intervals

- Melodic lines are characterised by large interval leaps and decoration such as exaggerated **vibrato**, **portamento** and trills.

Harmony:

- Although based on a theme by Bach, the music avoids tonal centres and traditional harmony, using instead **pitch** clusters and harmony derived from particular intervals.

Texture:

- The **orchestration** is often fragmented into individual instrumental families rather than large orchestral tuttis, with the motivic material passed around between them.

- Like Gubaidulina's melodic lines, the different sections of the orchestra use a wide range of colour: different string colours range through portamento, **ponticello**, **tremolando** and so forth, through to wind flutter-tonguing, muted brass and so forth.

Hans Werner Henze (1926-2012)

Hans Werner Henze and Germany

Hans Werner Henze was the most successful German composer working in traditional forms during the second half of the twentieth century. He was continental Europe's leading composer of opera, wrote ten symphonies and a vast output of music in all other genres. Highly expressive and romantic in character, Henze's music was intimately bound up with his own colourful life.

Henze grew up in Nazi Germany where he was obliged to become a member of the Hitler Youth (he was born in Gütersloh, North Rhine-Westphalia). He was conscripted into the German army and became a British prisoner-of-war.

Following the war, he initially worked as both a conductor and composer, but disturbed by the intolerance and homophobia of German society, he decided to move to Italy in 1953.

In the 1950s his music took on a new Italianate lyricism and warmth, as can be heard in the *Five Neapolitan Songs* (1956), though the emotional and sensual character of his music led him into conflict with the avant-garde composers such as Boulez, Stockhausen and Nono.

Hans Werner Henze

During the 1960s Henze became involved with politics, initially in Germany, eventually becoming a Marxist, making two visits to Cuba and leading to a series of directly political works such as *Essay on Pigs* (1969) and culminating in his opera *We Come to the River* (1976).

The 1980s saw a reconciliation with Germany, with the Berlin premiere of his Seventh Symphony in 1984 and a return to German subjects as the basis of his music.

After the premiere of his last symphony (the Tenth) in 2002, Henze suffered increasingly from illness, dying in Dresden in October 2012.

Find out more about Henze from the Guardian's guide at https://www.theguardian.com/music/tomserviceblog/2012/oct/29/contemporary-music-guide-hans-werner-henze

A brief snapshot of Germany and its music

In the years after the Second World War, from 1949, Germany was partitioned into two states: East Germany, controlled by the Soviet Union, and West Germany, controlled by the Allies: Britain, France and the United States.

The two halves of Germany were physically separated from 1961 by the Berlin Wall, with West Germany considering the East as an illegally constituted Soviet puppet state.

The Berlin Wall, a powerful symbol of the Soviet Union and the Cold War until its fall in 1990

West Germany was one of the strongest economies in the world during the second half of the last century (known as the '*Wirtschaftswunder*' or 'economic miracle'), while life in East Germany was significantly less successful with freedom much curtailed. Relations between the two halves of Germany were strained and extensive protests in East Germany in the late 1980s began to undermine the state. The Berlin Wall was broken through in November 1989 and Germany reunified in 1990 as the Soviet Union crumbled.

Main features of Henze's music

Henze's music passed through many different styles and changes: Stravinskyan **Neo-classicism** and some jazz influences in the late 1940s and early 50s; a new-found Neo-romantic lyricism from the mid 1950s onwards; a heightened violent and **dissonant Expressionism** married to political ideologies from the mid-1960s through the 1970s and then, from the 1980s onwards, a mature synthesis of many aspects of these styles.

Unlike many of his contemporaries, Henze's music is cast in classical forms: symphonies, concertos, string quartets, songs, operas and ballets. Music for the theatre is an important part of Henze's output; but besides opera and ballet, he also experimented with concepts of music theatre in the late 1960s and early 70s, particularly in works such as *El Cimarrón* (1969).

Melody lies at the centre of Henze's work, often taking the form of long arching complex chromatic lines. Henze's melodic lines and dissonant **harmony** are often derived from serial 12-note music, though this is used with great freedom: he said he used **Serialism** 'as a tool and never as an end in itself.'

Rhythmically, the music alternates between fast rhythmic extremes and slower static lyricism.

Most of Henze's music is orchestral: densely scored and multi-layered. It is highly expressive and dramatic in character.

EXAMPLE WORK:

Hans Werner Henze (1926-2012): Symphony No.7 (1983-84)

Henze wrote ten symphonies between 1947 and 2000; the seventh was his first 'conventional' four-**movement** symphony. For Henze's thoughts on it, see below under 'Hölderlin and the Seventh Symphony'.

The Seventh Symphony, for large orchestra, was premiered in West Berlin by the Berlin Philharmonic Orchestra conducted by Gianluigi Gelmetti in December 1984.

There are four movements:

- Tanz: Lebhaft und beseelt [Dance: Lively and happy]
- Ruhig bewegt [With tranquil motion]
- Unablässig in Bewegung [Incessantly in motion]
- Ruhig, verhalten [Peaceful, restrained]

The symphony lasts around 43 minutes and is published by Schott. It has been recorded on EMI by the City of Birmingham Symphony Orchestra conducted by Simon Rattle.

Henze's view of symphonic form was ambivalent:

'Old forms seem to me, as it were, like classical ideals of beauty, no longer attainable but still visible in the far distance, stirring memory like dreams.'

Hölderlin and the Seventh Symphony

Henze wrote,

'My Seventh Symphony is a German symphony and it deals with matters German. The first part is an Allemande – a German dance that gains increasing force and energy... The second... is relatively straightforward: I see it as a kind of funeral ode, a song of lamentation, a monologue. The third... is cast in the form a scherzo... While writing it I thought of the sufferings of Friedrich Hölderlin in [1770-1843] immured in the Authenried Asylum in Tübingen, where the treatment he received... amounted to nothing short of the most terrible torture. The final section is... an orchestral setting of Hölderlin's late poem Hälfte des Lebens ['Half of Life'].'

Henze suggests that the third **movement** conveys the torture that Hölderlin suffered, while the poem underlying the finale contains the following words: 'Where do I find flowers and sunshine and earth's shadows, when it is winter?'

Form:

- The symphony is in four movements: a lively dance-like opening movement; a slow second movement from which a rocking **ostinato** in the harp occasionally emerges; a relentless and incessant third movement, and a slow finale
- The opening movement, the composer writes, 'is a kind of *Allemande* in which two opposition elements attempt to tackle **sonata form** with two opposing themes.'
- The first, third and final movements all have the very clear shape of being constructed as a series of crescendos over the course of the whole movement
- The fourth movement contains a setting of a text by Friedrich Hölderlin, but the words have been removed; a process that can also be found in the last movement of Alban Berg's Lyric Suite.

Style:

- Stylistic influences include Stravinsky (possibly the Symphony in Three Movements), but also German composers who were active when Henze was a young man, such as Wolfgang Amadeus Hartmann (1905-63) or Wolfgang Fortner (1907-87).

Melody:

- There are several melodic styles used
- The ostinato often consists of short rhythmic melodic ideas that are repeated, though often with subtle variation
- In the second slow movement, the opening string melodies (combined **polyphonically**) are long and sustained, their general contour arching upwards and then falling back again, the lines often in dialogue with one another.

Harmony:

- **Harmony** is generally **dissonant** and harsh with a predominance of minor 2nds, major 7ths and minor 9ths.

Texture:

- The textures in all movements are nearly always dense and polyphonic

- At the outset, instruments are often grouped in duos and trios (bassoons, horns and a trombone, cellos and basses and so on) that overlap with one another

- The second **movement** also maintains this idea of groups or families of instruments: cellos and flutes, pairs of oboes, high and low strings, and so on.

Metre and rhythm:

- The opening movement maintains a rigid quaver pulse throughout. Simon Rattle recalled, 'It was very important to him that the first movement should dance... Henze meets *West Side Story*'

- In the first and third movements, the **rhythm** is driven forward by a number of overlapping **ostinati**; listen to the way (in the first movement) that the opening idea in the bassoons is soon overlaid by other ostinati (lower strings and brass, then upper strings, then clarinets and so on) until it disappears altogether in the process

- **Ostinato** is also present in the slow second movement where the harp has a regular rocking/rotating movement, emerging from the **texture** and then disappearing once again.

Witold Lutosławski (1913-94)

Polish Music and Lutosławski

Lutosławski was the most important figure in Polish music from the 1960s onwards. His music uses **aleatoric** techniques (rhythm not co-ordinated by barlines) and develops new ways of using **serialism**.

Lutosławski's life was dominated by politics. When he was five the Bolsheviks executed his father, and later he was captured by the Nazis and escaped, returning to Warsaw where he gave undercover secret concerts in cafés. After the Second World War he lived under the Communist regime.

In the late 1950s political pressure on him to conform was relaxed and he found the freedom to compose his own way, beginning with *Funeral Music* (1958) which launched his international career.

During the 1980s Lutosławski's music became more lyrical and concentrated more on **melody**, in common with many other composers in the 1980s.

Witold Lutosławski

In his later years he served on the Polish Cultural Council helping to achieve more freedom for the Polish people.

Find out more about Lutosławski from the Guardian's guide at https://www.theguardian. com/music/tomserviceblog/2013/jan/15/contemporary-music-guide-witold-lutoslawski

A brief snapshot of Poland during Lutosławski's lifetime

Lutosławski's life coincided with some of the most tempestuous years in Poland's history. After World War Two in 1945, Poland was seized by the Soviet Union who established a communist government. Initially Lutosławski was required to write music that served the people, but after 1956 a more liberal atmosphere could be felt. The formation of the independent trade union, 'Solidarity', in 1980 gradually eroded the dominance of the regime leading in 1989 to Poland's first democratic elections since the war. Solidarity's leader, Lech Wałęsa became Poland's president after the collapse of the communist regime.

Poland's first post-communist president, Lech Wałęsa

Main Features of Lutosławski's Music

Most of Lutosławski's music is orchestral; he claimed the orchestra was his favourite instrument. His orchestral style has a glittering colourful surface and **texture** is crucially important. Although often complex, his music is also very clear, dramatic and emotional.

Lutosławski pioneered the technique of 'controlled **aleatoricism**' where musicians play without precise rhythmic co-ordination: a sort of controlled chaos.

Harmony is at the centre of Lutosławski's music and is derived from his own serial 12-note method: the chords are rich, complex and often built from specific intervals (for instance, **augmented** 4ths and semitones in *Funeral Music*).

EXAMPLE WORK:

Witold Lutosławski (1913-94): *Chain 2* (1984-85)

Chain 2 is for solo violin and orchestra. It's a mini violin concerto in four linked movements written for the **virtuoso** German violinist Anne Sophie Mutter who gave the premiere in Zurich in January 1986.

It's one of three pieces called 'Chain' (*Chain 1*, *Chain 2* & *Chain 3*) composed between 1983 and 1986. *Chain 2* lasts around 20 minutes and is published by Chester Music.

It has been recorded by Anne Sophie Mutter and the BBC Symphony Orchestra conducted by the composer on Deutsch Grammophon 471 588-2.

A 'chain' ('Łańcuch' in Polish) is a musical form invented by Lutosławski in which phrases and sections of the music overlap, like a chain, instead of beginning or ending at the same time. He devised it because he wanted to find an alternative to classical forms.

Style:

- Hesitant, fragmented, nervous, unsettled
- Short fragments.

Melody:

- Most of the melodic material is given to the solo violin
- Short melodic motifs with rests in between are heard, often moving by step in semitones (listen to the opening of Section 1)
- More sustained, broader melodies (at the end of the first section for instance) have wider intervals (4ths, 5ths, 7ths)
- Fast-moving virtuosic passages for the solo violin.

Texture:

- The accompanying orchestral texture is fragmented with sudden brief bursts of activity
- The strings often have **rhythmically** repeated notes or sustained chords
- String **glissandi** are an important part of the texture
- The woodwind often have short irregular 'chattering' notes separated by short rests (for instance the flutes and bassoons in the first section).

Harmony:

- In Section 1, most of the chords (mainly in the strings) have four notes, usually sustained over a long period
- These are often derived from the 12 notes of the chromatic scale with the violin using the other 8 notes (listen in particular to the broad sustained melody in the violin towards the end of Section 1)
- In Section 2 the chords in the violin at the opening are made up of adjacent semitones in the section marked 'rude'. Later, in the section marked 'soave' they are now made up of major 2nds and 4ths and 5ths
- Later in the **movement** (at fig.35) there is a characteristic chord made of all the 12 notes of the chromatic scale.

Metre and rhythm:

- The whole of Section 1 is mainly unbarred, the moments of co-ordination being given to the players by the conductor. This is an example of Lutosławski's technique of 'controlled **aleatoricism**'
- The solo violin plays almost continuously, with entry points for the other instruments indicated at key moments in the soloists' part by large arrows at the top of the score
- The whole of Section 2, by comparison, is entirely metred.

Notation:

- As already mentioned, large sections of *Chain 2* (particularly sections 1 and 3) are examples of 'controlled aleatoricism'
- The way in which the score is laid out might be unfamiliar: when the players are silent, their stave is blanked out (rather than filled with rests). This is a way of writing scores popular from the 1950s onwards, particularly with Polish composers
- Players are often asked to repeat a short rhythmic figure or note using the usual repeat marks, but then followed by a long black line, indicating how long the note should be held for.

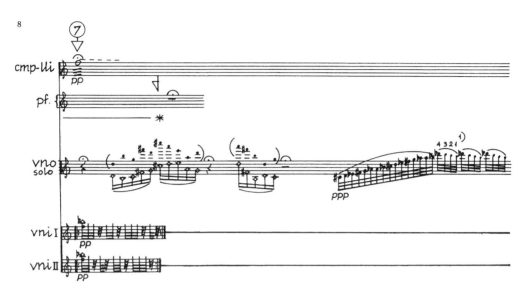

A section of the score from Chain 2. Notice how the score is left blank instead of being filled with rests when certain instruments are not playing

Kaija Saariaho (b.1952)

Finnish-born Kaija Saariaho (pronounced KY-uh SAH-ree-ah-ho) rejected contemporary music as she found it as a student in the 1970s, eventually moving to Paris where a new generation of 'spectral' composers were emerging. Since then she has evolved a unique sound world that fuses electronics and acoustic instruments seamlessly to create a new type of music.

Kaija Saariaho grew up in Finland 'without any kind of cultural background' and studied at the Sibelius Academy in Helsinki where she was the only woman in the composition class.

As a young composer she joined Finland's 'Ears Open' group along with composers such as Magnus Lindberg and Esa Pekka-Salonen.

When she heard the music of the French spectral composers Gérard Grisey and Tristan Murail, she moved to Paris where she discovered the rapidly evolving computer technology at the newly opened IRCAM (Institut de Recherche et Coordination Acoustique/Musique) at the Pompidou Centre.

She began to compose works that seamlessly merged live and electronic sounds, melting the division between the two worlds.

Kaija Saariaho shakes hands with the leader of the orchestra at a performance of one of her works

Mark-Anthony Turnage (b.1960)

Mark Anthony Turnage and England

Mark-Anthony Turnage is one of the leading composers of his generation. In the 1980s he emerged as a rebellious figure, fusing jazz, blues, funk and soul into his music at a time when serialism still dominated British music.

Born in Corrington, Essex, Turnage emerged in 1981 with his Miles Davies-inspired *Night Dances*.

While studying in Boston in 1983 he met Hans Werner Henze who later commissioned Turnage's first opera, *Greek* (1988), based on Steven Berkoff's play, set in the downtrodden east end of London. Its angry violence immediately established him as an *enfant terrible*.

Mark-Anthony Turnage

In the 1990s Turnage went on to produce a string of important pieces such as *Drowned Out* (1993), *Your Rockaby* (1994) and his second opera, *The Silver Tassie* (1997), based on World War 1.

Find out more about Turnage from the Guardian's guide at https://www.theguardian.com/music/2011/jan/22/mark-anthony-turnage-opera-composer

A brief snapshot of London during the 1980s

Turnage was brought up in Grays, Essex, with his family employed in local industries.

During the 1980s, he became particularly associated with the idea of working class identity and popular culture, including being known to be an Arsenal fan.

His opera *Greek* in particular associated him with the idea of protest within the Britain of the 1980s, with its politics dominated by the figure of the Prime Minister Margaret Thatcher who reversed the ideas of the Welfare State and Nationalised Industry.

Turnage lives in London with his family and has said 'I don't know if all composers work in that way, but I become obsessed with what I'm working on. I think about it all the time.'

Main features of Turnage's music

In Turnage's music the classical concern with form and development stands side by side with influences from jazz and blues. The music's melodic style is often jazz-inflected though the harmonic style might relate, for example, more to composers such as Henze or near contemporaries such as Oliver Knussen.

Turnage's orchestral writing is densely scored with lots of small details, though these often add colour to broad clear melodic lines. The mood of his music is often dark and related to death and loss.

EXAMPLE WORK:

Mark Anthony Turnage (b.1960): *Three Screaming Popes* (1988-89)

Three Screaming Popes is composed for symphony orchestra and was commissioned for the City of Birmingham Symphony Orchestra who premiered it with Simon Rattle conducting in October 1989. It is dedicated to Hans Werner Henze.

The piece lasts around 16 minutes, and is published by Schott.

It has been recorded by the City of Birmingham Symphony Orchestra conducted by Simon Rattle on EMI.

Three Screaming Popes was inspired by the paintings of Francis Bacon (1909-1992), regarded as the most significant British painter of the second half of the twentieth century.

Bacon made a series of paintings based on seventeenth century painter Diego Velázquez's portrait of Pope Innocent X (1650) in which the distorted figure of a pope is contained within what looks like a glass box.

In one of the paintings, from 1953, the figure appears to be screaming; this was one of the three images that inspired Turnage.

The music also takes its inspiration from Spanish dance (on account of Velázquez's nationality). Turnage writes:

‘My initial idea was to write a piece which distorted a set of Spanish dances as Bacon had distorted and restated Velázquez.’

You may view Velázquez and Bacon's paintings side-by-side if you search online for www.phaidon.com/resource/francis-bacon-pope-innocente-x-velazquez-comparison.jpg

Although the music is often harsh, Turnage has always maintained that the listener should not try to equate its sound with the idea of screams.

Style:

- The composer uses words to describe the music of the introduction such as 'a scrunchy brass chorale' and 'a bluesy **melody**'
- The music is made up of contrasts of long slow static passages and more energetic sections which suggest Spanish dance patterns.

Melody:

- The melodic lines tend to be jazz-inflected with flattened 7ths and major or minor 3rds
- Most of the melodic writing moves by step using tones and semitones, rising and falling with occasional rising intervals such as 6ths and 7ths at points of particular intensity

- Melodies are generally short, like extended motifs, contrasted with other ideas or **textures**, before being repeated

- The music often moves forward by alternating two short themes (as in the opening section)

- Melodic fragments are never literally repeated and are always slightly varied

- Listen to the opening two minutes: after the initial loud opening, note the recurring slow high **melody** in the oboes, soprano saxophones and E♭ clarinet followed by the chorale-like theme in the trumpets and horns and the way they alternate.

Harmony:

- The music is predominantly tonal, **rooted** in keys (the opening moves around E minor), but with a high degree of **dissonance**

- Melodic lines are usually strongly tonal, but surrounded by harmony made up of clusters and adjacent semitones (the opening chord, for example, contains most of the notes between B and E)

- The bass often consists of pedal notes or repeated tonal patterns

- The harmony often does not change for several bars at a time.

Texture:

- Orchestral textures are thick and heavy, with multiple doublings of melodic lines and pedal notes and harmonies made up of lots of multi-layered small **ostinato** patterns

- The instrumental colour is established by prominent use of two soprano saxophones, E♭ clarinet and bass clarinets (no 'standard' B♭ instruments) with trumpets muted for most of the work

- Textures often consist of extremes of either high or low instruments (or playing in high or low registers).

Metre and rhythm:

- There are two contrasting uses of **rhythm** in *Three Screaming Popes*: static slower sections and rhythmically driven faster sections, reflecting the influence of Stravinsky

- There are frequent changes of metre throughout the work

- In the slower sections, there is very little sense of pulse with irregular syncopated melodies or with the suggestion in the bass or accompanying parts of slow moving dance rhythms

- Faster sections are driven by ostinato and the use of **additive rhythm**.

Judith Weir (b.1954)

Judith Weir and Scotland

Judith Weir is the current (in 2016) Master of the Queen's Music – the first female composer ever to hold the post. Born in Cambridge to Scottish parents, she is one of the most inventive and original composers of her generation, often setting quirky and unusual texts and creating original formal ideas in her work.

A Night at the Chinese Opera performed by British Youth Opera

Story-telling has always been at the centre of Judith Weir's music: one of her first, most successful pieces, composed in 1979, was the opera *King Harald's Saga* – lasting just 10 minutes and written for a solo soprano who has to sing eight principal roles with no orchestra or even a piano to accompany her.

Since then, she has gone on to compose four full-length operas whose unusual subjects include *A Night at the Chinese Opera* (1987) and *The Vanishing Bridegroom* (1990).

Folk music, and the Scottish folk music with which she was brought up, is an important part of her work, bound up with her love of folk tales which can be found throughout her pieces.

Alongside composing music, Judith Weir has been Artistic Director of the Spitalfields Festival and has always been involved in educational work, from teaching **improvisation** to children, to being a visiting professor at various universities.

She was appointed Master of the Queen's Music in 2014.

> Find out more about Weir at www.judithweir.com and from the Guardian's guide at https:// www.theguardian.com/music/tomserviceblog/2012/may/28/judith-weir-contemporary-composers-guide

A brief snapshot of Scotland and its music

Scotland's economic situation has become progressively better since the 1980s due to the North Sea oil and gas industries as well as electronics manufacturing and the financial services sector. In 1997 a referendum led to the re-establishment of the Scottish Parliament and in 2014 an independence referendum was held, but was rejected by a majority of 55% to 45%.

Since 1945, music in Scotland has undergone an explosion of growth. This has resulted in the formation of the Edinburgh Festival, Scottish Opera, the Scottish Chamber Orchestra and St Magnus Festival along with the development of its other orchestras and ensembles.

Scottish music began to gain an international reputation in the 1950s with composers such as Iain Hamilton (1922-2000), Thomas Wilson (1927-2001), Thea Musgrave (b.1928) and Ronald Stevenson (1928-2015).

A new generation of composers began to emerge in the 1980s and 90s such as Judith Weir (1954), James MacMillan (1959) and Gordon McPherson (1965).

Notable composers who have settled in Scotland include Sally Beamish, and Sir Peter Maxwell Davies who moved to the Orkney Islands in the mid-1970s. Both composers have embraced and been influenced by Scottish culture and the richness of its folk music.

Main features of Weir's music

Judith Weir's music is instantly approachable: very clear with bright colours, largely tonal **harmony** yet with an undertone of irony and something more mysterious and difficult to pin down.

The music is modest and does not strive for highly emotional effects:

'... the crashingly loud side of music... is not the kind of music I generally like to write.'

The elements that make up her music are often very simple and made from everyday chords and melodic lines, but used in a new and original way.

Weir's melodic lines tend to be long and simple in their contours, influenced by the example of folk music.

Her music has many extra-musical influences and often takes texts as a starting point, including ancient Chinese texts, folk tales, **Romanticism** and nature.

Vocal music lies at the heart of Weir's output, but she has also written a substantial amount of orchestral and chamber music.

EXAMPLE WORK:

Judith Weir (b.1954): *Scotch Minstrelsy* (1982)

Scotch Minstrelsy for voice and piano was premiered in Glasgow in May 1982.

The composer has written that '*Scotch Minstrelsy* is a song cycle comprising settings of five (greatly abbreviated) Scottish ballads whose subject matter is almost exclusively violent happenings which take place against the beautiful background of the Scottish countryside. It was my intention to reflect this underlying irony in the way the words are set to music.' The title of the song cycle is deliberately ironic and refers to Sir Walter Scott's 1802-1803 three volume anthology of border ballads, *The Minstrelsy of the Scottish Borders.*

The titles of the five songs are:

- Bessie Bell and Mary Gray
- Bonnie James Campbell
- Lady Isobel and the Elf-Knight
- The Gypsy Laddie
- The Braes of Yarrow

Scotch Minstrelsy lasts around 14 minutes and is published by Novello. It has been recorded on Signum Classics SIGCD87.

Ballads are narrative stories in verse; they don't have any known authors and there are many variations of each, having been passed down by oral tradition since the Middle Ages. Ballads usually use the common dialect of the people and are heavily influenced by the region in which they originate. Scottish ballads are quite different to those from England and border ballads originated on the Anglo-Scottish border.

Style:

■ Folk-like melodic lines, generally simple, **diatonic** and **rhythmically** straightforward, but with unusual melodic and rhythmic inflections

■ Elaborate piano parts, rarely doubling the vocal part (but see the end of *Lady Isobel and the Elf-Knight* and the opening of the final song), and often seemingly in opposition to it, both rhythmically and harmonically

■ The piano parts are highly elaborate with detailed pedalling marked throughout (Note the opening of the whole cycle where the voice does not enter until bar 3).

Melody and word setting:

■ The melodic lines are long and flowing, arching upwards and then falling back, usually moving by step or using intervals no greater than 3rds or 4ths (though see the more dramatic leaps in *The Gypsy Laddie*)

■ The arc of the melodic line and its **cadences** follow the metre of the original ballads, though often broken by short rests

■ The word setting is largely syllabic with some occasional use of **melisma**.

Harmony:

■ The harmonic idiom is very wide-ranging, moving from simple diatonic moments through to chord clusters, **bi-tonal** chords and elaborate chromatic **polyphony**.

Texture:

The piano textures show a considerable range of different approaches throughout:

■ Much of *Bessie Bell and Mary Gray* is laid out as an elaborate closely-intertwined two-part invention (all notated on just one stave, but played using two hands)

■ Simple held notes building up into held chords are featured in the opening of *Bonnie James Campbell*, followed later by aggressive dense rhythmic chords

■ Widely spaced two-part writing in rhythmic unison characterises much of *The Gypsy Laddie*

■ *The Braes of Yarrow* (the final song) also features unison writing, but this time as the unison in the piano of just one line, one octave apart throughout. The voice part starts in unison with the piano, but gradually drifts apart.

Metre and rhythm:

■ The song cycle is rhythmically elaborate with many contemporary rhythmic devices.

■ The opening of *Bessie Bell and Mary Gray* is unbarred, with different groupings of notes including quintuplets and sextuplets, varying in phrase lengths. When bar lines do appear (from page 3 onwards), the groupings within the bar vary from triplet figurations to septuplets and irrational groups of 10 and 11

■ Despite the relatively simple nature of the vocal line, the word-setting often features rhythmic elements such as 'Scotch snaps' in *Bonnie James Campbell* or elaborate changes of metre in *The Gypsy Laddie*.

Relationship of Words to Music:

■ In *Scotch Minstrelsy*, Judith Weir's piano parts often seem to express the opposite of the meaning of the words, particularly in terms of the violent or unpleasant ends met by many of the characters.

- In the opening song the piano part seems almost independent of the meaning of the words, as if representing the flowing river next to the bower where Bessie Bell and Mary Gray hide from the plague. When, at the close, they die, the accompaniment, like the river, seems impervious to their fate

- In the other songs the death or fate of the various victims is never acknowledged in terms of dramatic musical gestures: Lady Isobel kills the Elf-Knight against the quiet *pianissimo* close of the third song and the fifteen gypsies are hanged against the gentle semi-quaver rustle of the close of the fourth song

- Only in the second song, *Bonnie James Campbell,* is the horror of death expressed in music itself.

Thomas Adès (b.1971)

Thomas Adès was born in London in 1971 and is generally regarded as the leading British composer of his generation. He is also a virtuoso pianist (he was runner-up in the BBC Young Musician of the Year in 1990) and a conductor.

He studied at the Guildhall School of Music, London, and then King's College, Cambridge, with the composers Alexander Goehr and Robin Holloway, graduating in 1992 with a double starred first.

He quickly established his name with works including his Chamber Symphony (1991), *Living Toys* (1994) and, in particular, his opera, *Powder Her Face*, based on the scandalous life of Margaret, Duchess of Argyll, (1996). In 1994 he was appointed Composer-in-Residence to the Hallé Orchestra.

Adès was appointed Artistic Director of the Aldeburgh Festival in 1999 (the festival was set up by Benjamin Britten in 1948) and Music Director of the Birmingham Contemporary Music Group (1998-2000). His orchestral work *Asyla* (1997) established his reputation, and Sir Simon Rattle later performed it in his first concert as Artistic Director of the Berlin Philharmonic Orchestra in 2002.

Thomas Adès holding his Composer of the Year Award at the Classical Brits 2010

In 2004, Adès's opera *The Tempest* (based on Shakespeare) premiered at the Royal Opera House, London, and simultaneously courted controversy and marked him out as a fully mature composer. Works he has produced since then include his Violin Concerto, *Concentric Paths* (2005), the orchestral work *Tivot* (2007) and *Totentanz* (2013). His latest opera, *The Exterminating Angel*, was premiered at the Salzburg Festival in August 2016.

Adès has a reputation for being reluctant to give interviews as a result of some unhappy experiences with the press early in his career.

He describes his working habits as 'chaotic'. He does not remember how individual pieces of music were written, and seldom listens to them afterwards, unless he has to conduct them. The hard work of bringing an idea to fruition on the page is almost forgotten when the piece is complete. 'When it's over, I can't recall the feeling while I was working on it,' he says.

Main Features of Adès's Music

Adès's music ranges through many different styles and eras, while always remaining recognisably his own. His opera *Powder Her Face* draws on popular music of the 1930s; *Asyla* on contemporary dance music; his piano work *Darknesse Visible* on the music of John Dowland, and so on. Tom Service has described this as the ability to 'make you hear things you thought you were familiar with as if they were completely new.'

This interest in renewing musical material can be found in, for example, his Piano Quintet (2000) where he re-visits the idea of **sonata form** and even begins the work in C major: 'I wanted to get a structure that would unfold at a sort of **Classical** rate but also contain complex metrical procedures,' he has said.

These metrical procedures use certain unusual time signatures that are often a feature of his music, such as $\frac{2}{6}$ or $\frac{4}{6}$ or $\frac{5}{6}$ and $\frac{2}{7}$, particularly in his Piano Quintet which has one of the most elaborate metrical structures in all his music.

Harmony is also a key feature of his music, and the ability to place traditional harmonies in an unfamiliar context.

Adès has now written three operas including *Powder Her Face* (1995), *The Tempest* (2004) and *The Exterminating Angel* (2016).

Find out more about Adès at www.thomasades.com, and from the Guardian's guide at https://www.theguardian.com/music/tomserviceblog/2012/oct/01/thomas-ades-contemporary-music-guide

SET WORK:

Thomas Adès (b.1971): 'Ecstasio', third movement from *Asyla* (1997)

Ecstasio is the third **movement** of *Asyla*. Like the third movement of many Classical or **Romantic** symphonies, it is based on dance music: in this case the dance music of the 1990s. Adès has referred to it as coming from both House music and Techno.

The notes below summarise some key points from the information provided in Eduqas's own extensive notes, which are available at http://resources.eduqas.co.uk/Pages/ResourceSingle.aspx?rlid=748
You will need to look at a score and the online analysis as well as the following.

Form: *Ecstasio* falls into three main sections. The first three are drawn from dance music: In Section A (bars 25-115), after the introduction, a single melodic motif is built up and repeated, mainly in 2 bar phrases, culminating in a large climactic section. Section B (bars 116-148) pulls back from this and builds up the tension again through the repetition of a simple 8 bar harmonic pattern. Section C and the coda (bars 149-221) form the work's climax: a repeated 1-bar phrase, which eventually disintegrates, the music becoming increasingly dense and quite different to what has gone before.

Melody: *Ecstasio* is driven forward by melody – a repeated 2-bar phrase for much of Section 1, a long rising 8 bar phrase repeated three times throughout Section B and an obsessively repeated 1 bar phrase throughout Section C. There is often very little in the way of **harmony**, with these melodic phrases supported by pedal notes.

Harmony and tonality: Most of the harmony in *Ecstasio* uses common chords or elements of them, but its harmony is never functional in a traditional way. It moves slowly, often with a harmonic **rhythm** of one chord to a bar, and sections build up over slow moving harmonies or groups of notes that can remain in play for very long periods. This lack of harmonic movement in the piece reflects the static harmony in dance music which is usually driven forward by rhythm. In terms of tonal centres, different sections have a very strong pull towards certain **pitches**.

The key centres might be shown thus:

Introduction	Section A1	Section A2	Section B	Section C	Coda
C♯ minor	F♯ minor – E♭	D major	D minor	D major	Moving to B minor

Rhythm: The opening tempo for *Ecstasio* is 130 bpm, which is the standard tempo for most dance music (the movement opens *alla breve* at 65 bpm, which is half of 130. It changes to 130bpm at bar 9). In the final bar of each 8-bar section there is frequently a change of time signature (these vary, but typically the change might be $\frac{3}{8}$ + $\frac{2}{4}$, $\frac{5}{8}$ + $\frac{2}{6}$ or $\frac{3}{4}$). Adès inserts these in order to slightly destabilise the regularity of the beat. In *Ecstasio*, Adès writes several **polyrhythmic** passages of considerable complexity. For instance, in the long bar 111 there are 8 bars of simple $\frac{4}{4}$ in the bass drum, against which is a different series of changing metres in the woodwind, brass and percussion that pass through $\frac{2}{4}$, $\frac{3}{8}$, $\frac{2}{6}$, $\frac{4}{4}$, $\frac{2}{4}$, $\frac{2}{6}$ and so forth.

Texture and sonority: Orchestral colour plays a large part in *Ecstasio*, creating the primal insistent world of dance music. The strings do not carry the main material and the musical line is often passed around the orchestra so that there is a constantly evolving series of sonorities. Adès uses pointillistic textures throughout, but a particularly notable passage can be found in Section A1 (bars 25-66). The two-bar repeated phrase is not given to any one instrument, but spread throughout the orchestra with multiple interlocking doublings.

Form:
Ecstasio falls into the following sections:

Bars 1-24	Introduction
25-83	Section A1

84-115	Section A2
116-148	Section B
149-184	Section C
185-221	Coda

Key Features

Introduction (Bars 1-24)

An introductory passage increasing in intensity and orchestral density.

Section A1 (Bars 25-83)

This consists of a 2 bar phrase (starting on an upbeat) for the whole orchestra, repeated throughout the whole section. It is constantly transformed by gradually adding notes and harmonies. The music is almost entirely divided into very clear groups of eight bars throughout, reflecting Adès's experience of the repetition of dance music:

> '[I've] noticed that in dance music today things are repeated 8, 16, 32, 64 times – it's very powerful indeed.'

Section A2 (Bars 84-115)

This continues the process from Section A1 and builds to the climax of the two sections. A radical transformation is made to the repeated phrase which is pared down to a new 5-note phrase, now subject to continual alteration through the use of **additive rhythm**, leading to a large **polyrhythmic** climax at bars 111-115.

Section B (Bars 116-48)

This section consists of a new series of harmonic progressions, repeated four times over a period of 32 bars, divided into four 8 bar sections in $\frac{4}{4}$ building to a crescendo.

Section C (Bars 149-84)

This is the climax of the movement and most simple in melodic and harmonic terms: a repeated one-bar phrase in D major.

Coda (Bars 185-221)

The coda moves the music towards a different sound world, building towards the music's final climactic chord. The section makes reference to Wagner's music drama *Parsifal* and the close of Act 2. This closes in B minor with a prominent C♯ **appoggiatura** in the oboe falling to the **tonic**, four bars towards the end. The final chord here appears to be a distorted collapsing together of these elements with an F♯ in the bass.

Sample questions relating to the set works by Adès and Beamish can be found on the Eduqas website. Go to www.eduqas.co.uk/qualifications/music/as-a-level/ and choose 'Digital Resources'.

Sally Beamish (b.1956)

Sally Beamish was born in London in 1956 and now lives in Scotland. She started composing music when she was four years old which her mother, who was a violinist, would play for her.

She studied at the Royal Northern College of Music, Manchester, and spent ten years as a professional viola player during which time she played with the Raphael Ensemble, the Academy of St Martin-in-the-Fields and was principal viola with the London Mozart Players. The years spent playing were very important when she eventually became a full-time composer: She has said:

Sally Beamish near her home in Scotland

'The single most valuable thing was learning how it feels to play someone else's music.'

Beamish switched from playing to composing around 1990 after having her first child: 'Playing the viola all the time I was miserable at not seeing the children enough, so the only thing to do was to compose.' The move to composing was hastened when her viola was stolen, and when she and her family moved to Scotland.

She quickly established her name in the early 1990s with the help of an Arts Council Composers' Bursary and by 1992 was receiving the equivalent of one performance a week and nine commissions in just one year.

In 1999, Sally Beamish became Composer-in-Residence with the Swedish Chamber Orchestra and this led to a contract with the Norwegian publishers, Norsk Musikforlag (who publish the set work, *Opus California*) as well as a relationship with the Swedish-based BIS record label. In 2002, her opera *Monster* was premiered by Scottish Opera. It is based on the life of the writer Mary Shelley who wrote the novel *Frankenstein*.

As a busy professional composer with a family, Beamish's working habits are disciplined and organised. For many years she worked in a potting shed at the bottom of the garden at her home in Sterlingshire, inspired by the rolling Scottish landscape, before moving to Glasgow in 2014.

Main Features of Beamish's Music

Much of Sally Beamish's music is informed by her practical experience as a professional viola player for many years before she took up composition in earnest.

A further important influence on her music was moving to Scotland in the 1990s which has become increasingly reflected in her style and has recently led to a collaboration between her, the Scottish Ensemble and traditional folk musicians.

Her melodic style also contains certain jazz inflections and **rhythms** which cross with Celtic influences.

The genre of the Concerto is an important part of Sally Beamish's output. She has composed more than ten so far, including three for her instrument, the viola.

Drama and musical theatre play a significant role in her music, including her one full length opera, *Monster* (2002), based on Mary Shelley's Frankenstein.

Find out more about Beamish at www.sallybeamish.com

SET WORK:

> **Sally Beamish (b.1956): String Quartet No. 2 (*Opus California*), Movements 1 ('Boardwalk') and 4 ('Natural Bridges') (2000)**

The notes below summarise some key points from the information provided in Eduqas's own extensive notes, which are available at
http://resources.eduqas.co.uk/Pages/ResourceSingle.aspx?rIid=748
You will need to look at a score and the online analysis as well as the following.

Form: The four **movements** of Sally Beamish's *Opus California* are based on four short extracts from the first movement **exposition** of Beethoven's String Quartet in C minor, Op.18, No.4 (one extract per movement). The link with California came about because the composer had recently visited the Cabrillo Festival in Santa Cruz.

'This quartet represents an 'opening-up' of my own language,' she has said, 'while offering a light-hearted angle both on the Beethoven and on the American experience.'

The original fragments of Beethoven are still recognisable to anyone who hears the two pieces side by side, but in Sally Beamish's hands the raw harmonies are transformed into a completely different emotional world: in the case of *Boardwalk*, the potentially tragic overtones of Beethoven now feel cool and streetwise, with rhythmic **syncopations** which suggest jazz or even popular music.

Harmony and **tonality:** Much of the harmonic movement in the first movement of *Opus California* stays very close to the opening section of movement 1 of the Beethoven Quartet, but its use of tonality and key centres is quite different. The harmony often suggests certain keys, but there is no traditional sense of **modulation** between them once the initial section is left: instead there is usually a sudden shift between keys at the beginning of a new section, or no settled sense of key at all.

In 'Natural Bridges', the use of both harmony and **melody** (through the use of intervals) is quite different to that in 'Boardwalk'. The use of intervals is very important melodically in this movement. Besides the **tritone**, the other important interval used is the 3rd (both major and minor). This and the tritone often make up the harmony in this movement.

Texture and sonority: Much of the first **movement** of *Opus California* uses the string quartet as Beethoven might have found it. The movement is almost entirely made up of two different elements: harmonic and melodic, often separated from one another (for instance, see bars 1-7 where the harmonic sections are quite distinct from the melodic ones). The melodic sections, at least initially, are often made up of smaller fragments of notes, passed between the instruments, only occasionally blossoming into fully-formed longer melodies (see bars 32-36 in violin 1 or bars 53-56 in the cello). These fragments are also strongly characterised by large expressive upward leaps, often using 7ths.

'Natural Bridges' is different in its approach to **texture** and **sonority**. There are three or four distinct textures that make up its character including pedal notes, triplet figures and the use of a **cadenza**.

Tempo, metre and rhythm:

The tempo for 'Boardwalk' is crotchet = c.120, which is slower than Beethoven's original marking of minim = 84. The whole movement is in $\frac{4}{4}$ and makes much of the various **syncopations** that can be felt within this metre including unequal divisions of the bar such as 3+3+2 or the use of unequal beats across the barline in 13-14: 3+2+2+2+3+2+2.

The tempo for 'Natural Bridges' is crotchet = 168, which is the same speed as Beethoven's original marking of minim = 84 (though not, of course, *Alla breve*). The syncopations that were so important in the first movement are scarcely present in 'Natural Bridges'. Instead this has a sharply defined crotchet pulse running through most of its sections allied to triplet movement which varies from regular to irregular.

Key Features

Structure of Movement 1: Boardwalk

'Boardwalk' falls into the following sections:

Bars 1-29	Section A
30-47	Section B (**Development**)
47-68	Reprise of Section A

Section A (Bars 1-29)

This whole movement is based on bars 1-4 of the first movement of Beethoven's C minor Quartet, Op.18, No.4

Bars 1-7 are based on bars 1-2 of the Beethoven and the four chords appear in exactly the same voicing as found in the original, over a pedal note of C.

The melodic line (starting at bar 3) is entirely derived from the final note of the decorative turn and final three notes of the first violin part in bar 1,

Beethoven bars 1-2

Beamish bar 5

subjected to octave displacement (B-C-E♭-D):

Beamish bars 6-7

Bars 8-15 are built from bars 3 and 4 of the Beethoven and are transformed in a similar manner. The remainder of the section is a varied repeat and elaboration of the material.

Section B (Bars 30-46)

This section is a brief **development**. It is very unstable in harmonic terms with no one key ever established. All the **harmony** is made up of altered seventh chords of differing varieties that are never resolved or settle in one key.

With the exception of the C minor **melody** in the first violin (bars 32-36); the emphasis is entirely on harmony.

Section A (Bars 46-68)

This is a **recapitulation** of the music of bars 1-29, beginning initially in G minor (the **dominant**) but returning to the home key at the close.

Structure of Movement 4: 'Natural Bridges'

This movement it is taken, the composer tells us, from 'the second bridge passage/coda' (approximately bars 70-77) of the Beethoven quartet.

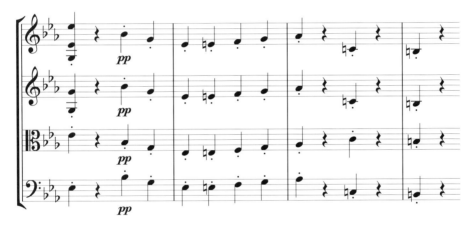

'Natural Bridges' falls into the following sections:

Bars 1-16	Section 1a
16-24	Section 2a
25-32	Section 1b
32-42	Section 2b
43-50	Cadenza
50-59	Development

60-74	Section 1c
74-80	Section 2c
81-93	Coda

Section 1a (Bars 1-15)

The movement opens with a repeating triplet idea in the viola over a **rhythmic** crotchet pedal of C in the cello. The initial viola rising triplet figure – A-B♭-E♭ – outlines the interval of a **tritone** – an interval that dominates this movement.

It is drawn from the opening notes of the Beethoven passage which also features the main intervals here: a semitone and 4th, making up a tritone.

Section 2a (Bars 16-24)

A repeated triplet figure in the three lower strings make up a closely-voiced 3-note chord (C-E♭-E) consisting of a major 3rd enclosing a semitone (the same 3-note figure heard in violin 1 at bar 9). This moves through 6 **transpositions** during this passage, all made up of transpositions of the same three notes (three of these in inversion).

Section 1b (Bars 25-31)

A varied repeat of bars 1-3 of Section 1a, now over a moving crotchet pedal (bars 25-28) and bars 9-11 (bars 29-31).

Section 2b (Bars 32-42)

A varied repeat of bars 16-24.

Cadenza & Development (Bars 43-59)

This passage combines and develops two ideas: the triplet figure outlining a tritone (heard at the outset) and a new rising figure (bars 50-51) related to the melodic top line of bars 32-40.

Section 1c (bars 60-74)

This section recapitulates Section 1a and makes a direct reference to the Beethoven.

Section 2c (bars 60-74)

A varied repeat of bars 16-24.

Coda (bars 81-93)

A return to the Section 1 triplet, extended and rising in a full unison along with an exact repeat of the Beethoven quotation as heard in bars 65-71. The movement ends with a final reference to opening of movement 1, closing on a unison C.

Practice Questions

Area of Study F: Into the Twenty-First Century

In the exam, you will be given **two** questions for this part of the paper, divided into between 5 and 7 parts (a-e or perhaps a-g), and each worth **15 marks**. The first question will be on one of your set works: *Ecstasio* or String Quartet No.2. The second question will be on an unprepared work. Here we have given you example questions for part 2, based on the non-set works already explored in this book, **but normally you would not be told what the work is that you are listening to**. Sample assessment papers which cover the set works are also available to download from the Eduqas website, and you should practise answering these as much as possible.

Sofia Gubaidulina: *Offertorium*

1. You will hear an extract from *Offertorium*. The extract covers approximately the first five minutes of the piece.

In an exam, the extract would be played **3 times** with a **1 minute pause** between each playing and a **7 minute silence** after the final playing for you to complete your answers.   **[15]**

You now have 30 seconds to read the questions below.

(a)   Identify the **type** of composition here (e.g. string quartet, orchestral work, concerto-type work).   [1]

    ....

(b)   Describe three elements of the **texture** in the opening section.   [3]

    ....

    ....

    ....

(c)   Tick the boxes below to indicate which **two** statements are correct.   [2]

The soloist enters immediately	
The soloist enters after the theme is passed around the orchestra	
The violin's melodic writing concentrates on outlining certain intervals	
The violin's melodic writing consists of long sustained melodies	

(d)   Describe the main characteristics of the composer's treatment of **texture** in the orchestra. How are groups of instruments treated?   [2]

    ....

    ....

(e)   Describe the orchestral texture prior to the entry of the violin.   [1]

....

(f)   Describe the use of pitches in the violin part for the first twenty seconds
        or so after its entry; where does it take the interval from?   [2]

....

....

(g)   Which **two** composers are referenced at the opening of the work and how? [4]

....

....

....

Hans Werner Henze: Symphony No.7

2. You will hear the first movement from Symphony No.7. The extract covers approximately
    the first eight minutes of the piece.

    In an exam, the extract would be played **3 times** with a **1 minute pause** between each
    playing and a **7 minute silence** after the final playing for you to complete your answers.   **[15]**

    You now have 30 seconds to read the questions below.

(a)   Tick **at least two** boxes below that describe the general **style** of the music.   [4]

Rhythmic	
Dissonant	
Ostinato	
Lyrical	
Transparent	
Dance-like	

(b)   Describe two elements of the **texture** in the opening section.   [2]

....

....

(c)   What two kinds of form does the composer mention in connection
        with this movement?   [2]

....

....

(d)   Tick one box which indicates the way in which this music was composed.   [1]

Diatonic	
Serial	
Aleatoric	

(e)   How would you describe the harmony in this movement?
      What kinds of intervals can you mainly identify?   [3]

....

....

(f)   Describe the texture of the opening ten seconds or so of the symphony.   [3]

....

....

Witold Lutosławski: *Chain 2*

3. You will hear an extract from *Chain 2*. The extract covers approximately the first
four minutes of the piece.

In an exam, the extract would be played **3 times** with a **1 minute pause** between each
playing and a **7 minute silence** after the final playing for you to complete your answers.   **[15]**

You now have 30 seconds to read the questions below.

(a)   Identify the **type** of composition here (e.g. string quartet, orchestral
      work, concerto-type work).   [1]

....

(b)   Describe three elements of the **texture** in the opening section.   [3]

....

....

(c)   Tick the boxes below to indicate which **two** statements are correct.   [2]

Most of the material is given to the violin	
Most of the material is given to the orchestra	
The orchestral writing is fragmented, nervous and unsettled	
The orchestral writing is sustained and melodic	

(d)   Describe the main characteristics of the composer's treatment of
      melody in the violin part. Is it consistent throughout or varied?   [3]

....

....

(e)   An important aspect of Lutosławski's style is '**controlled aleatoricism**'.
      Explain the meaning of the word aleatoric with examples of how it is used
      in his music.   [2]

....

(f)   Describe the elements you can hear and how they develop in the solo violin line
      for the first in the first 25-30' of Chain 2. What **intervals** predominate?   [2]

....

(g) What orchestral instruments enter around 15' into *Chain 2*? Describe so far as you can the texture they play. [2]

....

....

Kaija Saariaho: *Du cristal ...à fume*

4. You will hear the first movement from *Du cristal ...à fume*. The extract covers approximately the first seven minutes of the piece.

   In an exam, the extract would be played **3 times** with a **1 minute pause** between each playing and a **7 minute silence** after the final playing for you to complete your answers. **[15]**

   You now have 30 seconds to read the questions below.

   (a) Identify the **type** of composition **in the extract you have heard** (e.g. string quartet, orchestral work, concerto-type work). [1]

   ....

   (b) Describe three elements of the **texture** and **rhythm** in the extract. [3]

   ....

   ....

   ....

   (c) Tick two boxes that indicate the **harmonic** style of the piece. [2]

Serial	
Bi-tonal	
Static	
Spectral	

   (d) Describe how the **harmony** works during the extract. [3]

   ....

   ....

   ....

   (e) How does the title *Du cristal ...à fume* describe the form of the work overall? [2]

   ....

   ....

   (f) Listen to the first two minutes or so of the opening of *Du cristal...* How is a sense of movement achieved while a single chord is being sustained? [4]

   ....

   ....

   ....

Mark Anthony Turnage: *Three Screaming Popes*

5. You will hear the first movement from *Three Screaming Popes*. The extract covers approximately the first four minutes of the piece.

In an exam, the extract would be played **3 times** with a **1 minute pause** between each playing and a **7 minute silence** after the final playing for you to complete your answers. **[15]**

You now have 30 seconds to read the questions below.

(a) Describe two elements of the **melody** in the extract. [2]

....

....

(b) Identify the **type** of composition here (e.g. ballet, orchestral work, concerto-type work). [1]

....

(c) Tick the boxes below to indicate which statements concerning **rhythm** and **metre** are correct. [3]

The work is in $\frac{4}{4}$ throughout	
The music makes extensive use of ostinato	
There are frequent changes of metre	
The music is based on dance rhythms	
The music uses aleatoric rhythms	

(d) Give three examples of how the **harmony** works during the extract. [3]

1. ....

2. ....

3. ....

(e) Which **two** painters were involved in the inspiration for this work? [1]

....

(f) Listen to the opening chord of *Three Screaming Popes* and describe what features of it you can hear. [2]

....

....

(g) In the unison melody immediately after the opening chord, what instruments can you identify playing? [3]

....

....

....

Judith Weir: *Scotch Minstrelsy*

6. You will hear the whole of *Scotch Minstrelsy*. It is approximately 12 minutes long.

In an exam, you would not be given so long an extract to listen to, but the extract would be played **3 times** with a **1 minute pause** between each playing and a **7 minute silence** after the final playing for you to complete your answers. **[15]**

You now have 30 seconds to read the questions below.

(a)   Describe three types of piano **texture** used in the work.   [3]

....

....

....

(b)   Identify the **type** of composition here (e.g. opera, song cycle, cantata, choral work).   [1]

....

(c)   Tick the boxes below to indicate which types of **harmony** are used.   [3]

Chord clusters	
Spectral harmony	
Bi-tonal chords	
Microtonal harmony	
Diatonic harmony	

(d)   Describe how **melody** is used in this work.   [2]

....

....

(e)   Tick the boxes below that accord with the **rhythmic** style of the work.   [4]

Irrational groupings (quintuplets, sextuplets etc)	
Unison rhythm	
Additive rhythm	
Scotch snaps	
No bar lines	

(f)   Comment on the rhythm, texture and harmony of the piano part in the fourth song (*The Gypsy Laddie*).   [2]

....

....

Answers

Area of Study A

The Western Classical Tradition

AS level

1. (a) G major

(b) D major

(c) (1) Violins (2) Flutes

(d) Disjunct

(e) (i) Perfect (ii) Modulation

(f)

The dynamic at the start of the piece is *pianissimo*	False
The tempo of the extract is *Andante*	False
The ornament used in bar 9 is an acciaccatura.	True

(g) Dominant 7th

(h) (i) Minor 9th/compound minor 2nd (ii) Major 6th

2. (a) D major

(b) (i) A major (ii) Perfect

(c) and (d)

(e) 3^2; 9^2; 15^2

(f) 16^1

3.

Extract 1 (1774/5; Stamitz, Symphony in E♭)	Extract 2 (1822; Schubert 'Unfinished')
Dynamics: Clear graduation in dynamics; starts forte, but includes variation from ***pp*** – ***ff*** Also use of crescendo (e.g. sustained note in horns)	**Dynamics:** Wider dynamic range, more frequent gradation of volume; starts ***pp*** and builds; use of ***sfz***/crescendo/descrescendo
Orchestration/use of instruments: Begins tutti though small orchestra; oboes, horn, strings and continuo (though not terribly clear in the recording, it appears in the score and is implicit due to the date); double bass supporting harmonies; strings arco throughout; much string figuration; horns used for sustained notes/fanfare type ideas (due to limitations at the time); oboes melodic ideas (in 3rds) and offer contrast of colouring and 'dialogue' with horns towards end of the extract.	**Orchestration/use of instruments:** Larger orchestra; flutes, oboes, clarinets, bassoons, horns, trumpets, trombones, timpani (used sparingly in extract); 5 part strings, and begins with sinister phrase in cello and bass (lower strings); no continuo part; pizzicato evident in violas and lower strings (at start of string opening and later); in the first thematic idea, strings mainly used figuratively and thematic material initially in woodwind; cellos then violins present the second thematic idea, against syncopated accompaniment in clarinets, bassoons (and horns).
Tonality/Harmony: Major key; diatonic harmonies; many root position chords; use of dominant pedal (horns); includes modulation to the dominant key (B♭ major); chromatic rising scale evident in mid-section (strings); also use of diminished chord.	**Harmony:** Minor key to start; diatonic harmonies, but is more chromatic in the first passage; major key (relative-submediant) in second passage, again with some chromatic 'colour' to be found (Right at the end of the extract, listen out for harmonic changes/exploration).
Any other stylistic differences: $\frac{4}{4}$ or common time; texture is mainly homophonic though with occasional imitation of motifs; some unison ideas heard; devices such as use of sequence and 'echoing phrases' providing balance of ideas.	**Any other stylistic differences:** $\frac{3}{4}$ time; sonata form (two opening themes clearly differentiated); woodwind theme (played in unison) is very lyrical for a first subject; syncopated accompaniment for the second theme/melody dominated homophony; two thematic ideas very close together (i.e. short transition)

HAYDN's 'London' Symphony

4. (a) Tripartite structure

(b) Homophonic

(c) Clarinets

(d) Answers might include:

- Longer return of phrase 'a'
- Addition of solo bassoon
- Different harmonies

(e) 1795

(f) The middle section

(g) Answer might include:

- Starts in G minor
- Diminished chords in bars 40-41
- Higher dominant dischords and diminished chords in bars 43-44
- Followed by tutti section in D minor
- B♭ major reached in bar 46
- Stops on V7 chord in bar 55... and so on

(h) Answer might include:

- Return of 'a' is decorated with semiquaver sextuplets along with additional flute solo
- Some re-arrangement of parts
- Accompanying arpeggios in violin 2
- Further harmonic exploration (C minor, D♭ major)

MENDELSSOHN's 'Italian' Symphony

(a) An extended binary structure

(b) Monophonic

(c) (1) Transitory material (2) Coda

(d) 1833

(e) D minor

(f) Answer might include:

- Move away from home key to E major
- D major in bar 49 (with a variety of perfect cadences)
- Tonicisation of B minor/A major (bar 51)
- In 52, the harmonic progression is $V\frac{6}{4}$ – ii – $V\flat\frac{9}{7}$ – ready for return to D major in bar 53
- Diminished 7th chords in the final bar of the passage

(g) (i) Section A1

(ii) Answers should include:

- Now heard $\boldsymbol{ff}$
- Revolves around the note E
- In bars 59-61 key is now A minor
- Same scoring, and syncopation still evident
- Slight changes to the flute countermelody

A Level

1. (a) Pitch – bar 4¹ should be A above the stave; Rhythm – bar 15 should be quaver, crotchet, quaver.

(b) Dominant minor 9th

(c)

HAYDN's 'London' Symphony

2. (a)

Bars	Key	Cadence
3³ – 4	D major	Plagal cadence
19³ – 20	B minor	Perfect cadence

(b)

Minuet		Trio		Minuet (1-52 – no repeats)	
Section A (1-8)	**Section B** (+A) (17-52)	**Section A** (53-64)	**Section B** (+A) (65- 94)	**Section A**	**Section B** (+A)
(repeated)	(repeated)	(repeated)	(repeated)	Played without repeats	

(c) Answer might include:

- Violin 1 and solo oboe begin with an interval of a minor 3rd idea which is repeated, heard legato in the first violins, at first doubled in unison by the first oboe. After the previous D major at the end of the minuet, this unaccompanied motif (short example of a monophonic texture) feels as if the mode has simply changed from D major to D minor; in bar 55, the string crotchet chords (played pizzicato) bring a change of texture to homophonic, and of tonality to B♭ major (i.e. the flattened submediant; being a modulation to a key effectively a 3rd away from the tonic, it may be described as a tertiary modulation)

- The phrase-lengths of the melody are obscured by the continuous run of quavers; played legato, accompanied by pizzicato strings

- Orchestration has been reduced to one flute, bassoon and strings (no clarinets, brass or timpani), so a lighter texture. The bassoon joins in with the quaver idea at the end of bar 58, after which the music moves through a series of brief tonicisations: V7 – I in B♭ major at bars 59³–60; V⁶₅ – I in G minor at bars 61³–62; and finally, an imperfect cadence onto the dominant of F major at bar 63, in which key the section ends, with a perfect cadence in bars 63⁸-4. This modulation to the dominant as expected is more traditional than the minuet.

- The section is then repeated.

MENDELSSOHN's 'Italian' Symphony

(a)

Bars	Key	Cadence
7^3-8^1	A major	Imperfect cadence
45^3-46^1	D major	(Inverted) perfect cadence

(b)

Minuet	Trio	Minuet	Coda
Section A (bars 1-76) (includes a1, a2, a3 and codetta)	**Section B** (bars 77-124) (includes b, b1, return to b)	**Section A1** (bars 125-202 (Played without repeat of section)	**Section B1** (bars 202–end)

(c) Answers may include:

- Theme b1 – begins *mf*, with trumpets and drums added to support the fanfare, heard on a unison 'B' in woodwind, echoing the figure previously played by horns at the start of the trio

- Although the previous phrase clearly finished in E major, the omission of the rest of the chord here puts a question mark over the exact tonality. While the B (dominant pedal note) is sustained for just over two bars, the entire string section answers with a fanfare of their own, in antiphonal manner – and the harmonic progression now confirms the shift to E minor i.e. V^4_2 ➤ i^6_3 in that key (bars 93^3-94^3). This figure ends (still in strings), with an imperfect cadence in bars 95 and 96

- In bar 96, the fanfare rhythm repeats bars 92^3-95, but the answering response in strings tonicises the key of A minor, ending with an imperfect cadence in A minor

- The first fanfare given by brass and timpani (bar 100^3-104^1) is answered by strings with a new, repetitive motif

- Bars 104^3- 108 is based on bars bar 100^3-104^1, though violins and violas are an octave higher and the fanfare rhythm is heard only in trumpets this time, still supported by timpani.

Area of Study B

Rock & Pop

AS level

1. (a) 1975

(b) Inverted tonic pedal

(c) Glissando-like passages/quick scalic passages

(d) Electric piano/Fender Rhodes

(e) Lead vocal is doubletracked

(f) Relevant comments on the writing for strings could include:

- Longer note values in verse 2
- Chorus more chromatic
- Glissando at the end of verse 2
- Initially based on broken chords in the chorus
- Provides a countermelody to the vocal in the chorus

[One mark per relevant feature, up to a maximum of 2]

(g)

Bb	Eb	Bb/D	Cm

(h) Homophony

(i) Relevant comments on the bassline could include:

- Emphasises root notes of chords
- Mostly on-beat emphasis, except for introduction which is more syncopated
- Chromatic fills at the ends of the phrases
- Alternation between low bass and high fills e.g. line 11
- Use of acciaccaturas e.g. before verse 2

[One mark per relevant feature up to a maximum of 2]

(j) Relevant comments on the use of drum kit could include

Introduction:	Verse 1:
■ Four to the floor kick ■ Sixteenth / semiquaver closed hi hat patterns ■ Accented open hi hats	■ Snare and floor tom used together on beats 2 and 4 ■ Kick on 1 and 3 ■ Closed hi hat on each beat

[One mark per relevant feature up to a maximum of 2]

2. (a) (i) 1966

(ii) Relevant reasons could include:

- String-heavy arrangement
- Use of instrumental layering
- Raw and passionate vocal performance
- Clarity of recording/depth of field
- 'Wall of Sound'/dense production
- Extreme Panning

[One mark for a relevant comment]

(b) Modulation up a semitone

(c) Relevant comments on the vocal performances could include:

- Initially in harmony (lines 1-3)
- Mostly in fourths
- Octaves for the final line of the chorus (line 4)
- Call and response for the bridge (lines 5-11)
- Female vocal takes the lead between lines 6 and 8
- Male vocal leads in line 9-10
- Briefly together in octaves at the end of line 11
- Generally improvisatory in bridge
- Generally in higher register for both voices

[One mark per relevant comparison up to a maximum of 2]

(d) Relevant 'unconventional' pop instruments could include:

- Pizzicato violin/strings
- Harp

- Celesta

[One mark per relevant comparison up to a maximum of 2]

(e) Relevant comments on sense of build could include:

- Drum fills playing quavers on snare drum in line (both kits)
- More spacious vocal arrangement
- String glissandi/tremolo
- Contrasting chord progression
- Use of higher vocal register e.g. line 11
- Use of higher register in string section e.g. lines 11 into 12

[One mark per relevant comparison up to a maximum of 2]

(f)

Suspended 4th	
Major 7th	✔
Diminished 7th	
Neapolitan 6th	

(g) Imperfect

(h) Relevant comments on the style could include:

- String orchestration
- Backbeat emphasis/snare and tambourine on 2 and 4
- Layered instruments e.g. drum kits
- Call and response vocals
- Lyrical melody lines
- Use of horn section
- Lyrics about love and love lost
- Dense production style/wall of sound

[One mark per relevant comparison up to a maximum of 2]

A Level

1. (a) Relevant comments on the use of harmony could include:

- Harmonic sequence
- (Starts) major
- Ends with a suspended chord

[One mark per relevant comment up to a maximum of 2]

(b)

vi	ii	V	I

(c)

Diminished 7th	
Neapolitan 6th	
Suspended 4th	✔
Major 7th	

(d) Relevant comments on the use of lead/backing vocals could include:

Verse:

- Lead vocals **only** for line 1
- Both in unison for 'I heard her say' in line 2
- Backing vocals are a 3rd below for end of line 2 'from each other'
- Lines 3 and 4 are a repeat of this structure, with all of line 4 harmonised and an extra backing vocal layer on 'from each other'

Chorus:

- Some backing vocals are in unison with the lead vocal (line 8, 10, 11)
- (mostly) a 3rd below (line 9)
- Lead vocal has a short riff at the end of the chorus (line 11)
- Doubletracking (same singer)

[One mark per relevant comparison up to a maximum of 3]

(e) Relevant comments on texture and instrumentation could include:

Introduction:

- Sustained string notes
- Synth bass plays root notes
- Piano plays chords along with melody
- Repeated piano block chords (before verse)
- Staccato string broken chords (before verse)

Pre Chorus:

- Strings play a chord at the beginning of the pre chorus
- Electric Piano is added
- Vocals added

- Backing vocal parts sing in harmony/unison

[One mark per relevant comparison up to a maximum of 2]

2. (a) Relevant comments on the opening passage could include:

- Improvisatory in character
- Tremolo strummed guitar
- Descending sequence
- Two lead guitars in octaves
- Modal
- Chromatic descent at the end

[One mark per relevant point up to a maximum of 3]

(b) Relevant comments on the texture could include:

- Generally melody-dominated homophony
- Sense of heterophony with guitar playing simpler version of vocal melody during lines 1 and 2

[One mark per relevant point up to a maximum of 2]

(c)

I	vi	IV	I

(d) Relevant comments on the music's stylistic origins could include:

- Improvisatory character (e.g. opening guitar passage)
- Organised as verse/refrain
- Lyrical themes associated with Ireland
- Electric guitar introduction imitates uilleann pipes
- Modality

[One mark per relevant point up to a maximum of 2]

(e) Answers must compare the stylistic features of the second version with the first musical extract and could contain comments such as:

Similarities in both excerpts:

- Similar structure (verse/refrain)
- Similar lyrics with slight differences/ developments

- Chord progression is the same

In extract 1:

- Extended improvisatory introduction
- Instrumentation includes drum kit and bass guitar
- Introduction on lead guitar is not used in extract 2
- Half-time feel when compared to extract 2
- Some close harmony in refrain (3rds and unison)
- Introduction guitar phrase acts as link between refrains and verses
- Predominantly straight rhythms

In extract 2:

- Shorter introduction
- Introduction features the fiddle
- General sense of heterophony around verse melody
- Tin whistle improvisation around vocal melody
- Accompaniment includes banjo, mandolin and acoustic guitar
- Vocal is delivered in call and response style with group singing refrain
- Rhythms are generally swung

[This indicative content is not exhaustive and all valid alternatives should be considered]

Musical Theatre

Test yourself answers

Here are the answers to the test yourself questions you have found as you worked through the musical theatre chapter:

Richard Rodgers

(1) Starts in a minor key, then moves to the tonic major

(2) AABA (32 bar song form)

Leonard Bernstein

(1) Triplet rhythms, flattened sevenths, extended chords (7ths and 9ths), syncopation, (glissandi on strings, swing rhythm)

(2) Octave

Stephen Sondheim

(1) It starts with one solo voice, (monophonic), then two other voices enter **canonically** creating a **contrapuntal** style. The three voices sing **homophonically** (in harmony); then follows a unison passage on 'won't you walk me through your pretty garden', there is three-part harmony on 'pretty please', then more unison singing, with one voice singing an octave lower. The harmony on the last note includes the third of the chord.

(2) Syllabic writing, lines 1 and 2 are the same, lines 3 and 4 are the same. Each line begins with a dotted rhythm. Each line starts on the tonic and ends on the dominant degrees of the scale. Lines 3 and 4 begin the same as the start of lines 1 and 2 but an octave higher. There is largely stepwise movement in the melody.

Andrew Lloyd Webber

(1) $\frac{7}{8}$ or $\frac{7}{4}$

(2) Moves between a minor key and the relative major

Claude-Michel Schönberg

(1) **Tremolando** strings, clarinet melody, 4 bar introduction, French horn, woodwind (flute and oboe) keyboard/harp arpeggiated chord before vocals start.

(2) Syllabic, **melisma** on two note 'can', alto voice, low register, melody moves by step, some repeated notes and ascending and descending intervals of a 3rd.

Stephen Schwartz

(1) The time signatures are irregular, or change every bar:

$\frac{6}{4}$ (or $\frac{3}{2}$) + $\frac{4}{4}$ + $\frac{3}{4}$ + $\frac{4}{4}$ + $\frac{6}{4}$ (or $\frac{3}{2}$) + $\frac{4}{4}$ + $\frac{3}{4}$ + $\frac{7}{8}$

(2) 3rds/6ths

AS Level

1. (a) Tenor

(b) (i) $\frac{4}{4}$ (ii) $\frac{12}{8}$

(c)

The bass line is chromatic	
The bass line moves by step	
The bass line uses a tonic pedal	✔
The bass line has triadic movement	

(d) Answers might include:
- Syllabic
- Parlando style/speak-singing
- Recitative style
- Monotone/based on one note
- Centred on tonic note
- Uses same note as bassline
- Note changes on the word 'time' up a minor third

[1 mark per relevant comment to a maximum of 3.]

(e) Answers might include:
- Starts in minor (Bb minor)
- Line 3 tonic major (Db major)
- Line 4 modulation up a semitone and to the minor (D minor)
- Line 9 'new' tonic major (D major)

[1 mark per relevant comment with line number to a maximum of 3.]

(f) Answers might include:
- Line 1: Lower brass (trombones) and lower strings play semibreve notes (one note per bar). Timpani adds movement at the end of each bar, all on tonic note. Horns and lower strings

play a descending 4 note idea (one per bar) gong added at the end of the line.

- Line 2: woodwind added, crescendo on the word 'time'

- Line 3: cymbal roll, strings add quaver movement

- Line 4: **_ff_** chords at cadence point from brass – before line 5, a 4 bar instrumental introduction (horns melody with trombones an octave lower, string tremolando and timpani rolls)

- Line 5: violins play rhythmic pattern and double vocal melody

- Line 6: as line 5 with brass quavers at end/fanfare style brass

- Line 7: as above

- Line 8: cymbal roll on 'look', timpani plays at cadence into line 9

- Line 9: violins constant quavers (12 per bar) flute on 2nd and 3rd beats, drum without snare adds triplet crotchet rhythm on 3rd and 4th beat

- Line 10: 5 note descending chromatic line trombone and lower strings with timpani

- Line 11: chromatic as before but horns added

- Line 13: horns add fanfare idea after 'town'

- Line 14: woodwind now playing constant quavers (12 per bar)

- Line 15: horns playing long sustained notes (dotted minims) on 1st and 3rd beats, timpani dominant to tonic on 'they' and 'all'

- Line 17: on 'name' trumpets now play vocal melody from line 5 previously heard in violins.

[1 mark per relevant comment with line number to a maximum of 4.]

(g) Claude Michel Schönberg

2. (a) Soprano

(b) $\frac{4}{4}$

(c)

Perfect cadence in a minor key	
Plagal cadence in a minor key	
Perfect cadence in a major key	✔
Plagal cadence in a minor key	

(d) Answers might include:

- Syllabic setting all the way through

- Wide range for voice (line 1 & 2, A below middle C, compared to top G in line 8 on the word 'strength', or any other similar example showing wide range)

- Use of repetition between line 1 and line 2

- Line 3: ascending triplet figure moving by step with answering phrase using same rhythm in a descending more triadic figure

- Use of long sustained notes (line 4 on 'die' and on 'try' in line 8)

- Repeated note idea at start of line 5, 6 and line 11

- Triadic writing (line 5)

- Triplet rhythms line 7 and 8

- Crescendo to forte (or similar) dynamics coupled with highest range lines 7-10

[1 mark per relevant comment to a maximum of 3.]

(e) Answers might include:

- Line 1: minor key (G minor) – tonic minor

- Musical interlude (or line 3): modulation to major (G major) – tonic major

- Line 5: modulation to B♭ major (original key's relative major)

[1 mark per relevant comment with location included, to a maximum of 3.]

(f) Answers might include:

- Line 1: flute and oboe melodic ideas, sustained strings but pizzicato from lower string (cello or keyboard harp sound)

- Line 2: sustained warm string sound, synthesiser chord at end of line
- Four bar musical interlude: sustained strings with keyboard playing 'music box' type sound on the melody
- Line 3: strings double vocal line legato
- Line 4: 3 note ascending idea from French horns, trombone added
- Line 5: brass and strings (trombone prominent) descending 5 note motif on horns while vocalist holds note
- Line 6: strings and horns
- Line 7: cymbal roll at start of line brass prominent
- Line 8: timpani playing repeated notes on the dominant
- Line 9: timpani plays dominant to tonic notes strings and brass
- Line 11: strings play softly, horn plays on 'good-bye' and keyboard (harp) flourish to end.

[1 mark per relevant comment with location to a maximum of 4.]

(g) (i) Andrew Lloyd Webber

(ii) 1985 (accept 1970-2000)

A Level

1. (a) (i) $\frac{3}{4}$ (ii) $\frac{6}{8}$

(b) French horn

(c)

At line 17 there is a tonic pedal for 12 bars	
At line 17 there is a dominant pedal for 12 bars	✔
At line 17 there is a sub-dominant pedal for 12 bars	
There is a perfect cadence between lines 8 and 9	✔
There is a plagal cadence between lines 8 and 9	
There is an imperfect cadence between lines 8 and 9	

(d) Comments might include:

- Lines 1-4 A♭ major vocal line but harmonised by E♭ and B♭ bass notes, suggesting a mixolydian mode on E♭ (examiner would accept major or modal)
- Lines 5-8 F major/change of key to a major key a 3rd below
- Line 8 into 9 a perfect cadence into G major (modulation to a new major key)
- Line 15 modulation up a semitone to A♭ major
- Line 17 a dominant pedal and a perfect cadence into line 18

(e) Answers might include:

- Syllabic writing throughout
- Lines 1-4, solo tenor voice uses a wide range
- Line 5, voices sing different parts overlapping (contrapuntal)
- Line 8, singing in harmonies
- Line 9-16, unison singing
- Line 17 starts in unison, extra lines added
- Line 18, harmonised chord (six part)

2. (a) (i) $\frac{7}{4}$ (ii) $\frac{3}{4}$

(b) Soprano and Tenor

(c)

Augmentation	
Ostinato	
Riff	
Sequence	✔
Stretto imitation	✔

(d) Answers might include:

- Tonic and dominant harmonies
- Dominant pedal used throughout lines 17-19 apart from first and last bars (Line 17 'Oh happy we' and line 19 'how we agree')
- Perfect cadence line 19 on 'a-gree'

(e) Answers might include:

- AABAC structure, all sections major except 'B' section which is in relative minor

- AABA or 32 song bar form (1 mark)
- C section at end 'coda' or similar (1 mark)
- A = major, B = minor (relative) C = tonic major again (1 mark)

(f) Answers will present any correct and appropriate musical and stylistic features of extract 2, including observation of any possible comparison with extract 1.

Both extracts:

- Tenor and Soprano soloists
- Both use harmony between voices (extract 1 only at the end)
- Major tonality is most common
- Diatonic harmonies
- Contrapuntal movement at end
- Both singers finish on a unison tonic note
- Both extracts have short simple melodic phrases based on four bars
- $\frac{3}{4}$ time signature used in both extracts
- Vocals end with a perfect cadence

Differences in extract 2:

- $\frac{3}{4}$ time signature only, no changes
- Higher key (A♭ major, extract 1 is G major)
- Tempo much slower
- Extract starts with both singers in unison
- Repeated note idea in the melody in lines 1, 2 and 3
- First three lines based on a simple melodic idea created around three and/or four pitches
- Vocal range (tessitura) is higher
- Harmonies between voices 3rds and 6ths from line 3
- Tenor has staggered entry on 'now we start'
- Tenor has melodic interest in line 5, soprano has upward scale from sub-dominant to tonic
- Range of dynamics used f to pp
- Strings accompaniment lines 1 and 2, violins sustained, cello with quaver movement

- Line 3 strings only tremolando
- Line 4 woodwind join on 'one hand' dotted minims (flute, 2 clarinets and bass clarinet) at the end of the line cello has two crotchet notes pizzicato
- Line 5 double bass joins strings and two clarinets
- Line 5 slower than previous lines
- Music 'outro' 9 bars
- Violin solo featured very high range
- Use of tonic pedal note at the end through last 8 bars/IV-V-I cadence/ V7-I chords used in instrumental below violin solo/ tritone A natural use in E♭ chord creating/augmented 4th
- Cello, bassoon, clarinet and flute all have augmented 4th figure
- Pause on the last tonic major chord/ Celeste added
- Rallentando penultimate bar

Area of Study D

Jazz

AS Level

1. (a) Dixieland

(b) Reasons might include:
   - Sound – early recording
   - Instrumentation – cornet, soprano saxophone (clarinet), trombone, banjo, piano
   - Time feel – strong two in a bar feel (cut time: ¢), rolling swing quaver banjo accompaniment
   - Improvisation – collective improvisation, call and response/ polyphony/weaving
   - Performance techniques – heavy vibrato on cornet and saxophone, trombone glissandi, saxophone (clarinet) plays elaborate arpeggiated material.

2. (a) 1940s

(b) 1. Reeds play arpeggiated material in unison (homophonic)

2. Brass pick up the theme in octaves

3. Drums play the 10 to 2 pattern on hi-hats

(c) The A section is a 12 bar blues

(d) i. Reeds – melody is made up of arpeggios in harmony

ii. Brass – syncopated stops providing harmonic content

iii. Rhythm section – drums continue 10 to 2 pattern, walking bass four in a bar, guitar comps four in a bar, piano comps but is quite faint.

3. (a) Bebop

(b) Reasons could include:

- Fast $\frac{4}{4}$ swing feel
- Angular, syncopated melody
- Lots of phrases and sub-phrases end with the two quaver bebop rhythm
- The 'head' is played in unison
- Drums heavily accent some phrases of the melody ('dropping bombs!')

(c) *I Got Rhythm*

A Level

1. a) Answers might include:

- *One O'Clock Jump* starts with rhythm section only and piano solo (improvisation)
- *In The Mood* is tightly orchestrated with minimal 'solos'
- *One O'Clock Jump* features tenor saxophone solos either side of a trombone solo trading 'twos' with the drums
- Both orchestrations have backing figures often working antiphonally, for example the brass stops (punctuations) in *In the Mood*
- The trumpets use 'Derby' mutes in *One O'Clock Jump*
- Both pieces have varying textural devices split between the instrumental families, such as legato arpeggiated melody in the reeds (saxophones), rhythmic backing figures in the trumpet section and glissandi pedal points in the trombones

- Both pieces are based on a 12 bar blues form
- Both pieces belong to the swing era
- Both pieces are examples of a big band
- *In The Mood* is designed for dancing whereas *One O'Clock Jump* is more a 'listening' piece.

2. (a) Modal

(b) (i) The double bass

- Walking bass in the A sections
- Rhythmic pedal point in the B sections

(ii) The drum kit

- Strong 10 to 2 feel on the ride cymbal
- Stick on rim of snare drum on beat 4

(c) AABBA – each section is eight bars

(d) Answers could include:

- The piece has an upbeat $\frac{4}{4}$ swing feel
- The melodic content of section A is based on a simple two bar rhythmic motif that is repeated and developed
- The melody follows a simple stepwise contour that is harmonised in parallel but within the mode
- The rhythm is crotchet beats 1 and 3 followed by the 'Charleston' rhythm
- Section B is in a different mode
- Section B has a smoother (more legato) rhythmic feel which is performed out of phase

3. (a) Five

(b) Trumpet, tenor saxophone, alto saxophone, piano, trumpet

(c) Points may include:

- Tempo – *Flamenco Sketches* is about 60bpm (ballad tempo)
- Trumpet is muted in *Flamenco Sketches* with 'harmon' mute but open in *Milestone*
- Drummer uses brushes on *Flamenco Sketches* and sticks on *Milestones*
- Improvisations are more diatonic in *Flamenco Sketches* with a greater sense of each musician exploring the sound of each mode

- In *Milestones* the solos have a sense of harmonic movement provided by sequencing (the use of patterns) even though there are no 'changes' in the chart. This is especially true in the alto saxophone solo (Cannonball Adderley)

- Shifts to the next tonal centre in *Flamenco Sketches* are anticipated by the soloist creating cadential lines.

4. (a) Cool

(b) Reasons may include:

- The sound of the saxophone is pure with little vibrato

- There are fewer accented syncopations in the lines than bebop

- Extended melodic (linear) explorations in the improvisation

- Improvised counter-melodies from other frontline instruments provide simple harmonic support

5. (a) (i) Classic blues – *St. Louis Blues*

(ii) Parker blues – *Blues for Alice*

(iii) Jazz blues – *Billie's Bounce*

(iv) Country blues – *Oh, Black Betty*

Area of Study E

Into the Twentieth Century

Set work – Poulenc

1. (a) B minor

(b) Play in (parallel, compound) 6ths

(c) Any of the following would receive marks:

- F# major (in LH)

- C major (in RH)

- Tritone/diminished 5th relationship between chords

- Based on octatonic scale

- Polychordal

- Functions as dominant 7th to B in bar 23

(d) **One** mark would be given for each of the following comparisons or any statement that makes the specified difference explicit:

- Bar 23 in first inversion/bar 35 in root position

- Bar 23 is a B minor chord/bar 35 is a B major chord

- Bar 23-4 is *p* /bar 35-6 is *fff*

- Piano part is much fuller and covers a much wider range in bars 35-6

- The oboe and bassoon alternate the melody in 23-4/oboe and bassoon play together (in octave unison) in 35-6

(e) One mark would be given for each relevant comment that is (where possible) supported by bar numbered references to the score. The following are examples of relevant content but are not an exhaustive list:

- Some sense of contrasting material at bar 23, **but**

- Some motivic links back to A section and the contrast is not that great

- The movement climaxes in the middle of this section at bar 35

- The A section material only comes back briefly at the end and in F major/minor

- The octatonic F#/C dominant in bars 21-22 makes bar 23 sound like the beginning of a new section

- Unusual tonal scheme (B♭ at beginning, B at bar 23, C at bar 45, F at bar 52)

- Relevance of this tonal scheme to semitone rise from A in first movement to D♭ in third movement

Set work – Debussy

2. (a) B minor

(b) G major 7th

(c) B octatonic/diminished (7th) scale

(d) One mark would be given for each point:

- Lots of divisi

- Variety of playing techniques including arco

- Tremolo in basses and lower cello part

- Pizzicato

- All instruments low in their register

- All marked *pp* or less

(e) Identify

Bar number in extract	Bar number from 11-28	Difference
Bar 94	11	Register/ Instrumentation /addition of G harmony
Bar 99	23	Just this two-note fragment at the end rather than whole idea/ texture much more sparse

(f) One mark would be given for each relevant comment that is (where possible) supported by bar numbered references to the score. The following are examples of relevant content but are not an exhaustive list:

- Bar 1 – B minor/octatonic
- Bar 5 – Octatonic
- Bar 11 – B minor
- Bar 14 – Pentatonic
- Bar 21 – G acoustic
- Bar 29 – B minor
- Bar 31 – C major
- Bar 33 – Whole tone
- Bar 37 – Octatonic
- Bar 43 – Octatonic
- Bar 57 – B minor
- Bar 64 – (D♯ minor) pentatonic
- Bar 80 – Octatonic

Unprepared work

3. (a) Monophonic

(b) Octave unison/octaves

(c) Any of the following:

- The next phrase starts with the same contour
- **But** the intervals are different (the first two are minor rather than major thirds)
- **But** the rhythm is slightly different

- The last section starts with a more distant echo of the same idea (major third followed by minor second)
- There is no exact repetition of this idea (or any other melodic idea)

(d) Any of the following:

- End is more tonal
- End is more consonant
- End is more triadic
- Ends on a major triad
- Harmony is more full at the end (compared to more contrapuntal texture at opening)
- Harmonic rhythm is slower at the end

(e) Expressionist

(f) Berg

(g) Marks would be given for discussion of any relevant Expressionist work. Of those covered in this study guide either Schoenberg's *Erwartung* or Berg's *Wozzeck* would be most appropriate. The following content is indicative:

- Chromatic melodic lines with some awkward intervals
- **But** the intervals in this example are not as extreme as in either *Erwartung* or *Wozzeck*
- Low level of melodic/motivic repetition
- Lack of triadic harmony (although some in *Wozzeck* as in this piece)
- Harmony is mostly atonal
- Lack of functional/cadential progressions
- Structure of melody follows expression of emotion of the words rather than formal phrase structure

Unprepared work

4. (a) Strings only

(b) (1) Octave unison at the opening

(2) **Then** chords in rhythmic unison/ homophonic/homorhythmic

(c) Marks would be given for any of the following:

- Repeated rhythmic idea

- Dotted/dotted quaver and two demisemiquavers or equivalent
- Pedal
- Mostly in octave unison (some added notes on occasion)
- Lower strings

(d) Marks would be given for any of the following:

- Starts with unison rather than octave unison
- Repetition of last two notes (of main melodic idea, becomes quite aggressive)
- Ends with a pizzicato

(e) Stravinsky

(f) Neo-classical

(g) Marks would be given for discussion of any relevant Neo-classical work. Of those covered in this study guide either Stravinsky's *Concerto for Piano and Winds* or (less so) *Pulcinella* would be most appropriate. The following content is indicative:

- Description of rhythm and shape of melody
- Use of ornaments
- Use of common practice harmony with added/wrong note modifications
- Conventional/straightforward textures
- Instrumentation

Area of Study F

Into the Twenty-First Century

Sofia Gubaidulina: *Offertorium*

1. (a) Concerto or concerto type work with solo violin

(b) Answers could include:

- Fragmented texture passed around the orchestra
- Different families within the orchestra used one at a time rather than in full tuttis

- A wide range of colours are used such as portamento, ponticello, tremolando, wind flutter-tonguing, muted brass
- String glissando

(c)

The soloist enters immediately	
The soloist enters after the theme is passed around the orchestra	✔
The violin's melodic writing concentrates on outlining certain intervals	✔
The violin's melodic writing consists of long sustained melodies	

(d) Different families within the orchestra used one at a time rather than in full tuttis

(e) Unaccompanied notes passing round the orchestra/performers play one, two or three notes at a time/the melodic line is fragmented

(f) The violin plays only a semitone which it takes over from the orchestra

(g) Bach (through the use of his theme from *The Musical Offering*) and Webern (through the quotation from his orchestration of the Fugue (*Ricercare*) from the *Musical Offering*).

Hans Werner Henze: Symphony No.7

2. (a)

Rhythmic	✔
Dissonant	✔
Ostinato	✔
Lyrical	
Transparent	
Dance-like	✔

(b) Marks would be given for the following answers:

- Dense
- Polyphonic
- Instruments grouped in twos or threes

(c) Sonata form and allemande

(d)

Diatonic	
Serial	✔
Aleatoric	

(e) The harmony is generally dissonant and harsh with a predominance of minor 2nds, major 7ths and minor 9ths

(f) Marks would be given for the following answers:

- Duo for two bassoons
- Bassoons moving in small intervals
- Two interlocking bassoon parts

Witold Lutosławski: *Chain 2*

3. (a) Concerto or concerto type work with solo violin

(b) Elements could include:

- Fragmented with occasional bursts of activity
- Extensive use of string glissandi
- Rhythmically repeated notes and/or sustained notes in the strings
- Irregular chattering notes in the woodwind

(c)

Most of the material is given to the violin	✔
Most of the material is given to the orchestra	
The orchestral writing is fragmented, nervous and unsettled	✔
The orchestral writing is sustained and melodic	

(d) It is varied. Answers might also include:

- Short melodic motifs with rests, moving by step in semitones
- Sustained, broader melodies with wider intervals (4ths, 5th, 7ths)
- Fast-moving virtuosic passages for the solo violin

(e) The word aleatoric applies to music in which some element of it is left

to chance or to the performers to determine. In the heard extract the solo violin plays almost continuously with entry points for the other instruments indicated at key moments in the soloists' part by large arrows at the top of the score.

(f) A tremolando/trill is followed by a series of rapid 2-note figures (in 4ths); a short figure is heard eight times: a long note followed by three short ones (semitones), not always at the same pitch.

(g) Two low flutes playing detached notes, tubular bells playing tremolando all supported by a pizzicato note in the strings.

Kaija Saariaho: *Du cristal ...à fume*

4. (a) Orchestral work with electronics (not concerto – this applies only to the second half)

(b) Answer may include:

- Tone colour
- Ostinato
- Lack of metre

(c)

Serial	
Bi-tonal	
Static	✔
Spectral	✔

(d) The harmony of the first seven minutes originates from the opening bell chord: the orchestration constantly changes, highlighting different elements of the chord and its details.

(e) The title describes the two different halves of the piece: crystal denotes order, symmetry and structure in the first half while smoke is unpredictable, always changing and capricious in the second half.

(f) The texture is kept moving through repeated notes from different instruments, the entry of new instruments, crescendos and diminuendos, thickening and thinning of texture.

Mark-Anthony Turnage:
Three Screaming Popes

5. (a) ▪ Jazz inflected, mainly moves by step
with occasional rising intervals such
as 6ths and 7ths

▪ Short motivic melodic lines

(b) Orchestral work

(c)

The work is in $\frac{4}{4}$ throughout	
The music makes extensive use of ostinato	✔
There are frequent changes of metre	✔
The music is based on dance rhythms	✔
The music uses aleatoric rhythms	

(d) (1) Tonal but with a high degree of
dissonance

(2) Pedal notes and repeated ostinati in
the bass

(3) Predominance of semitones and
clusters

(e) Diego Velázquez and Francis Bacon

(f) Answers may include:

▪ A diminuendo

▪ Repeated notes (trumpets, horns,
lower strings, percussion)

▪ Adjacent tones and semitones

▪ All instruments in the middle range
creating an indistinct blurred sound

(g) Oboes, soprano saxophone, E♭ clarinet,
euphonium (approximate identification
is acceptable – ie. clarinet, saxophone,
low brass)

Judith Weir: *Scotch Minstrelsy*

6. (a) Answers may include:

▪ Widely spaced two-part writing in
rhythmic unison

▪ Unison writing one octave apart

▪ Elaborate closely-intertwined two-part
invention

▪ Simple held notes, building up into
held chords

(b) Song cycle

(c)

Chord clusters	✔
Spectral harmony	
Bi-tonal chords	✔
Microtonal harmony	
Diatonic harmony	✔

(d) Answers might include:

▪ Simple folk-like melodic lines

▪ Long and flowing, arching upwards
and then falling back

▪ Moving by step or using intervals
no greater than 3rds or 4ths

▪ Often broken by short rests

(e)

Irrational groupings (quintuplets, sextuplets etc)	✔
Unison rhythm	✔
Additive rhythm	
Scotch snaps	✔
No bar lines	✔

(f) Right and left hands in rhythmic unison,
but different pitches used in both hands.
The texture uses extremes of register
(left hand low in the bass clef and right
hand high in the treble). The harmony
uses a wide variety of intervals, including
many major 2nds and semitones.

Glossary

Accented. A note given special emphasis, either because of its prominent position or because it is marked with a symbol such as > to indicate that it should stand out.

Acoustic scale. A seven-note scale starting on C containing the notes C, D, E, F♯, G, A and B♭. It differs from the major scale in having an **augmented** fourth and a minor seventh.

Adagio. A **tempo** marking which means that the music should be played slowly. Also used as the name for a passage or **movement** of music played in this manner.

Additive rhythm. This is a repeated **rhythm**, 'displaced' either by adding notes to or subtracting notes from it – this is a well-known technique and can be found in Stravinsky. The term can also used to refer to music in which each bar is divided into different or unusual note groupings. For instance, Bartok's *6 Dances in Bulgarian Rhythm* (from his *Mikrokosmos*) have time signatures such as [**3+3+2**] and [**4+2+3**].

Alberti Bass. An accompaniment pattern in which the notes of a chord are repeatedly sounded in the order low, high, middle and high again. It is named after an obscure Italian composer who was addicted to the device.

Aleatoric. Music in which some element is left to chance or to the performers to determine.

Allegro. Italian for 'cheerful'. A **tempo** marking.

Allegretto. A **tempo** marking which is slightly slower than **allegro**, and therefore a fairly brisk speed.

Anacrusis. One or more weak-beat notes before the first strong beat of a phrase. Often called a 'pick-up' in jazz and pop music.

Antiphony. The alternation of different groups of instruments and/or singers.

Appoggiatura. A **dissonant** non-chord note, approached by a leap, that resolves by moving usually by step to a chord note. It is like a suspension but without the preparation. Appoggiaturas are sometimes written as small notes like ornaments.

Articulation. how smoothly or detached the notes of a piece are played, for example **staccato** and **legato** are types of articulation.

Atonal. Western music without a note that acts as a home **pitch** to which all other notes are related. This means, in particular, that atonal music avoids major and minor keys (and also **modes**).

Augmented. an augmented interval is one semitone larger than a major or perfect interval: for example, C-F♯ is an augmented 4th, E♭-C♯ is an augmented 6th.

Augmented 6th chord. A chromatic chord based on the 6th degree of the scale (or the flattened 6th degree if the key is major) containing the note an augmented 6th above it. The chord also contains a major 3rd above the **root** and may include a perfect 5th or augmented 4th above the root. The chord resolves when the two notes forming the augmented 6th move outward by a semitone to the dominant.

Backbeat. A term used in pop music to describe accenting normally weak beats (eg. beats 2 and 4 in $\frac{4}{4}$ time).

Baroque. Music written in styles typical of the period 1600-1750.

Bi-tonality. The use of two different keys at the same time, produced perhaps by different instruments or parts.

Blue notes. A term used in jazz and blues for a note (usually the 3rd, 5th or 7th degree of a major scale) that is made more expressive by slightly lowering its **pitch**.

Book musical. Distinct from a **through-sung** musical, where there are no spoken lines, and the entire story is told through song and music, a book musical integrates music and dance fully into a script in order to tell a story as a coherent whole.

Break. A term used in pop and jazz for an instrumental solo within a song.

Cadence. The last notes of a phrase, suggesting a point of repose. If harmonised, the chords can define the degree of completion more exactly, into a perfect, imperfect, interrupted, plagal or Phrygian cadence.

Cadenza. An extended passage for the soloist in a concert, usually unaccompanied and virtuosic. Traditionally, the cadenza is a decoration of the **cadence** at the end of the first movement just before the coda.

Cakewalk. A dance originally developed by the African–American community on slave plantations as part of dance competitions at the end of which the winning couple would be presented with a cake. Associated with early jazz and **ragtime**.

Canonic. Music in which a **melody** in one part fits with the same melody in another part even though the latter starts a few beats later.

Chain form. In the work of Witold Lutosławski, music where one strand begins before the previous one has ended.

Chromaticism. A word meaning 'coloured' used to describe notes outside the current key or **mode**. They are added for colour and do not cause a change of key. Accidentals are not, however, necessarily chromatic.

Circle of fifths. A series of chords whose **roots** are each a 5th lower than the previous chord. In practice the series would soon drop below the lowest note available on most instruments, so the bass usually alternates between falling a 5th and rising a 4th, producing the same series of **pitches**.

Classical. A term often used for any sort of art music, but more specifically and properly referring to music written in styles typical of the period 1750–1825.

Cluster chords. Chords containing three or more adjacent notes separated by a semitone. These are **dissonant** chords without resolutions and are not found in functional **harmony**.

Comping. Improvising a jazz accompaniment.

Continuo. Abbreviation of 'basso continuo' An essential part of instrumental music in the **Baroque** era comprising a bass instrument (cello, bassoon, etc.) and a **harmony** instrument (harpsichord, organ, lute, etc.) to provide the backdrop to the rest of the musical **texture**.

Contrapuntal. A texture that uses **counterpoint**.

Col legno. An instruction for a string player to produce the notes by using the back of the bow (i.e. the wooden part).

Country music. A genre of popular music that originated in the Southern United States in the 1920s. It takes its **roots** from Appalachian folk music and blues.

Counterpoint. The simultaneous combination of two or more melodies with independent **rhythms**. There may be some imitation between the parts but counterpoint can also be non–imitative. A whole **movement** may be **contrapuntal** or the music may alternate between contrapuntal and other **textures**. The term is often used interchangeably with **polyphony**.

Cycle of fifths. See **circle of fifths**.

Cyclic form. A form in which a theme or **melody** occurs in more than one movement of a piece of music, as a unifying device: sometimes at the beginning and the end, and sometimes in every movement in a different guise.

Da capo form. A **ternary form** in which the first, 'A' section of a piece of music is a complete musical entity, ending in the tonic key, and could in principle be sung or played alone. The second section contrasts with the first in its key, **texture**, mood, or tempo, and the third section would be marked 'da capo' meaning 'from the head' – an instruction to begin at the beginning again. In a da capo aria, the singer would usually add ornamentation to the second iteration of the 'A' section **melody**.

Development. The central section of **sonata form**. The term is also used more generally to describe the manipulation and transformation of motifs and themes in any sort of music.

Diatonic. Notes that belong to the current key: the opposite of **chromatic**.

Diminished 7th. An interval notated as a 7th that is one semitone smaller than a minor 7th, such as E to D♭. Also a chord based on this interval, and made up of superimposed minor 3rds (or their enharmonic equivalents), for example E–G–B♭–D♭.

Dissonance. A combination of notes that produces a clashing sound when played together (the opposite of consonance).

Divisi. An instruction to divide a single section of instruments into multiple subsections. This often applies to the violins of the string section in an orchestra, but in choral music, for example, the soprano section might divide at times into first and second soprano.

Double time. In jazz, using note values twice as fast as previously but without changing the pace of the chord progressions. Often used during **improvised** solos.

Doubletracking. An audio recording technique in which a performer sings or plays along with his or her own pre-recorded performance, usually to produce a bigger sound than can be achieved with a single voice or instrument.

Dominant. The 5th degree of a major or minor scale (for example, D is the dominant in G major).

Dominant 7th. A **triad** on the **dominant** (the 5th degree of the scale) plus a **diatonic** 7th above its **root**. In C major the dominant chord consists of G, B and D. The dominant 7th chord is G, B, D and F.

Dynamics. How loudly or softly the music is played; the volume of the music, indicated by dynamic markings such as *piano* and *crescendo*.

Entr'acte. A piece of music performed between acts of a musical or opera, like a short **overture** to the second half.

EQ. Short for equalisation, EQ changes the relative volume of the frequencies in a recording; this could relate to an individual track, instrument or a whole mix. An EQ unit is made of a number of filters, which increase or decrease the volume of audible frequencies from bass to treble.

Expressionism. An early 20th Century style characterised by the expression of inner fears and obsessions, often through distorted or violent artistic ideas.

Exposition. See **sonata form**.

Feedback. An audio phenomenon that occurs when the sound of an output is captured or recorded by the input, creating an infinite loop and a characteristic 'howl' that is often used as a musical effect in rock music styles. It can be intentionally created by playing a loud note on an electric guitar close to the amplifier.

Flanging. An electronic effect, sometimes used with electric guitars, that creates a distinctive sweeping sound. Originally it was produced by slowing down one tape recorded in relation to another by pressing on the flange of the tape spool.

Fluency. A fluent performance is one without unwanted stops-and-starts or hesitation. It is something examiners will be especially looking out for. A performance that lacks fluency throughout is likely to incur quite a harsh penalty!

Fugato. In the style of a **fugue** but not in strict fugal form.

Fugue. A musical form in which a main theme is taken up and developed by each of the parts in turn.

Glissando. A slide from one **pitch** to another.

Golden Section. A geometrical proportion that divides a line with a longer side and a shorter one. Many contemporary composers have used the proportion to mark climactic points or moments of significance in their music. It can be applied using Fibonacci numbers (where each number is the sum of the previous two: 1, 2, 3, 5, 8, 13, 21, 34, 55, and so on.) So, in a piece 34 bars long, the Golden Section falls either at the end of bar 21 or bar 13.

Graphic notation. The representation of music using visual symbols which are not traditional musical notation. Commonly found on vocal scores by composers such as John Cage.

Harmonics. On string instruments (including the harp and guitar), a very high and pure sound produced by placing a finger lightly on a string before plucking or bowing.

Harmony. The combination of chords used in a piece of music. To study harmony we concentrate on the vertical aspects of the music (the chords, and how they change) though the horizontal aspect (i.e. how the individual voices or instruments move, called 'voice leading') is also important.

Hemiola. A **rhythmic** device in which two groups of three beats ('strong-weak-weak, strong-weak-weak') are articulated as three groups of two beats ('strong-weak, strong-weak, strong-weak').

Heterophony. A **texture** in which simple and elaborated versions of the same **melody** are heard together.

Homophonic. A musical **texture** in which one part (usually the uppermost) has the melodic interest, and the other parts accompany (as opposed to a **polyphonic** or **contrapuntal** texture, in which all the parts are melodically interesting).

Homotonal. A piece of music is homotonal if all of its **movements** are in the same key.

Idée fixe. Also called **leitmotif**.

Impressionism. A style particularly associated with late 19th and early 20th Century French music. Just as Impressionist paintings often blur objects and explore the effects of light, so Impressionist music frequently blurs **tonality**, using chords primarily for the atmosphere they create rather than as functional **harmony**, and exploring unusual and delicate tone colours.

Improvisation. A performance in which most or all of the music is made up on the spot.

Intonation. This refers to accuracy of **pitch**, whether on an instrument or voice. Like **fluency**, it is something an examiner will be expecting in a good performance. Wind and string players in particular often need to retune during the course of a performance, since the overall pitch of instruments, even when in tune at the start, can be affected in the course of the performance by such factors as temperature or prolonged playing. Lack of intonation will result in notes that are sharp or flat.

Klangfarbenmelodie. A technique which splits the **melody** or musical line between several instruments.

Legato. Notes that are performed smoothly, without gaps between them. The opposite of **staccato**.

Leitmotif. A recurring theme, usually a melodic phrase but sometimes an interval or **rhythm**, used throughout a composition and associated with a particular character, idea or event.

Maximalism. A movement within **Modernism**, and the opposite of minimalism, in which everything is expanded, such as the size of the orchestra, and the length of musical works.

Melisma. Several notes sung to one syllable.

Melody. The element of music created by single notes being played successively, creating a horizontal dimension on the stave when written down, commonly known as the tune.

Microtones. Intervals smaller than a semitone, frequently used by contemporary composers. They are often divided into quarter tones (half of a semitone), but may also be divided in other ways.

Middle 8. The central 8 bars of a piece or song, in pop and jazz music, also known as the 'B' section, within a common 32-bar AABA song format. Also used for a similar part of a non-32 bar form of piece, so not always actually 8 bars long.

Minuet and trio. A minuet is an elegant dance in $\frac{3}{4}$ time, found mainly in music of the **Baroque** and **Classical** periods, and in conjunction with a trio often forms a **movement** of a symphony or other large work.

Mixolydian mode. a type of **mode**. A scale that can be found by playing an octave of white notes on the piano from G to G. It can be **transposed** to start on any note, for example, a mixolydian scale on C is C–D–E–F–G–A–B♭–C.

Modes/modal music. A mode is a type of scale: Church or Greek modes consist of 7 **pitches**, but other types have different numbers. Major and minor scales are types of modes but the term is usually reserved for those such as the **mixolydian** or dorian.

Modernism. A cultural movement of the early 20th Century that rejected tradition in order to create new forms of expression that in music are often complex and **dissonant**.

Modulation. The process of changing key.

Moment form. Originating in music by Karlheinz Stockhausen, a form of music defined as a 'mosaic of moments' where many independent units of music are put together in such a way that a narrative line is expressly avoided.

Monothematic. A musical composition constructed on a single theme or **melody**, which unites the **movements** of a **sonata** or **symphony**.

Monophonic. A **texture** consisting of a single unaccompanied **melody**, which may be performed by a soloist or by many people performing in unison or in octaves.

Motto theme. A theme or **melody** which recurs throughout a composition – similar to a **leitmotif** or **idée fixe**.

Movement. An independent section in a longer piece of music such as a symphony.

Multiphonics. a technique on an instrument that can only play one note at a time (a **monophonic** instrument) in which several notes are produced simultaneously. They are usually found in music for woodwind using new fingerings or different embouchures.

On brass instruments they usually consist of simultaneously playing the instrument and singing into it.

Narrative form. Music which tells a narrative and uses that story as the organising basis for its form.

Neapolitan 6th. The first inversion of the major triad on the flattened second degree of a scale. In the key of E minor, this is a chord of F major in first inversion.

Neo-classicism. An early 20th Century style that combined forms and techniques from the 18th Century with a more modern approach to elements such as **rhythm**, **harmony** and instrumentation.

Octatonic scale. An eight-note scale. Most often, this refers to one in which the notes ascend in alternating intervals of tone and semitone or vice versa.

Orchestration. The dividing of musical line, **melody** and **harmony**, between the instruments of an orchestra.

Ostinato. A **melodic**, **rhythmic** or chordal pattern repeated throughout a substantial passage of music. In popular music and jazz a melodic ostinato is known as a riff. A ground bass is a type of ostinato.

Overture. A piece of orchestral music played at the beginning of (or before) the first act of an opera or musical theatre work.

Pantonality. Twelve tone music, or that which gives equal importance to all notes rather than prioritising them by a hierarchy in which the **tonic** and **dominant** of a key take precedence. It is the term that Schoenberg preferred to 'free **atonality**' to describe his **dissonant** pre-serial music.

Parlando. From the word 'to speak', **recitative**-like singing.

Passacaglia. An early 17th Century form of music, often featuring a bass **ostinato** and written in a slow triple time.

Pastiche. A piece of music (or other art form) which imitates the style of another work, artist or period.

Pentatonic scale. A scale of five **pitches**. You can find one such scale by playing all the black notes on a keyboard.

Phaser. An effect that creates a sweeping sound through modulating the phase of a waveform using an all pass filter, causing changing interference patterns. It is often used on electric guitars and electric pianos, and gives a slight sense of movement to the sound.

Pitch. How high or low a note sounds. For example, in an ascending scale the pitch of the music rises, and notes lower down on the stave have a lower pitch.

Pizzicato. A direction to pluck notes on a string instrument.

Plainchant. Also called 'plainsong', a body of chants used in early Western church liturgies. Characteristically slow and with a relatively narrow range of **pitches**.

Pluralism. Pluralism suggests a number of different approaches or styles, both in music generally and within a musical piece, rather than just one kind of style. It is a particular feature of the musical world since 1980.

Polyphony. A musical **texture** in which two or more parts move independently of each other, creating a layered effect of several different strands.

Polyrhythm. A polyrhythm is where two different metres or musical pulses are played simultaneously. A very simple example would be two beats against three; or four against five.

Ponticello. A bridge on a stringed instrument.

Portamento. A musical term and instruction to slide from one **pitch** to another.

Programme music. Music that is intended to tell a story or suggest a specific image.

Rāga. In Indian music, a melodic line or **mode**.

Ragtime. A style of music developed in the 1890s and onwards, characterised by a syncopated melodic line and regularly **accented** accompaniment, and played primarily on the piano.

R&B. Short for Rhythm and Blues, a style of music developed in the United States primarily by African Americans, soulful and often with much vocal **improvisation**.

Recapitulation. See **sonata form**.

Recitative. A rhythmically free vocal style used for dialogue or narrative in opera and occasionally musical theatre. It is usually minimally accompanied and followed by a more traditionally 'sung' aria.

Renaissance. A term referring to music written in styles typical of the period 1400–1600.

Reverb. Used in recording and short for reverberation, reverb mirrors the sound of a room and creates a sense of ambience. Heavy reverb can make it sound like a track was recorded in a very reflective room, like cave or bathroom, whereas a dry signal (with no reverb) will sound more artificial or 'close'.

Rhythm. To do with time rather than **pitch**. Rhythm concerns the length of the notes and rests in a piece of music, how long they last, and how they are combined to create different patterns in time.

Ritornello. A structure used for large-scale **movements** in the late-**Baroque** period. An opening instrumental section (called the ritornello) introduces the main musical ideas. It is followed by a contrasting **texture**, although usually based on similar material, that features one or more soloists. Sections of the ritornello, often in different keys, then alternate with solo textures until the complete ritornello (or most of it) returns at the end in the **tonic** key. The fragmentary nature of most of the ritornello sections gives the form its name - ritornello means 'a little return'.

Rococo. An elaborately ornamental late-**Baroque** style.

Romantic. A term referring to music written in styles typical of the period 1825–1900.

Root. The note that corresponds with the letter-name of a chord. For example, the root of a chord of C is always the note C, no matter which of its **pitches** (C, E or G) is the bass note.

Rubato. This word literally means 'robbed' and refers to shortening some beats and lengthening others in order to give an expressive, free feel to the pulse – 'stealing time'. The use of rubato is particularly associated with piano music of the late Romantic period, and with jazz.

Serialism. Music based on manipulations of a chosen order for the 12 degrees of a chromatic scale. Other musical elements such as note lengths and **dynamics** are occasionally treated in the same way.

Scat. **Improvised** vocal music used in jazz, in which meaningless sounds are produced, often imitating the sounds of instruments such as the trumpet.

Scherzo. A light, vigorous piece of music, often replacing the **minuet** as the third **movement** of a **sonata** or symphony.

Skiffle. A genre of music with roots and influences in jazz, blues and folk, often played on improvised or home made instruments, such as the washboard.

Sonata form. The most common structure for the first **movement** (and also often other movements) of sonatas, symphonies, concertos and chamber music in the **Classical** period and later. The essence of sonata form is the use of two contrasting tonal centres (**tonic** and either the **dominant** or another closely related key such as the relative major) in a first section called the **exposition**; the use of a wider range of keys to create tension and excitement in a central section called the **development**; and a **recapitulation** in which the music from the exposition is repeated in the tonic key.

Sonata–rondo form. A blend of **sonata** and rondo form in which the second theme, or 'B', occurs twice: ABACABA.

Sonority. Quality and resonance of sound.

Spectralism. See the section about Kaija Saariaho on page 259 for a detailed discussion of Spectralism.

Sprechstimme. Also called 'Sprechgesang', a form of singing which is a cross between singing and speech. The tone quality of speech is heightened or lowered according to **pitches** marked on a musical score.

Staccato. Notes that are performed shorter than printed so that each is detached from its neighbours. Often shown in notation by dots above or below the notes affected. The opposite of **legato**.

Stretto. The telescoping of imitative parts so that entries come closer to each other than they originally did.

Stride piano. Characteristically when the left hand plays a single bass note or intervals of an octave, seventh or tenth on beats one and three (the 'on-beats') and strides up to a chord on beats two and four (the 'off-beats').

Strophic. A song that uses the same music for every verse, as opposed to one that is through-composed.

Subdominant. The 4th degree of a **diatonic** scale.

Submediant. The 6th degree of a **diatonic** scale.

Symphonic poem. See **tone-poem**.

Syncopation. A **rhythmic** device in which emphasis is given to a moment that does not fall on the beat: an offbeat or weak-beat **accent**.

Synthesiser. An electronic device with a keyboard that allows the player to add digital effects and to manipulate the sounds produced.

Tāla. **Rhythmic** patterns as used in Indian music.

Tempo. The speed of the music. This is often indicated by a tempo marking at the beginning of a piece or passage of music.

Tenuto. From the Italian for 'to hold', this musical direction usually means that the player should hold a note slightly longer, or sometimes slightly louder than its stated value. A form of emphasis.

Ternary form. A three-part structure consisting of a middle section flanked by two identical or very similar passages. The form can be represented by the letters ABA, or, if there are differences in the A section when it returns, ABA[1].

Texture. The effect resulting from the relationship between the various simultaneous lines in a piece of music. Specific textures include **monophonic**, **homophonic**, **polyphonic**, **heterophonic** and **polyrhythmic**.

Thematic transformation. A technique in which a musical theme is developed by transforming it in some way, for instance by **modulation**, **transposition**, inversion, or playing a retrograde (backwards) version of it. Transformation in terms of note lengths could involve **augmentation** or diminution.

Theme and variations. A piece of music which takes a **melody** or theme and reimagines or reworks it in terms of key, tempo, **rhythm** etc over the course of a number of 'variation' movements.

Through-sung musical. A musical without dialogue, in which all of the story is told visually and through songs and music.

Time-based notation. Music in which normal **rhythmic** values are dispensed with and measured in seconds instead.

Tonality. The use of major and minor keys in music and the ways in which these are related. Not all music is tonal, some is **modal** and some is based on non-Western scales such as the **pentatonic scale**. Western music that uses neither keys nor modes is described as **atonal**.

Tone-poem. Also called a '**symphonic poem**', a one-**movement** piece of orchestral music which evokes some other non-musical source such as a poem or painting.

Tonic. The first degree of a **diatonic** scale, otherwise known as the key note.

Transposition. The movement up or down in **pitch** of a whole passage of music or piece.

Tremolando. See **tremolo**.

Tremolo. A musical effect that refers to a very quick repetition of a single note (on bowed or plucked string instruments) or of two alternating notes (on keyboard instruments).

Triad. A chord of three notes: a bass note and notes a 3rd and 5th above it.

Tritone. An interval of three tones, such as B to the F above.

Tutti. 'All' – the full ensemble, or a passage of music intended for the full ensemble.

Underscore. Music which is played quietly under dialogue, in a musical theatre show, for example.

Vamp. A term used in pop music and jazz for something similar to an **ostinato** in classical music. A repeating phrase which is played as an accompaniment, it can be, for example, used as an intro until the **melody** instrument or voice comes in.

Variations. A musical structure in which the main theme is varied a number of times (A, A[1], A[2]).

Vibrato. A performing technique in which the **pitch** of a note wavers rapidly to give the sound greater vibrancy and resonance.

Virtuoso. A highly skilled instrumentalist or singer, capable of performing technically difficult ('virtuosic') music.

Wah wah. An effect produced by brass instruments when the player alternately applies and removes a mute, and on an electric guitar when the player controls output from the amplifier with a pedal.

Walking bass. A bass line in which the notes are all on the beat, and move mainly by steps instead of leaps.

Whole-tone scale. A scale in which every note is one whole-tone step above or below its neighbours.

Music credits

English Lyrics by Herbert Kretzmer.
© Copyright (Music & Lyrics) 1980 Editions
Musicales Alain Boublil.
English Lyrics © Copyright 1985 Alain Boublil
Music Limited (ASCAP).
All Rights Reserved. International Copyright Secured.

Children Of Eden
Words & Music by Stephen Schwartz
© Copyright 1991 Williamson Music Company.
Administered by Hal Leonard LLC.
All Rights Reserved. International Copyright Secured.

All That I Love (from "Martin Guerre")
Words by Alain Boublil & Stephen Clark
Music by Claude-Michel Schonberg
© Copyright 1998 Bouberg Music Limited.
Administered for the United Kingdom & the
Republic of Ireland by Alain Boublil (Overseas)
Limited. Administered for the USA by
Alain Boublil Music Limited (ASCAP)
c/o Joel Faden & Company Incorporated.
All Rights Reserved. International Copyright Secured.

All I Ask Of You (from 'The Phantom Of The Opera')
Music by Andrew Lloyd Webber
Lyrics by Charles Hart
Additional Lyrics by Richard Stilgoe
© Copyright 1986 Andrew Lloyd Webber
licensed to The Really Useful Group Limited.
All Rights Reserved. International Copyright Secured.

A Weekend In The Country
(From "A Little Night Music")
Words & Music by Stephen Sondheim
© Copyright 1973 Rilting Music Inc.
Administered by Hal Leonard LLC.
All Rights Reserved. International Copyright Secured.

Candide
Words by John Latouche
Music by Leonard Bernstein
© Copyright Jalni Publications Incorporated.
Universal Music Publishing Limited.
All Rights Reserved. International Copyright Secured.

Caravan
Words by Irving Mills
Music by Duke Ellington & Juan Tizol
© Copyright 1937 EMI Mills Music Incorporated, USA
Lafleur Music Limited.
All Rights Reserved. International Copyright Secured.

Anthropology
Music by Charlie Parker & Dizzy Gillespie
© Copyright 1948 Music Sales Corporation/Atlantic
Music Corp. Music Sales Corporation for World
excluding USA. Music Sales Corporation and
Atlantic Music Corp for USA.
All Rights Reserved. International Copyright Secured.

How High The Moon
Words by Nancy Hamilton
Music by Morgan Lewis
© Copyright 1940 Chappell Co. Incorporated.
Warner Chappell North America.
All Rights Reserved. International Copyright Secured.

The Rite Of Spring
Music by Igor Stravinsky
© Copyright 1913 Boosey & Hawkes Music
Publishers Limited.
All Rights Reserved. International Copyright Secured.

Erwartung, Op. 17
Music by Arnold Schoenberg
© Copyright 1909 Universal Edition AG (Wien).
Universal Edition (London) Ltd.
All Rights Reserved. International Copyright Secured.

Variations For Orchestra, Op. 31
Music by Arnold Schoenberg
© Copyright Universal Edition AG (Wien)
Universal Edition (London) Ltd.
All Rights Reserved. International Copyright Secured.

Classical Symphony in D, Op. 25
Music by Serge Prokofieff
© Copyright 1917 Hawkes & Son (London) Ltd.
All Rights Reserved. International Copyright Secured.

Concerto For Piano And Wind Instruments
Music by Igor Stravinsky
© Copyright 1923 Boosey & Hawkes Music
Publishers Limited.
All Rights Reserved. International Copyright Secured.

Trio For Oboe, Bassoon And Piano
Music by Francis Poulenc
© Copyright 1926 Edition Wilhelm Hansen AS,
Copenhagen. Chester Music Limited.
All Rights Reserved. International Copyright Secured.

Offertorium
Music by Sofia Gubaidulina
© Copyright 1980 Sikorski Hans Musikverlag GMBH-
Co/Boosey & Hawkes Music Publishers Limited
All Rights Reserved. International Copyright Secured.

Chain 2
Music by Witold Lutoslawski
© Copyright 1988, 1996 Polskie Wydawnictwo
Muzyczne SA, Kraków, Poland. Transferred to Chester
Music Ltd. © Copyright by Chester Music Ltd for
the World except Albania, Bosnia and Herzegovina,
Bulgaria, China, Croatia, Cuba, Czech Republic,
Estonia, Hungary, Latvia, Lithuania, Macedonia, North
Korea, Poland, Romania, Serbia and Montenegro,
Slovakia, Slovenia, Ukraine, Vietnam and the
Commonwealth of Independent States (CIS).
All Rights Reserved. International Copyright Secured.